Self-Care for Black Women

5 Books in 1

A Powerful Mental Health Workbook to Quiet Your
Inner Critic, Boost Self-Esteem, and Love Yourself

Layla Moon

Table of Contents

Book #3: 365 Powerful Positive Affirmations for Black Women 163

Book #4: 365 Badass Positive Affirmations for Strong Black Women 197

Table of Contents

Table of Contents

Table of Contents

Table of Contents

Table of Contents

Table of Contents

4 FREE Gifts

To help you along your spiritual journey, I've created 4 FREE bonus eBooks.

You can get instant access by signing up to my email newsletter below.

On top of the 4 free books, you will also receive weekly tips along with free book giveaways, discounts, and so much more.

All of these bonuses are 100% free with no strings attached. You don't need to provide any personal information except your email address.

To get your bonus, go to:

https://dreamlifepress.com/four-free-gifts

Spirit Guides for Beginners: How to Hear the Universe's Call and Communicate with Your Spirit Guide and Guardian Angels

Guided by Moon herself, inspired by her own experiences and knowledge that has been passed down by hundreds of generations for thousands of years, you'll discover everything you need to know to;

- Understanding what the call of the universe is

- How to hear and comprehend it

- Knowing who and what your spirit guides and guardian angels are

- Learning how to connect, start a conversation, and listen to your guides

- How to manifest your dreams with the help of the cosmic source

- Learning how to start living the life you want to live

- And so much more…

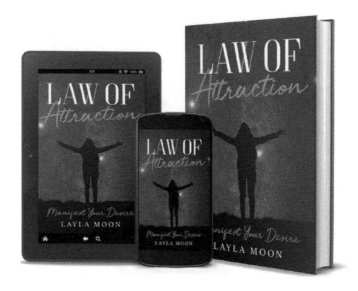

Law of Attraction: Manifest Your Desire

Learn how to tap into the infinite power of the universe and manifest everything you want in life.

Includes:

- Law of Attraction: Manifest Your Desire ebook

- Law of Attraction Workbook

- Cheat sheets and checklists so make sure you're on the right path

Hoodoo Book of Spells for Beginners: Easy and effective Rootwork, Conjuring, and Protection Spells for Healing and Prosperity

Harness the power of one of the greatest magics. Hoodoo is a powerful force ideal for holding negativity at bay, promoting positivity in all areas in your life, offering protection to the things you love, and ultimately taking control of your destiny.

Inside, you will discover:

- How to get started with Hoodoo in your day-to-day life

- How to use conjuration spells to manifest the life you want to live

- How casting protection spells can help you withstand the toughest of times

- Break cycles of bad luck and promote good fortune throughout your life

- Hoodoo to encourage prosperity and financial stability

- How to heal using Hoodoo magic, both short-term and long-term traumas and troubles

- Remove curses and banish pain, suffering, and negativity from your life

- And so much more…

Book of Shadows

A printable PDF to support you in your spiritual transformation.

Within the pages, you will find:

- Potion and tinctures tracking sheet

- Essential oils log pages

- Herbs log pages

- Magical rituals and spiritual body goals checklist

- Tarot reading spread sheets

- Weekly moon and planetary cycle tracker

- And so much more

Get all the resources for FREE by visiting the link below

https://dreamlifepress.com/four-free-gifts

Book #1

Emotional Self-Care for Black Women

A Powerful Mental Health Workbook to Silence Your Inner Critic, Raise Your Self-Esteem, and Heal Yourself

Introduction

When you think of an emotional black woman, the first thing that probably comes to mind is a woman who is angry, bitter, and raging at the whole world. Either that or our minds draw up the vision of a black woman crying pitifully. We don't see emotions in a positive light and unfortunately, I can't say it's our fault. A few years ago, I shared the same sentiments. Sadly, the messages around me reinforced this imagery I had of what an emotional black woman is supposed to look like. I thought crying was the ultimate expression of a woman's emotions. And so do a lot of people, which is why we strongly try to deter our black brothers from finding emotional expression in their tears. We tell them it is womanly and therefore, "weak."

As we fight for gender equality in today's climate, the freedom to cry freely is gradually being frowned upon as well. We have prospective life partners saying things like, they "don't like their women emotionally weak." And when you translate that in 'regular speak,' they mean they don't want a woman who is tearful or expresses herself in any of the ways I mentioned earlier. The problem is not people having standards for what they want in a potential partner. The problem is the narrow perspective we have when it comes to the colorful range of human emotions and feelings, that we assign emotions to specific genders or dictate how each of us should react to these emotions. And worse still, we made it the general definition of what it means to be an emotional black woman.

This is the reason I felt inspired to write this book. I am hoping that at the end of the book, that picture of who we think an emotional black woman is will change. I do this with the expectation that certain important concepts that we have assigned negative labels to will be seen in a new light and will empower us with the knowledge to help us thrive and grow in our respective endeavors.

At the end of this chapter, I want you to understand what emotional health is and what it means to care for your emotional health. The idea that a strong black woman is someone who has succeeded in shutting down her emotions or someone who does not display emotions in ways that are considered weak should be burned and destroyed forever. That narrative is costing us our peace and happiness. We need to care about our emotions.

What is Emotional Self-Care?

I came across the word self-care in a Hollywood movie. The way it was sold to me was basically taking a bath in a tub surrounded by candles, petals, and all that stuff - which is nice, but far from the whole truth. Self-care is way more than having a nice soak in the tub. It is in your attitude towards yourself. It is in your interactions with other people. It is in the words you silently say to yourself when no one else is listening. When your emotional health is neglected, your inner critic assumes control by default. The voice becomes the loudest and if you do not consciously check your inner critic, the message will be negative, and that negativity will consume you.

A quick internet search tells us that emotional self-care is a conscious effort towards identifying and nurturing your true feelings, your conscious inner state, and your emotional intellect. If I was going to phrase this in a cool way, I would say emotional self-care is the quaint art of giving a f**k. As women, we spend a lot of time and effort trying to get other people to care about our feelings when we fail to do the same for ourselves. We shut ourselves down emotionally and expect some knight in shining armor to come and rescue us. This expectation is ridiculous because we are actually in possession of the key to the chains that hold us down. The only way to help ourselves grow emotionally and to maintain stable emotional health is to start caring about our feelings. And to do that, this process must happen in three phases.

Phase One: Correctly Identify Your Feelings

A lot of us have negative emotional flare-ups, but we tend to focus more on the circumstances that created the flare-ups rather than our reaction to those circumstances. From my understanding, emotions are the symptoms of what is going on inside our heads...mentally. When you get a cold, you manifest symptoms like fever, headache, and so on. To treat it, you don't start chasing the environmental factors that probably led to your cold. Instead, you focus your treatment on what is going on with your body.

Emotional self-care works in the same way because when you have an emotional flare-up (whether negative or positive), you must try to identify what you are feeling and why you are feeling it and then determine the next course of action to ensure that you are in a more positive emotional state. We should aspire to manifest more positive emotional flare-ups than negative ones. That is the end goal (I think it should be).

I am not saying that life is meant to be a bed of roses. That is unrealistic. I am saying that when you build your emotional health through self-care, you reach a point where there is very little in life that will cause you to break to a point where you feel that life is no longer worth it. This point is called emotional resilience, and it is at the core of everything we are going to talk about in this book.

Phase Two: Nurture Your Feelings

I struggled with this phase for the longest time because of my one-track mind. I assumed that nurturing my feelings was akin to fanning the flames of a burning bush; letting it grow, burn, and eventually consuming you. As I reflect on my thoughts from some years ago, I have to admit that I was kinda crazy. Thankfully, contrary to my crazy world of imagination, it simply means understanding what you are feeling and understanding which actions will pacify you. Let me break that down. I struggled with anger a lot. As a black woman living in a world that is clouded by racism, it is difficult not to be angry. One moment you are enjoying life, and then some person or event comes and squashes that moment like a bug because of their prejudices against your skin color. Worse still, you feel helpless to react.

That sense of helplessness feeds anger and I had a lot of it. When I realized that I had to learn to nurture my feelings, I kept thinking, "Am I supposed to grow this anger?" Thankfully I didn't act on that line of thought. Instead, I sat down and processed my anger. Beyond the helplessness, I needed to understand why I was angry. This helped me realize that my anger was mostly because I felt like my rights were being violated. It was during this process that I also understood that anger is not the negative emotion we have painted it out to be. It is the way you act when you're angry that brings about negativity.

When I understood that my fundamental rights as a human being were being trampled on and that this is what inspired my anger, I was able to channel that rage into more positive forms that yielded better results (this did not happen overnight). These actions pacified my anger and I learned to embrace my anger because it made me more aware of myself as a woman. Through it, I understood the things I could tolerate in a relationship. It also helped me build clearer boundaries in my relationships. We'll get into this later.

By nurturing your emotions, you develop a better understanding of yourself which will, in turn, help you build better relationships with others.

Phase Three: Conscious Effort

This phase is present from the moment you decide to practice emotional self-care because it requires conscious effort. I am sad to say this, but the reality is that a lot of us are not raised with the knowledge of emotional self-care. We are groomed to survive the physical hardships of this world, but most of us are not lucky enough to have the kind of foundation that helps us prioritize our emotional health. And so, to get into the practice of emotional self-care, we need to make a conscious effort. Another reason conscious effort is important is because of our mental programming. We see the world through our society's lens, which also influences our perception of self. However, nine times out of ten, we are not who society says we are.

It is our duty to take the time to get to know ourselves, understand our visions, and build our goals. All this requires a level of self-awareness and conscious effort to make it happen. As you become more self-aware, you still need to apply more effort to get rid of the preconceived notions you have about how life is supposed to be or how you are supposed to react emotionally in different situations. For example, as black women, we are conditioned to believe that a relationship where love hurts is the one that proves your womanhood. This should never be the case. We deserve men who love us, respect us, and treat us like the queens that we are. However, if you don't make the conscious effort to apply this knowledge in your relationship with yourself as well as the ones you have with other people, you find yourself repeating old negative patterns that bring pain and hurt.

How Does Emotional Self-Care Impact Us?

From my personal experience, I didn't start living - and I mean really living - until I started practicing emotional self-care. Up until that point, I felt as though I was living my life for other people on their terms. I was so afraid to write a book because I was worried about what other people were going to think about me. I stopped myself from taking risks and going on adventures because I allowed the views and opinions of other people to dictate what should or shouldn't be done with my life and my money. But that is just scratching the surface of what you stand to gain when you imbibe the culture of emotional self-care. There are so many benefits but I am only going to focus on 3 of them.

1. Freedom to be you.

We all know those crazy house rules; girls should be this... girls should not do that ...and so on. With emotional self-care, you can break free from those stupid rules and focus on yourself. It is through this that you can understand what your true limitations are and most importantly, unveil your amazing potential. When you invest in your emotional health, you cast yourself in a new light, where you find that those things that were thrust on you or taken away from you because of your gender might hold the key to unlocking the life you dream of.

Sometimes, the freedom you gain is simply finding validation in your emotional expressions. You may discover that you are not the crazy girlfriend they said you were. You were simply expressing your emotional need, which is crucial to your existence in any relationship.

2. Emotional Intelligence

Emotional intelligence goes beyond your ability to recognize other people's emotions. How you act on the knowledge that you have defines the level of your emotional intelligence. Through emotional self-care, you are able to develop a deeper understanding of emotions, and this gives you a greater ability to connect with people who might be going through similar circumstances. And it is through these connections that you are able to develop deeper bonds with people, giving you the chance to build more sustainable relationships.

3. Self-awareness

Without proper emotional self-care, it is almost impossible to determine how well you know yourself. If you simply accept the labels that people throw on you based on their limited understanding of who you are, you are depriving yourself of the opportunity to explore the depths of your personality and everything that comes with being you. One major contributor to poor self-esteem is an absence of self-awareness. When you don't know who you are, you accept whatever is given to you, and often, you get the crumbs that fall off the table. This negatively impacts your self-esteem.

Why is Emotional Self-Care Crucial for a Better Life as a Black Woman?

The crusade for better emotional self-care for black women should have started hundreds of years ago. Right now, as the world veers into chaos thanks to the raging pandemic and other disturbing social factors, it is even more important for us black women to band up together and look inwards for the solutions that the world needs today. The starting point for any tangible solution in any given society is self-reflection. Being a black woman in today's world means a lot of things to different people, but factually speaking, our role in society is crucial. We hold up families and empires, and their continued existence is dependent on us getting it right with ourselves.

We have put everyone else ahead of ourselves and this has been to our detriment. We have become more broken than ever, and broken people only end up breaking other people. Through emotional self-care, we can start putting those pieces back together and mending those areas of our lives that require it. We need deep healing in our community, and as women of color, that inner hurt has a lot to do with the negative messages we have been raised with or around. Through conscious efforts on our part, we can become more self-aware. This will help us grow into our power and potential and through this power, we can begin initiating the transformation we want to see in the world around us today. It is time to come out of denial. It is time to shed the lies. But most importantly, it is time to take up our rightful places in society. And the fact is, we can only do that from an emotionally healthy place. Having this in mind, let's explore emotional health in detail.

The Core Layers of Emotional Health

The entire purpose of this book is to bring your complete focus to yourself. No other chapter in this book will demand this of you more than this first chapter. Here, we are looking inwards, and you need to brace yourself for information you might be subconsciously aware of but are not emotionally ready for. We tend to avoid these topics because we don't like how they make us feel. But we must understand that emotional self-care is about acknowledging your feelings and tending to them. These feelings are not always going to be pleasant but it's okay. Life is not all sunshine and rainbows. We have days where the clouds are dark and scary, but those days bring us the rain that turns the land lush and green.

With a better understanding of self, you can turn those dark and unpleasant emotions into pointers that direct you on a path that is more ideal for you and the life you want. When I started my emotional self-care journey, one of the things that helped me was having a vision of what my end goal was. I wanted a life where I was happier because I was doing the things that I loved and experiencing those things with people who love me just as much as I loved them. I found that paying attention to the causes of those negative emotions I was experiencing helped me to identify the things I really wanted in my life and the things that I had outgrown. And I believe that this was how I was able to get to the point where my life is everything that I wanted to be.

Side note; I need you to constantly remind yourself that having the life that you want doesn't mean having a perfect life. The objective is having a life that is so amazing that even on dark days, it fits right into the pattern of things. By acknowledging what is important to you, you allow yourself to develop positive solutions to the things that might be causing you emotional problems. When we deny ourselves what we want without developing self-awareness, the problem doesn't fade away or disappear. It simply builds up to a point where it becomes toxic. It is like covering a can of spoiled milk. Just because it's covered up and tucked away in a corner doesn't mean that the milk stops being bad. It just gets worse. The same thing happens to our emotions when we don't tend to them properly.

In this chapter, we are going to look at the three core aspects of emotional health. We will start with self-awareness, which is knowledge of who you are. We will then explore self-esteem, which emphasizes how you feel about who you are. And finally, we have self-efficiency, which is basically how you service your feelings about yourself based on the knowledge you have about your identity to improve your life and make it better. Is this making you scratch your head a little bit? Hang in there. Everything will become clearer in a bit as we address these core areas one by one.

Self-Awareness

When you put aside your title at work, your relationship status, and whatever wealth you may or may not have accumulated throughout your entire existence, ask yourself, who are you? Many of us, for a lot of wrong reasons, have attached our identity to the things that we own, the people we associate with, and the work we do. These are all important in their own way. The relationships you have provide you with the unit you need to thrive. The work you do gives expression to your skills and talents. The things you own are basically your way of expressing delight and joy. However, no matter how grand, amazing, or terrible all these things are, they cannot give depth or definition to your identity. That is something that comes from within.

We live in a world that is obsessed with labels, but we shy away from the most important label all of us carry - the label of self. These other labels that we choose to carry come with expectations. There is the single mum label, the patient wife label, and the independent woman label, just to mention a few. While these labels may fit us perfectly, we tend to attach more meaning to the social expectations that come with these labels. For example, there is a societal expectation of what a successful woman should look like. As a result, many of us are unable to identify as successful because we feel that we don't fit into that image of success. This is where self-awareness comes into play. It is imperative that you know what your goals are in life.

I am not talking about goals that you inherited from your parents or people that you looked up to. I am talking about goals that give you a sense of purpose and a sense of accomplishment. These are goals that tend to your innermost needs and desires. They come from a place of selfish expectations. The word 'selfish' used to make me cringe before, and that was because I only associated it with negative emotions. However, when you start your self-reflective journey and look inwards, you cannot honestly do a good job of it without being a little selfish. This means disregarding the messages you have been groomed with right from when you were a child and focusing solely on your needs and wants. It is from this place that we can now define what our goals are. It is from here you can truly paint a picture of what you want your future to look like, and it is here that you will begin to see the blessings you already have.

So, take the time to get to know yourself. Don't rush the process. Don't sweep anything under the rug. Ask those pertinent questions. Be honest in your answers and layer by layer, you will reveal the person hiding behind the unnecessary labels.

Self-Esteem

Knowing who you are is one aspect of your journey. How you feel about this person you now know is a completely different story. Your self-esteem is basically your feelings towards your perception of self. If you don't feel good about who you are, you are bound to experience poor self-esteem. Poor self-esteem is not a direct result of the absence of certain things in your life. It is the dissatisfaction or our inability to truly accept the real and honest version of ourselves. It is possible to accept who you are and then decide to make changes so that you can grow into the person you want to become. However, if you focus solely on becoming a totally different person without trying to be more self-aware and understanding who you are, you may end up constantly making changes and never being satisfied.

Up until a few years ago, the beauty of being black was not deeply appreciated. In the media, people with light skin color were being appreciated over their counterparts. I remember being completely unaware that a particular country had people with darker skin shade until I visited. My misinformation was largely due to what was portrayed in the media. It wasn't surprising to find that brown boys and girls in that country felt the need to undergo cosmetic procedures to lighten their skin. As black women, we are constantly made to feel like we are not good enough no matter how hard we try. The struggle to succeed has become so 'normal' that we think it is okay for black women to work twice as hard as their colleagues just to get less than half of what they deserve.

The acceptance of unfair practices as the norm shouldn't minimize our self-discovery journey, but it does a terrible number on our self-esteem. We are made to feel like we should be competing against our peers when our only competition should be ourselves. Imagine running a race where everything is about the person running beside you. The crowd is waving their flags and chanting their names. Even the people officiating the race seem to be rooting for everyone but you. It gets to a point where you feel that the race is about them and you are invisible. That is what happens when you are not self-aware. You become invisible to the point where your self-esteem is non-existent. You need to stop and embrace every feeling you have about yourself...Good, bad...everything. This will help you embrace the idea of loving yourself at your worst and at your best. That is where the idea of unconditional love stems from. You don't need to be someone or something to appreciate your unique qualities. It is through the acceptance of every aspect of yourself that you can start building a healthy self-esteem.

Self-Efficiency

When you know who you are and how you feel about who you are, the next logical step on that journey is taking actions to get where you want to be. This is what self-efficiency is about. I used to think that self-efficiency was about performing some form of service for other people. Or being resourceful enough. However, in this context, it is much more than that. By understanding the knowledge you have gained about yourself and the feelings you have about that knowledge, you can take the necessary action to create the future you desire. Let's say you have become aware of your unhealthy eating habits and when you look at yourself in the mirror, you see the outcome of those eating habits. But instead of hating yourself for it, you come up with an actionable plan that will help you work towards the body you desire. This is what self-efficiency is about.

On your journey to becoming emotionally healthier, you need to learn to cater to your emotions. Catering to your emotions does not mean indulging in every feeling you have. Self-efficiency helps you cater to your emotions using knowledge as opposed to instinct. We do some things instinctively, but self-efficiency is about putting considerable thought into the actions we intend to take before we take them.

Practicing self-efficiency in emotional self-care can be as simple as letting go. Using the example of unhealthy eating habits, letting go of the repressed emotions you are trying to drown out with food is a self-efficient/sufficient act. It allows you to use your knowledge of the cause of the bad habit, and make changes by letting go. It also serves your self-esteem because you are no longer powerless to the urge to eat whenever you have an emotional crisis. Instead, you are putting yourself in a position of power by taking the right steps to become a much better version of yourself.

For me, self-efficiency is about staying true to my happiness, connecting myself to actions, thoughts, and words that empower me and make me feel visible in my world. Being self-sufficient is allowing yourself to be confident in your choices and goals. To be truly self-sufficient, you must let go of any past trauma that has defined you - it could be a mistake that you made or something that was done to you as a child or even as an adult. Holding on to pain makes it difficult for you to uproot the things in your life that have kept you caged in, and they will keep empowering your inner critic. Your inner critic convinces you that you can't do this or you shouldn't do that because of "imagined" reasons or experiences. Holding onto emotions like guilt only give your inner critic more material to use against you.

As we wrap up this chapter and move on, here is a task for you:

1. Do the work. Don't procrastinate. Don't try to rush it. Just do the work.

2. Embrace yourself. Literally. Hug yourself and be grateful for being you.

3. Let it go. The hurt, the disappointment, all of it. Let it go.

When you complete these tasks, you will find yourself at the end. The best part of the process is falling in love with who you are and the person you are becoming.

CHAPTER TWO

Building Your Perception of Self

After undergoing intensive self-evaluation, you may find yourself wanting in some areas. Just because you are meant to embrace every facet of who you are does not mean that you are perfect and without flaws. This acceptance is a critical part of the process of loving yourself unconditionally as self-love is not and should not be attached to certain expectations of one's self. However, self-improvement is an important part of the self-love journey. The love you express towards yourself doesn't involve just being kinder to yourself, but also wanting better for yourself.

This brings us to the subject of this chapter - building your perception of self.

Your perception of self will define your self-esteem. One of my favorite Instagram accounts features a duck that acts like a dog because it was raised among 5 dogs. When the duck is with his 5 brothers, the only people who think it's a duck are you and I. While the self-delusion of this sweet duck is not exactly a fine example, it highlights how your perception of self can inflate your confidence and help you stand strong against other people's opinions. When it comes to your identity, you are the only person with the right to control the narrative. People are entitled to their own opinions, but the person whose opinions ultimately define you is you.

In this chapter, we are going to learn how to separate your identity from other people's perceptions of who you are. You will shed those layers of your identity that are built on lies and other false representations. Raising your self-esteem is important. When you look into the mirror every day, does your reflection represent everything you are or everything you despise? The way you feel indicates how high or low your self-perception meter is.

By the end of this chapter, I want you to be able to think highly of yourself. Stop coming up with excuses to be anything less than the best. You deserve so much better, but you can't expect other people to do what you have failed to do for yourself. If you are ready to give your image a boost, let's start with the most obvious part: uncovering the lies.

Uncover the Lies

As black women, our identity is masked under layers of images projected onto us by other people. You start as daddy's girl. Then you become Paul's woman. If things go according to plan, you become Rebecca's mother. These kinds of tags are also found in official places. Your name is not enough for people. They put you in a box because it helps them feel like they've figured you out.

Instead of investing the time and effort it takes to know someone and then figuring them out, people prefer to identify you using official titles such as Ronson's PA or the company's accountant. These are not essentially wrong when you look at them from a very simple context. However, by placing these labels on you, there is also an expectation of how they think you should think and behave.

These expectations become the lies we use to clothe ourselves and they form an integral part of our identity. We no longer look at our situations logically because we believe there is a standard that has been set and we are supposed to live up to them based on the identity given to us. To be a daddy's girl, you are expected to depend on your father for virtually everything because the idea of an independent woman being a daddy's girl is unheard of. In the same way, the personal assistant of a prominent male figure is expected to bend to her boss's will even when they cross her personal space and, in some cases, abuse the employee/employer relationship. When you find yourself at a crossroad where your morals or value system do not align with the expectation of the identity you have been given, you start questioning yourself rather than the social ideals that put you in that box.

Questioning the social ideals that have put you in a mental quagmire helps you uncover what is real about you and what isn't. This is where you start questioning the reason people expect you to behave and speak a certain way because you are a black woman. You can be a daddy's girl and still be strong, fierce, and independent. It is possible to be a daddy's girl and not bow down to the patriarchy that expects you to be a helpless damsel-in-distress. Whatever position you occupy in society, the burden of responsibility falls on you to define how you interpret that role. Yes, there are standard expectations pertaining to the duties we are expected to perform. However, those roles should not form your identity. Understand your limitations physically and mentally, and then use that to determine how it plays into your identity. Don't let people push their own version of your identity on you.

Embrace the Truth

Have you ever entered an empty home and felt the presence of the people who were there before? My grandfather used to tell me that if you clear out a house and don't fill it up afterward, it will echo what was there before you took it out. In other words, if your sole purpose was to get rid of certain items in the house and you don't replace those items with the things you want, there will be an echo of what was there before. The only way to counteract it is to replace it with something else. In the same way, if you get rid of lies about yourself and you fail to fill up the empty spots with the truth, you will find yourself echoing the lies that were there before. Understand this; when you are in this mental warfare involving what society thinks of you vs what you think of yourself, truth and lies are the most utilized weapons. In the previous segment, our focus was uncovering lies, especially those involving social expectations based on the boxes placed over us by people in our immediate environment.

In this segment, you are encouraged to not only uncover what the truth is, but to embrace it. There is a general cliché; the truth hurts. This is only true to some extent. The truth is only harmful when its sole intention is to hurt the recipient of that truth. Now, this is a self-assessment task, and the objective is to empower yourself. Therefore, the truth you uncover during this process will not hurt you, but empower you. The process of increasing your self-power requires a little bit of unpleasantness, but not the kind that brings about pain. It simply takes you away from your comfort zone. When you confront yourself with certain truths about your identity, you may have to think uncomfortable thoughts. The only reason those thoughts are uncomfortable is because you were raised in a specific way, and the truth might force you to go against what you believe are your ideologies in life.

The truth forces you to broaden your perspectives. It gives you more than one view at a time and it is from these different perspectives that you get more information about the person you are. It's like having a high-performance computer in the hands of a person who is clueless about computers. They will use it for basic tasks, and the computer will never be utilized to its full potential. But in the hands of a tech whiz, that computer becomes a massive instrument for doing amazing things. That's what knowing the truth about yourself does. This in turn will help you build up your perception of self.

As strange as the truth may seem and as uncomfortable as it may feel, you need to put yourself in a frame of mind to accept this new truth. For example, women have been called the weaker vessel for years simply because society says so. However, when you look at your journey through life and the things that you have accomplished up to this point, you will find that there is power in being a woman. This truth may not feel comfortable to other people. It may not even feel comfortable for you, but if you are going to learn the new truth, you must embrace it.

Rebrand your Identity

Whenever I think of rebranding and identity, the first image that comes to mind is that of the Coca-Cola bottle. This is a brand that has been around for over a century, and they consistently put themselves out there. It is almost hard to believe that this was a drink invented by a doctor, exclusively sold in a pharmacy and that at one time it was believed to cure coughs. As the times evolved and policies changed, the company rebranded and made itself to be a drink that contained happiness. Whether this is true or not is not up for debate. This was a story they sold us, and the entire world bought into it because Coca-Cola is now a global brand. That is the power of rebranding your identity: you tell people your story, not the other way around.

So far, you have uncovered lies about who you are and exposed some truths about yourself. The next step in this journey is to merge the truth with your expectations for yourself. Word of caution - this is not where you go overboard with your ideas. What do I mean by going overboard? You may want to lose some weight. That is something to aspire to, but deciding to lose 50 pounds in 3 days is going overboard. You are free to dream. There is no need to put a limit on what you can be. Just make sure that the new identity does not end up breaking you in the process. If you are going to set a body goal or beauty goal, make sure that you are doing it for yourself. This is very important because we've just left a place where our identity was shaped by the opinion and perspectives of other people. Now that you have a chance to rebrand, don't repeat the same mistakes.

So, how do you rebrand? First of all, sit down. Take a minute and think about the woman you want to become. Picture how she lives her life every day from the moment she wakes up. Think about what time this woman wakes up, the kind of activities she indulges in from sunrise to sundown. Think about how she dresses and while you are picturing these things, imagine how you'd feel while doing those things. This is important because you are entering into a new age within yourself where your happiness is the priority. If you are going to live your life on your terms, your rebranding should be about becoming a person who makes you feel even better about yourself. The key to achieving this is to ensure that this new image is built on the truth about yourself and the things that trigger positive emotions. It should never be about what people think you should look or live like.

CHAPTER THREE

Attain Emotional Balance

Emotional balance in my opinion refers to the ability to effectively manage your emotions in an honest and healthy way. People think that not reacting to your emotions makes you emotionally balanced. Or the fact that you don't feel negative emotions speaks to your emotional maturity. This is all wrong. We are human. One of our defining markers as human beings is emotions. We are made to feel and experience life as it happens to us. And sometimes, we need to react to these emotions to fully explore the experiences around us. Failure to do so creates an imbalance in your emotional life and where there is an emotional imbalance, it is difficult for you to step into your identity as a powerful black woman who has healed from the trauma and is ascending into her awesomeness.

When I defined emotional balance, I used two words that the hallmark of true emotional balance; 'honesty' and 'healthy.' You need to be honest about what you are feeling and then ensure that you are reacting to those feelings in a healthy way. But before you can be honest about what you are feeling, you must be aware. And that is a theme that you will find throughout this book. You cannot afford to live your life in a default setting where you act and react on instinct. It is even worse when you realize that the instincts we are acting on were written in our DNA millions of years ago. This was at a time when life was completely different from the way it is now and the secondary foundation for our instinct is the environment that we find ourselves in. So, when you rely on instinct you are relying on outdated survival strategies biologically embedded in us. This means that you may not be acting on what is best for you.

In this chapter, I am going to explore what it means to be fully aware of what we feel. This includes asking the necessary questions of 'what.' Questions like, what am I feeling? Why do I feel this way? Through the answers that we get, we may be able to uncover the underlying fears that have held us bound and empowered the inner critic within us. When we are aware, we become honest about our feelings. It is crazy that we have made it okay to deny what we feel based on some social expectation placed on gender. For example, men are not supposed to cry and women are too emotional. So, because we want to avoid these labels, we deny our feelings. But no more. To attain emotional balance, you must be honest with what you are feeling and learn to react to those emotions healthily.

Confront your Fears

One of the craziest things I learned on my journey was the fact that fear is not a negative emotion per se. It is how we react to it that creates a negative experience. There is no true emotion that is negative. It is our reaction to them that causes the negativity. If you react to positive emotions like love and happiness negatively, you will get a negative outcome. And yes, it is possible to react to love negatively. However, this is not the subject of this chapter. Our focus is on this thing called fear. Oftentimes, when we are planted in an environment that takes us out of our comfort zone, the first emotion that emerges is fear and this fear has a way of pushing us to exercise caution before making a decision. Ultimately, it is about protecting your interests. When you understand that fear comes from a place of self-preservation, you start building a different attitude towards it.

You should realize that by protecting yourself, you are limiting yourself from fulfilling your potential, which means that fear has taken control. In such a scenario, fear is no longer serving you. It has become a hindrance. To counteract this, it is important to explore the fears that you have entertained in your life. Sometimes fear is a result of direct or indirect experiences. When you exercise caution in your dealings, pause to ask critical questions such as 'the whys.' Why are you doing this? Why are you not doing that? When you understand the reason behind your action, fear no longer becomes a barrier but rather an ally on your journey. You get to understand just how far you need to exercise caution. Is it going to take you to the first three steps or the next 50 steps? If you find that your fears are based on irrational things or outdated theories, then it is time to reevaluate your choices so that you can take the bold steps that you need to get to the next level.

People like to use grand terms such as slaying your dragons to define confronting your fears. It makes it seem as though you are doing something monumental, and this can hinder you from taking a step. The best way to approach this is to question yourself. Asking the right questions forces us to change perspectives and leads us to a credible reason. And until you can accurately identify a reason that resonates with your being, you must keep pushing forward. The scariest step is the first step you take. When you take that first step and realize that the fears are not what you made them out to be, it becomes easier to take the next step and the next one until you get to a conclusive end. Another fear you need to conquer is the fear of failure. A lot of black women hold themselves back because they are afraid of what will happen if they fail. You need to understand that failure is not a defining experience. It provides you with lessons if you look beyond the pain or negative emotions evoked by that failure. My mentor always told me that the fear of failure is the cage for potential. If you really want to be the woman you think you are meant to be, you must let go of this fear.

Take Down Those Emotional Walls

As women, when we experience a negative emotion because of heartbreak, betrayal, or disappointment, we resolve to shut down emotionally because we feel if we have our emotional walls up, nobody can hurt us. In theory, this sounds good. Take away the emotions and you take away the pain that these emotions cause. But the trade-off is that it deprives us of the privilege and joys of truly living life. Without emotions, we become empty entities who are just existing; unable to connect on a deeper level with the people around us. Yes, betrayal is painful. When you love someone and trust them and then they turn around and stab you in the back, that pain hurts like nothing else. But guess what? That is part of our experiences as humans.

Is it possible to live a life without heartbreak? Probably. But you would have to be the most cautious person in the world or the luckiest. However, if you spend your life protecting yourself from heartbreaks, you end up protecting yourself from other important emotions like genuine kindness, love, or happiness. You would find it difficult to let people into your life. It is the people that you let into your life who will give you rich memories to last you a lifetime. If you are going to silence your inner critic, you need to learn to take down those walls. it is scary to put yourself out there in a world that seems vile and full of hate. But you need to understand that there is also love out there. There are also people who will fill your life with so much enjoyment that you will thank the pain you experienced in the past because it led you to this point.

The truth is you deserve to live a life of joy. You deserve to love and be loved. You deserve to be in relationships with people who honor you and respect you. But those kinds of situations can only happen when you let yourself be loved. When you put up an emotional wall, you shut out the rest of the world. You may successfully shut out those negative emotions you are trying to avoid but you will certainly also shut out happiness. I am not saying that you cannot find happiness within. But if you are going to accept the truth, you must accept all of it. And one important truth is that we rely on our fellow humans for a full and healthy life experience. Just remember that letting down those emotional walls does not mean you have to be stupid about the choices you make. We will get to that in a subsequent chapter where you learn about setting healthy boundaries in any relationship. But for now, accept that opening yourself up is the only way you are going to be able to receive what you are expecting.

Be Vulnerable

One of my favorite movies to watch with my girls is *friends with benefits*. It is a movie that showcases the need for vulnerability in our relationships. These two people came together because they felt an immense attraction to each other. However, because of their past relationships and the negative experiences they had, they decided they wanted a relationship where emotions were strictly regulated. They were just going to be two people smashing whenever they felt the urge but without the emotional complications that come with relationships. The problem with this arrangement from the onset was the fact that they were friends first. When you are friends with someone, there is an emotional connection. It is a wasted effort to attempt to enter a 'situationship' with a friend.

It is like saying you are going to buy your favorite cake in the world, store it in the fridge and not eat it. Especially when you refuse to stock your fridge up with any alternative food. It is a disaster waiting to happen. Being vulnerable in today's world is often interpreted as being weak. People think that being vulnerable sets you up for disappointment. Yet when they get into relationships, they expect people to be able to read their minds, know what they want, and offer it to them. This is impossible. Being vulnerable is about expressing your expectations to others. It is as simple as that. Now, being vulnerable doesn't mean loving someone to stupidity. That is just dumb behavior. Let's say, for example, you sign up on a dating app. On such platforms, you will find all kinds of people; people who just want to have sex, people who want to have conversations, and even people with more sinister objectives.

Being vulnerable on such a platform is not putting up your house address and your monthly income details so that people know you for what you have. That is crazy. The right way to be vulnerable is to let people know what you expect out of whatever relationships you form. Sure, some people may want to prey on this information you have provided so that they can get what they want from you. We will talk about this in another chapter. But for now, remember what we said about the fear of failure and how that cages your potential. When you decide to withhold information that is critical to the success of any relationship you build because you are afraid that someone is going to take advantage of it, you are killing the potential to find a prospective date. This applies to other areas of your life. Being vulnerable is essentially putting your intentions out there and having the courage to stick to your principles by only settling for what you want. Nothing more and nothing less. Being vulnerable is a different kind of strength and as we go into the next chapter to discuss the darkness within, you will understand just how powerful being vulnerable is.

CHAPTER FOUR

The Battle Within

To become an empowered black woman who not only survives the world we live in today but thrives amid the chaos, you must look inward for strength. However, because of our messed-up backgrounds, crazy experiences, and even crazier self-imposed expectations, there is a war raging within that must be won if we are going to give ourselves a chance in this life. This war is borne out of an emotional conflict that arises when our sense of self clashes with the projection of other people's expectations of us.

In this chapter, we are going to look at three major sources of this battle: anxiety, depression, and anger. Almost every black woman that I know has had their life's experiences clouded by one or all these emotions.

We are made to feel like there are specific things we must have and without them, we cannot be considered wholesome. For example, a woman in her thirties, unmarried, and without children is often regarded as incomplete, and this lack of completeness makes us feel like failures. By our own standards, we can call ourselves successful and accomplished women. But in the presence of other people, our accomplishments diminish because there is an expectation of who we should be, and this leaves us worried. As if our black girl struggles aren't enough today, our pain is often silenced. There are cases of black women who go missing for months and years before law enforcement agencies take the reports seriously. This lackadaisical attitude towards our welfare and absence of safety damages us physically and emotionally. And worse, because we are often put in this situation by the very people who are supposed to have our best interest at heart, this creates another form of anxiety.

However, I want you to know that because this is a common experience doesn't mean that it has to define your personal experience as a black woman. Yes, there are social prejudices, injustices, and other things that we will talk about in this book. But for now, you should put the focus on yourself, your journey, your experience, and how you can tackle what is going on within. This way, you can get to the light that is inside you and through that light, illuminate your essence and share that light with the rest of the world. That is the objective of this book. At the end of the day, I want to see you shine. I want to see you rise above your fears, your failures, and whatever limitation society has placed on you. I want you to be able to open your mouth and tell the world, "I am a successful black woman," and mean it with every fiber of your being. To do that, we must tackle these three emotions that have eaten into the heart of our community as black women.

Anxiety

Anxiety has become a buzzword in our world. It is so common for people to use the word that you would be forgiven for assuming that it is a trend. However, as "trendy" as it may sound, anxiety is something that has been around for eons. The major difference between past and present anxiety is that it is documented a lot more now. Also, people own up to their anxiety. But what exactly is this anxiety? And how/why is its impact on the black community, particularly its women, so vital to your transformation journey? Before we get into it, let me remind you that I am no expert on the subject. I am coming at it from my experience as well as those of people close to me. The clinical data on anxiety can be found on the internet, in books, and so on. Anxiety in lay terms from the perspective of someone who lived with it for years and learned to manage is what you are going to get here. So, with that in mind, let us get into it.

In my opinion, anxiety is the body's exaggerated response to worry and concern. However, it is not as simple as it sounds. Nothing ever is. When you are anxious, your biological fight or flight response is activated. Your emotions are so alert that they initiate a physical response. That worry and concern are expressed as elevated heart rate, short breaths, and other accompanying physical symptoms. It is interesting to note that this fear is not always based on reality. It is often either your mind reliving an experience or anticipating a negative outcome. I am not great at social interactions. I love being around people, but the thought of talking to people verbally or nonverbally makes me anxious. The root cause of my anxiety was tumbling down on stage when I was 7. Every time I get thrown into a social situation, I fear that I am going to end up falling flat on my face. In essence, my anxiety is not based on real-time events. Generally, anxiety latches on to fear, amplifies it, and then cripples you from the inside.

In our community, we believe in actual events. When you are anxious because there is the presence of real danger or cause for concern in your environment, you get sympathy from people. But reacting to the concern without any physical evidence to support the cause for your worries will attract criticisms and harsh judgments that will further trigger your anxiety. Many black women have to appear strong. We are encouraged to suppress our fears when the only outcome is the massive growth of those fears leading to years of emotional torture. The objective shouldn't be to ignore your fears, but refusing to let them control your actions. We must teach ourselves to explore our fears. Uncover their source and the rationale behind them. Listen to your body. Don't judge yourself based on what you think other people are going to think or say. Most importantly, don't doubt yourself. Your fears and concerns are real. But they should not take control of your life.

Depression

Life is full of ups and downs. This is a slogan that you have probably come across. Depression kind of works the same way, except there are more lows than highs. Being sad occasionally is perfectly normal. It is a natural response to the pain of loss. And loss is something we all deal with at some point in our lives. The gravity of loss we experience will determine how much grieving we go through. But our ability to effectively manage our sadness. Without this ability, when we hit those low points in life, our reaction to it would drag us even lower. Depression is like a constant dark cloud on what should be a bright and sunny day. Some people have described it as a constant weight on their shoulders. Like drowning with weights attached to the feet. It is a horrible description but the sense of helplessness that comes with it makes it even worse.

Our community is riddled with losses. Preventable but painful losses nonetheless. The racial injustice and prejudices which make day-to-day living tedious has become "acceptable." In fact, some people go as far as justifying such treatment being meted out to people they consider different. When you take into consideration the challenges that come with life generally and being a black woman, the odds are stacked against you. This creates a perfect environment for overwhelming sadness that may transform into depression. Because virtually everyone is experiencing the pain of loss, we are unable to console each other, much less ourselves. As a result, we slowly become masters in the art of mourning. We learn to cope with the pain but rarely learn to heal. Sadly, we pass on this lifestyle of mourning to the next generation, and the cycle continues. This doesn't have to be your story.

Overcoming depression is not about getting over your pain. It lies in true healing. The cliche, "time heals all wounds" cannot be true if you do not use the time to initiate the steps to healing. Burying your pain can provide reprieve but it does not give you the necessary skills to efficiently manage pain, loss, and grief. If you are going to get past that negative inner voice, you must learn to manage your reaction to the downs and low points in life. Grief or loss management is an essential life skill to reach our full potential. I wish that life was all roses and no thorns. But if you only mentally prepare yourself for the good parts in life, you leave yourself exceptionally vulnerable when those not-so-great parts come along.

Anger

Anger is an emotion that has gotten a negative rap. People feel that anger is something that shouldn't be experienced at all when in reality, it is crucial for a healthy life experience. Anger is a biological way of letting you know that someone has violated your rights. It doesn't always mean that you are right. It just means that you have certain subconscious lines and someone may have crossed them, making you angry. Anger is not bad. As I said, I don't believe in negative emotions. However, our reaction to these emotions is what we qualify as negative or positive. When you flare up in anger and aggressively attack other people, your anger becomes negative. But when you learn to manage anger effectively and react to it appropriately, your anger becomes a powerful ally.

Our current perspective regarding anger is fueled by what we have witnessed in our community. We see anger in its raw and excessive form. This makes it difficult for us to understand this complex emotion and learn how to manage it. We are not supposed to silence our anger or pretend it's not real. At the same time, we are not supposed to give in to the rage that we feel every time it comes over us. In our community, we frown upon the concept of anger management because we believe it connotes weakness. Ironically, it is the excessive display of rage that is often applauded, especially in men. In women, it is entertained. They call us spicy for being expressive with our anger until we slight them. Then they call us bitches. Neither of these attitudes is healthy. We need a more beneficial approach to addressing our anger.

As a black woman, I understand your anger. We have been unjustly treated by society. The men that are supposed to love and protect us end up abusing us and this has created a lot of anger. Not to mention the anger that we inherited from the pains our ancestors experienced. We have a lot of healing to do as a community. But before we get to that point, we need to start by healing individually. The healing process begins with understanding how to manage your feelings, especially anger. It is okay to be angry but don't let it get to the point of rage. In the process of managing your anger, you should try not to put the expectations of other people before your feelings. Yes, anger should be controlled. But don't forget that anger lets you know when your personal space or lines have been violated.

It is important to react (in a healthy way of course) so that you can set those boundaries and maintain a space that is conducive for your mental and physical health. Don't entertain the antics of other people simply because you want to manage your anger. Be rational in your reaction but ensure that you do acknowledge that emotion, its cause, and perhaps the solution. And speaking of causes, one of the underlying root sources of the anger that is embedded deep into our community today is the racial wall that has forced us to live like outcasts within our own community. People look at us and resort to their prejudices and biases before getting to know us. This has led to unfair treatment and a lot of injustice. I don't have to outline the struggles we have had to face in various societies simply because of the color of our skin. The next chapter educates us on how to manage social expectations based on skin color and gender. It doesn't excuse the behavior or attitude society has towards us. It simply educates us on how to function and thrive under those ugly circumstances.

CHAPTER FIVE

The Race War

Humans are communal by nature. We are biologically programmed to share our spaces with each other. However, some conditions must be met for this to happen. One of those conditions is sharing similarities. We erroneously believe that to tolerate and live peacefully with each other, we must look, think, and act alike. Anyone different from us is an outsider and therefore not deserving of the benefits of being a part of a community. As disheartening as this sounds, this is not even the worst part. For some reason, we have decided that certain qualities merit a person having or being worth more than others. These qualities are embedded in the color of our skin, the size of our wallets, and even in the language we speak.

The idea that one race is inherently superior to another has led to world wars. And even though we have extinguished the flames of the last three wars, the battle continues. There are people who feel that they are entitled to specific benefits simply because their skin has a lighter hue. They strongly believe that people with darker skin color are inferior and next to animals. Therefore, they shouldn't be a part of society. This led to the birth of a system that actively antagonizes people of color. This is ironic because we live in a society that is diverse and evidently, one that has benefited immensely from our diversity. Yet, some people feel that those benefits should be allocated to white people.

There have been several attempts to raise awareness about this injustice. Our ancestors as well as people who have noticed the absurdity of this race war have protested for hundreds of years. But still, it prevails in society. The statistics that highlight the impact of the racial war against people of color are mind-boggling and baffling. Our community has suffered losses, pains, heartaches, and severe mental breakdowns. Despite speaking out against people who choose to oppress us, not much has changed. Granted, things aren't the same as they used to be, but change has been terribly slow. However, some people have managed to thrive under such conditions without losing their sense of self and integrity. In this chapter, we are going to learn how to do the same.

Damaging Social Misconceptions

Our first opinion of self is developed during the first few years of our existence. The people we interact with and the community we live in plays a huge role in defining our perception of self. I talked about this earlier and now you'll see how this plays out. There are a lot of damaging social misconceptions about being a black woman. And because these things are repeated in the content we consume, it is not surprising that many of us absorb these messages and use them as our identity. I am going to talk about three of some of the most damaging social misconceptions about women of color.

1. Tolerating Abuse is a Mark of Strength

Black women are inherently strong. This is one of our superpowers. We are physically, emotionally, and mentally strong. However, the definition of that strength has been miscommunicated to us. When we are put in relationships, one of the things that is expected of us is long-suffering with emphasis on the last part. A woman of virtue is described as a woman who endures all the excesses of her husband in the hopes of having his love as a reward for her endurance.

Loyalty is preached in relationships but in our community, it is a lopsided expectation in the sense that women are expected to be loyal to their men. But the same loyalty is not required from the men. A lot of black women are put in relationships where their partners abuse them physically, mentally, and emotionally and the moment she says she's had enough she is bullied for her decision because society feels she is not displaying strength. This kind of collective thinking has left a lot of women trapped in marriages and relationships that degrade them and make them question their instincts, their emotions, and their sanity. This abuse empowers that negative inner voice we are trying to get rid of. True strength lies in one's ability to relentlessly pursue their goals regardless of the obstacles in their way. It is your ability to rise above your circumstances, not in your ability to endure the cruelty of others.

2. Black Women Are Inferior Species

I am happy that black women are beginning to rediscover the magic we carry within. However, the scars left behind by centuries of racial abuse have embedded the concept of black women being inferior in the minds of a lot of people, including members of our community. Our beauty, our culture, our features, and everything about us is ridiculed because of the color of our skin. With years of reinforcing the same message, it is not surprising that many of us have accepted the idea that we are inferior to women with different skin colors.

We feel that to be accepted, we need to change the way we look and modify our features so that we can blend in with the rest of the world. This is wrong. You are beautiful.

You are powerful. Your beauty is the stuff poets write about. If you go to the Bible and read the Songs of Solomon, he was talking about a beautiful black woman. Do you see the lyrics used in that piece? It describes beauty like no other. You need to start seeing yourself in a different light. Woman, you are beautiful.

3. Black Women Are Bound to Fail.

My favorite quote of all time is, "Whether you can or you can't, you are right." Because of the way society has been set up, social structures support people with skin tones different from ours. Meaning that from the moment they are born, they are given the right resources to help them get to their destination effortlessly. People of color, on the other hand, are deprived of basic necessities, making our journey twice as hard and more likely to fail. However, you need to understand that the absence of those resources does not automatically determine the outcome of your life. You are the biggest factor that determines how far you go in life. Yes, it would be easier if you had those resources at your disposal. And yes, we need to work twice as hard just to get by. But that is where our inherent strength comes to play.

While we are working together towards building a society that provides equal opportunity for every one of us, we must forge our own path under the tough circumstances laid out before us. Our strength must be channeled into furthering ourselves mentally, physically, and financially. Just because we were handed a tough lot in life does not excuse us from trying to be better than we were before. The idea that you are bound to fail simply because society has robbed you of your rights is damaging. Correct that by recognizing what you have and channeling it for your greater good.

The Crippling Effects of Racism

Racial discrimination is something that people of color are intimately familiar with. It is a part of our daily experience. So, I am going to spare you the problems and focus on the areas that are related to the reasons you bought this book.

1. Negative Stress

Racial discrimination triggers stressors in our environment that make it difficult for us to truly live on terms that are favorable to us. Picture this; you are in the middle of a beautiful day. The weather is perfect, your co-workers are all on their best behavior, you are feeling fly in your favorite outfit...in fact, everything is going swimmingly well. And then suddenly, an angry white person calls you a dressed-up monkey. It doesn't matter how amazing your day was. Everything goes downhill from this point onwards. Your tongue starts to feel like a thousand needles are stuck into it, there is a sinking feeling in your stomach and your sweat glands start overcompensating. This is negative stress. It has a paralytic effect.

2. Self-Sacrifice

To survive this harsh climate, we have been forced to put other people's thoughts and opinions before and above our own. This kind of lifestyle has been so glorified that any thought of deviating is met with labels such as selfish or self-serving. The reason for accepting this way of life is to either form alliances that aid our survival or establish a safe environment for us to survive. In other words, we trade our identity so that we can have access to the most fundamental human right; the right to live. The racial profiling that is prevalent in society has caused many of us to sacrifice ourselves leading to distortion and dissatisfaction with who we are. When you are out of touch with your true self, your ability to reach your full potential is grossly limited.

3. Self-Reliance

This sounds like a good thing, and in some ways it really is. But when it happens under our current social conditions, it can have a crippling effect on communal growth. Self-reliance entails depending on yourself. As humans, we all need to have this basic life coping skill. However, if it is borne out of an environment that generates deep mistrust in other people, it becomes a hindrance rather than a step in the developmental process. We are communal by nature. A few pages ago, I talked about how our formative years are defined by the community. You can thrive alone, but you need a tribe to truly enjoy life. Over-dependence on self can lead to mental and physical isolation. The shared community space becomes a poisonous well that keeps breeding distrust leading to some of the social ails that are evident in black communities today. This holds us back as individuals and as groups.

Finding Your Place in Society

Given everything we have learned so far, finding your place in society is key for the next step on your journey. And to do that, you must exercise some form of awareness. To know the problem is to solve it. If you have or are exhibiting any of the characteristics listed in this chapter, you have created awareness in part. You still need to do a lot of research and perhaps seek psychological counseling to help you understand why you act the way that you do. Just make sure that in your search, you don't work with people who either try to justify the unfair treatment you have experienced or minimize your pain. You have come too far to go back to the diet of lies and poor palliative measures drummed up by people who want to be heroes. Be aware of the truth, of who you are, of where you have come from, and the reasons behind each of these truths. Don't worry about where you are going. That is another step on this journey.

The next step is to accept the truth. Again, this is something I talked about earlier, and is a prerequisite for this part of the journey. Embracing the truth about who you are allows you to create pathways for the solution. The longer you deny the truth, the tighter the cycle that keeps you trapped to the point where the web of lies becomes your life. The truth is not always easy to accept. Sometimes, it is unpleasant. The idea that we are victims of a society that was supposed to help us become victors is not something that is easy to swallow especially when you lay that knowledge against the background of racism. That we missed out on several opportunities simply because of the color of our skin is enough to make any sane person boil with anger and resentment. But that is the truth, plain and simple. It doesn't mean that society is out to get you and ruin you. This is a system that has been in place for hundreds of years. Until the fabric that makes up society is changed, that is just the way the machine works.

However, you are not a machine. You are human. You are a woman, and you are black. That means a lot. Regardless of the psychological messaging you may have been fed, you have a place in society. You are important. You matter. Not just to the people who brought you into this world or who nurtured you, but to the world. Your role might be small, but without that void being filled up, the world would be 'less.' But with your presence and with you working in your power, the world becomes richer. It took a long time for me to get this message. I felt like I was too insignificant to matter to anyone. It was like if I vanished today, there was no one who really cared. This thought made me feel trapped. I didn't want to die because I was afraid of how isolated my death would be. But at the same time, living was tough because I still felt isolated.

Sometimes it feels that way especially when you are put in a competitive environment where it feels like everyone else is doing better than you. Imagine your legs tied up with a rock attached to it and then being forced to run a race (under threat of death) against people who are driving cars. Sounds impossible right? This is the reality for black women today. This is why it is remarkable that some of us even succeed at all. I believe that this speaks to the strength and magic of being a black woman. You need to key into this. If you continue to walk in the light of your truth and in the understanding of your worth, you will realize that you have a place. At the end of this book, you will also find your voice. For now, you are going to take things into the next chapter where we talk about finding purpose in who you are.

CHAPTER SIX

Expanding and Finding Purpose in Your Blackness

I used to be strongly offended when people started sentences with the phrase, 'you black people' or 'you black women.' It was almost as if somewhere along the line, I became a collective and my identity was irrelevant. But over time, I understood that I have prejudices of my own (we will get to that soon). I also learned to understand that people who phrased things like this were often prejudiced. They have a vague notion of what a particular set of people are supposed to look and act, and they impose this on everyone with similar features. Sometimes, their notions are based on prior experience, but they refuse to individualize that experience. Rather they use the lessons from that experience to characterize every person they meet. It is kinda like the same way people travel to one country in Africa, visit a specific locality, and declare that entire Africa is the same as the place they visited. It used to drive me crazy.

This was until I had a conversation with someone who I consider a mentor. According to her, when you have a negative experience, your brain subconsciously analyzes the environment and points out what it considers the key instruments for initiating that trauma. This becomes your trigger. So, whenever you are put in an environment where those key elements pop up together in a specific pattern that your brain interprets as dangerous, it triggers an alarm. When this behavior or thought process is repeated constantly, it becomes your truth. People have associated black culture with negative triggers. They see a man with long dreads and feel that he cannot be professional. They see a woman with a big, curvy body and analyze it to the point where the woman is sexualized against her will. Our music, dressing, and even the way we socialize have been given negative labels, making it difficult for us to freely associate with our blackness.

This chapter is about learning to take charge of that narrative. Changing people's perceptions of you is a task that will take a very long time. However, changing your perception of yourself is something you can start working on right now. Not only will it enhance your experience in life generally, but it will also help you embrace every aspect of who you are. It will help you find purpose in who you are. If you have been running away from yourself because of what other people think about you, this is the part where you stop, take a closer look, embrace it, and start believing in it. Your blackness should not be defined by society. You are the only one that should determine what being black means to you. You have been given the necessary tools to get started on that journey. The magic and strength that come with being black are already in your veins. Now is the time to use it to propel yourself forward and achieve your full potential.

The Truth About Being Black

Here is a simple assignment I want you to carry out. Get on your browser and search the phrase, 'black women are...' Leave it at that and then click search. Chances are your top 10 searches are going to contain negative commentaries about black women. I did it and my search results included conversations about how women are advancing in the marketplace, but women of color are lagging. There was also talk about how black women are victims of sexual assault, abuse, and so on. This is the image they have of you and me as black women; victims that can be taken advantage of. They don't tell you that one of the richest self-made women in America is a black woman. You don't get to see that kind of representation. Instead, they try to project what they want you to see in yourself. Thankfully, there is a way to combat these lies, and that is by using the truth.

Social activists use the word "representation" a lot, and there is a reason for that. When you see yourself reflected in a positive light in society, there is a ripple effect that trickles down to those in grassroot environments who may be stuck in tough conditions without hope. But when they see someone like them doing great, they can be inspired and be given hope/strength to push further. You need to start being more proactive when it comes to building or creating black women's representation in your life. Here is what I mean. Start by looking at a list of people who inspire you. Go over their track record. Let their proven success be a positive trigger in your mind. You will get a lot of negative news about an experience a black woman is having somewhere. Don't let that be your only representation in the media. For every negative message you get, replace it with a positive one.

Black women are doing amazing things, and they didn't start today. Whether in the field of science, activism, media, or religion, you will find powerful and influential black women who pioneered change during their time. The problem is not that black women are not present in these situations. It is the lack of reporting, or rather underreporting, that has undermined their efforts. While we wait for the world to get off their seats and do what is needed, it is our job to be proactive in searching out these women and giving them the credit that they deserve. This is not just for the people who are getting these accolades. It is also for us to validate our power, strength, and brilliance. But most importantly, it is to help pave the way for those who are coming after us so that they might look up and see the light that will lead them to their next destination. We must start teaching ourselves and the next generations that we are more than our circumstances. This is the truth about being black. We are more than our skin. We are bigger than our limitations and we are definitely not the people society paints us out to be.

Why Your Blackness Should Be Celebrated

The celebration I am talking about here is not the collective one we hear about like the holidays dedicated to our heroes. I am referring to the private celebrations. We know that there is black history month dedicated to educating and celebrating the history of black people. But celebrating your blackness is about acknowledging things about you that are linked to your roots. The way you talk, the texture of your hair, the color of your skin; all these things weave a biological story about where you come from, and you should celebrate it. History has not always favored black people because the people who wrote history were biased. However, you are the one in charge of your narrative. And yes, you may be biased toward yourself, but I will take that over destructive self-criticism any day. The point is you have a chance to rewrite your story. Are you going to focus on the scared black girl that everyone thinks you should be? or the strong black woman that you are?

Girl, you have survived extreme odds to get to this point. The fact that you are sitting with this book in your hands is a testament to what you have had to go through. Don't ever take your victories for granted no matter how little they are, especially on your quest to heal and find your confidence. You must learn to celebrate your wins. We think that until we hit those huge milestones in our lives, we haven't accomplished much. This kind of thinking will make you feel like a hamster on a wheel. You just push yourself and spin round and round for no absolute purpose. But when you enjoy each moment and savor every win, you empower yourself with confidence, making it easier for you to walk with your head held high because you are aware of who you are and what you have achieved. You know the doors you had to break down to create opportunities for yourself and you know that you are going to open doors for other black girls. This is worth celebrating.

Most importantly, you are going to celebrate your blackness because those things that people taunted you about have now become your most prized features. Some people say that black people dress funny. Well, that fashion sense is what you are going to celebrate today. Even if you don't dress the way society thinks black people should be dressing, it is still okay to celebrate and recognize it. This is a big part of where you are coming from, and is a part of who you are. Your strong black features like your nose, your eyes, your lips, and your body are things you are going to celebrate. It is time for you to take a bold step towards the mirror, look into it as you strip off all your clothes and tell yourself, "Damn, I am beautiful." Celebrate the color of your skin whether you are brown or black. Being a black woman means you come in different colors, shapes, and sizes. Celebrate this difference. Celebrate the ways that your body and features contribute to the diversity among black people. Celebrate your name. Whether it is the more 'acceptable' names or the ones that we are known to answer. This is who you are. There is no shying away from it. Embrace it and don't just embrace it. Celebrate it.

Gain Mastery Over Your Narrative

This last part of this chapter is a pivotal defining moment for you because until you take this step, the rest of the chapters in this book are going to be futile. It is time for you to take charge of your narrative. You must first learn to make peace with who you are. Whether you are big or skinny, whether you are a deep shade of black or a lighter shade of black, you must disassociate your sense of worth from these physical markers and then work towards accepting yourself as you are. Even if you intend to make changes in the future such as probably losing weight, the first step in that process is learning to love yourself. If you starve yourself of self-love because you feel you are now at a place where you think you should be, you create a template for the relationships you are going to have with other people because you are subconsciously sending the message that until you jump a certain hoop, you are not worthy to be loved.

For this reason, you must tell your story differently. You have heard a lot of things about yourself. Some of it has been positive. Some of it, negative. Now this is where you key into those positive reviews you have gotten about yourself and then tune out the negatives. Focus on positive feedback. Let that message stir up that good vibe inside you. Use the emotions that come from it to inspire a new list of positives. Let this become your affirmation. I am strong. I am beautiful. I am powerful. I am wise. These are just a few of the affirmations you can use to change your narrative. You are not what society says you are. I have said this several times in this book, but the reason I repeat it is that these false narratives have been repeated from the day you were born. And to counteract it, we must repeat the truth. You are your own person and that is perfectly okay.

At some point in this journey, you will experience a broad range of emotions. You might start out with sadness before experiencing boiling rage. This is okay. Identify those emotions and acknowledge them. Let them stew up a little so that you can understand where your pain is coming from. The moment you get clarity, you should find a way to channel those emotions. Either through journaling, working out, or even just taking a nice long walk on a sunny day. I baked my feelings. Find what works for you. This will help you purge the negativity surrounding these emotions and help you see a brighter path. It is from this path that you can now begin the next phase of your journey.

In the next chapter and the chapters after it, our focus is going to be on you as an individual and as a woman. So, approaching that with a clear head and stable emotion is important. If you find yourself struggling to move on from the information you have absorbed in these past chapters, you might want to talk to someone about it. That is another thing we have to learn to embrace in our community - prioritizing mental health. It is part of changing the narrative. Your mind is just as important as your body. So, when you find yourself struggling mentally, don't hesitate to seek help. It doesn't make you weaker, and fighting your pain alone doesn't make you stronger. While we learn about our history, we will uncover the mistakes that people who came before us have made. We have paid the price by growing up under the consequences of their actions. However, we don't have to live with those consequences or let them determine our stories going forward. We can heal ourselves so that the impact can flow down to the people who come after us.

CHAPTER SEVEN

Identify Your Worth

The only person that can determine your worth is you. People will have an opinion of what they think you should be worth, but it will always be just that; their opinion. What stands out is what you say about yourself. In this chapter, our main objective is to help you determine your worth. In this context, we are not looking at what you should expect to be paid at your job or business. We are working on developing a strong idea of how you feel you deserve to be treated. Confidence comes from knowing who you are and what you are worth. You can walk into any room regardless of the atmosphere and still feel bold enough to be yourself while making the people in the room feel comfortable being around you. Knowing your worth is not undermining the worth of others to establish yours. It is having a keen sense of awareness.

Some people have built their confidence around breaking down the confidence of other people. This is a temporary fix and is only going to lead you to the path of bullies in society. True confidence comes from taking all the necessary steps and putting in the work and that is what we are going to try and do in this chapter. When you are trying to build your confidence after healing from trauma, one of the first things that goes out of the window is your sense of self-worth. Depending on what spectrum your personality lands on, whether you are narcissistic or reclusive, that worth could be overinflated or underestimated. Neither works well for your image, especially when you plan on working with other people.

Eventually, we will get to the part where you figure out how to deal with your personal struggles while working with other people. For now, we are trying to build a solid image for you from the inside out. This is an area where people usually make a grave mistake. They start by trying to build confidence from the outside in. Nothing wrong with that, but it doesn't last long. When you start the process from the inside, you build a solid foundation that can carry you through the toughest circumstances. Confidence that relies on external factors is very superficial. Things like making your hair, getting new clothes, working on your body size, and so on are all external factors. I am not saying that it is not important. Of course, it plays a role. But if you don't work on the stuff that is inside, all that effort you put on the outside is going to be wasted. On that cheerful note, let us begin.

Who Are You?

As black women, our identity is hidden under layers of labels and social tags given to us by society. It is almost as if from the day we made our debut on earth, the rest of the world decided that we weren't good enough from the start. Our hair is meant to be styled a certain way to be presentable. Anything less is considered wild and untamed. They control our speech and our ability to procreate (the latter was done in some form). But no matter how much they try to silence us, that black girl sauce comes through on the other side making more people want to be like us. This is a clear demonstration of the fact that we have something inside of us that is worth emulating. The best part? This thing that we all share is unique to each of us. What sister girl A has is different from what sister girl B has and so forth.

You just need to find out what your own brand of black girl magic is. Remember, we are different, but we all bring something to the table. The next line of action is figuring out what your "it" factor is. To do this, silence those voices in your head that tell you who should be and who you shouldn't. Especially when those voices create conflict every time you make a simple decision. Voices that say things like girls are not supposed to do this, girls don't do that, and so on are only there to bring you down. They speak based on the repeated negative messages they have received for the most of their life. These voices don't know the real you. And as of right now, you don't know who you are either. So, if you wanted to get to know a person better, what would you do? Ask questions. Start with the simple stuff like the 'what' type of questions. What do you like? What is your favorite color? What inspires you? The list is endless, but keep at it.

After these types of questions, you move on to the 'why' questions. Why do you like cheese so much? Why do you prefer morning runs to nighttime workouts? These questions will help you probe deeper into your mind. The deeper you go, the more intimate knowledge you will uncover. Another way to get to know yourself better is to teach yourself to rely on your instincts. No matter how much programming we undergo, there is a biological language that your body never forgets and that is your instincts. The more you use your instincts, the more reliable it becomes until it is one of the more reliable voices in our heads. Your instincts will snitch on your partner when they start cheating on you. The same instincts alert you when something is off. And when you want an extra shot of confidence, guess what? Your instincts. In very simple terms, ask yourself questions, but don't question your judgment.

Raise Your Standards

We have already established the fact that you deserve the best in life. However, just because you deserve it doesn't mean you are going to get it. You still need to require it. The reason a lot of people disrespect you is because you have not made it a requirement for them. In the book, "Think like a man, Act like a woman," one of the common questions that people asked was why their men hadn't taken their relationship to the next level. The response that Steve Harvey gave was that the women in that position have not made it a requirement. What does this have to do with anything we are talking about? Basically, if you want to enjoy the best of life, you need to raise your standard, and the standard is not limited to material things. Just because we talk about raising standards today doesn't mean that tomorrow you will be required to wear only designer outfits. I said it before, the outward stuff is superficial and can only take you so far. It is the stuff that goes on inside that we need to build on.

Raising your standard is determining within yourself to demand better treatment. When people talk down on you, you don't engage them or entertain them. You put them on ignore. This will let them know consciously and subconsciously that if they want your attention, they need to do better. When you tolerate behavior that does not elevate you or befit your status as a black queen, you open the door for all sorts of disrespect. This is not just from men. It could also be from your fellow women. And it is not limited to romantic relationships. It happens in workspaces and social spaces as well. There are people that carry themselves with such grace and dignity that before you approach them, you find yourself adjusting your outfit so that you are presentable. Those people have created a standard with their expression, their movement, and speech. You know that you have to do better if you want to say something to them much, less expect them to respond.

In raising our standards, we also need to learn to change the narrative. People have concluded that black women who have standards are either difficult or materialistic. The reason is one of two things; the women in question were either unable to communicate what they wanted to achieve at the end of the day or they misunderstood what raising their standard means. This is why I talked about the designer outfit. You must understand that raising your standard doesn't mean you automatically become difficult to work with. It means that you choose people who choose you. If people are going to be reasonable with you, then you are going to be reasonable with them. People should not present unruly behavior and expect you to negotiate under such circumstances. You may lose some social or financial benefits here and there simply because you choose to stick to your standards. But in the long run, it will pay off. Eventually, word goes around that this woman does not take it from anyone.

Improve Yourself

Raising your standard is not a one-way street where you expect other people to treat you the way you want to be treated but release yourself from any responsibility in that process. You will also need to put in that work to help you elevate yourself to that level in your relationship. Here is what I mean, when you step into a work environment and you want the respect of the people on your team, you must mentally prepare yourself for the expectation that you are bringing something to the table. When you have nothing to offer, it is difficult for people to respect you. I know that this sounds unfair but that is the environment that we live in. The purpose of this book is not to help you create a fair and balanced world. It is the help you thrive in a world that is unfair and unbalanced. When you step into any environment, you have to come 'correct.' What do I mean? Whatever skill sets you to have on your resume must be twice as impressive. Never make the mistake of having a resume that is better than you are in person.

I am not saying that you should undersell yourself so that when you apply in person, you are better. I am saying you should improve yourself every single day. It is a lot of hard work, but this is the kind of hard work that pays off. Let say that you are in the tech field. Make sure that your fingers are on the pulse of everything related to the tech world. You don't need to be a master at everything but having more than basic knowledge of your field of expertise can make you a vital addition to any team in any organization. And when people see value in you, they automatically respect it. In the same way, your appearance speaks volumes about who you are as a person. As much as it is superficial, we cannot deny that we live in a superficial world. Most people judge a book by its cover because the simple truth is people are not that invested enough to want to flick past the cover of the book in other to get to the content unless they see a perfectly packaged cover that appeals to their visual senses.

Putting in the required work in developing available skills sets, learning valuable new things, and contributing to improve what you do is the internal work. Polishing your dress sense can provide a confidence boost and even give you access to a different crowd. Talk to a stylist if you are not sure about your current outfit combination. For the most part, your instinct will guide you in this department because you'll be drawn towards outfits that reflect your personality. This is key because no matter how dressed up you are, if it does not align with that inner personality, there is going to be a mix and match type of situation. It would be like putting gold on the snout of a pig. People can immediately sense when you are not authentic. Again, dressing in designer outfits from head to toe will not fix this. This is why you need to put all the ducks in a row so that by the time you're ready to put yourself out there, it all makes sense. Work on yourself internally and then progress to that outward expression of self. The combination of both would create a powerful black woman image that automatically commands the respect you deserve. Get this right and the next phase will be easier.

Our next chapter is going to focus on another core area that defines us as black women, and this is our friendships. Black women are known for their sister girls who uphold them during tough times and hype them up when their confidence is low. We have unique friendships that just bring joy to the heart whenever you witness it. But you have to be strategic in building those kinds of friendships and that is what we will be working on.

CHAPTER EIGHT

Build Your Circle

Show me your friends and I will tell you who you are. This is an old saying that rings true to this day. My mentor is fond of saying, 'your net worth is defined by your network.' Connect with the right kind of people and you will go very far in life. But if you link up with the wrong set of people, the only place you are going to be is down. We want to advance ourselves. At the start of every new year, this is our resolution; to be better than the person we were the previous year and that's fine. However, one key area we don't put the work into is our inner circle. These are the people you turn to when you have those tough questions you cannot answer yourself. These are the people who bring opportunities to your doorsteps. I remember attending a business seminar a long time ago. One of the speakers said something about us being 6 degrees away from the solution to our problems. This 6-degree stems from your inner circle.

In essence, you know a person who knows a person who might know the person that can get you what you are looking for. The relationships you establish that go on to form your inner circle require a special kind of treatment. This is not just about managing your peers. This is about how you are reflected in and by this group of people. These are not your 'yes men' or minions. Neither are they the ones who stamp out an idea every time you present it. They are the fire to your raw gold material. They will purge out those impurities and bring out the best in you and you will do the same thing for them. We all want those kinds of relationships. Girlfriends that we can call anytime, any day. Our ride or die bitches* as we like to say. So, in this chapter, we are going to explore what it takes to get these people into your inner circle as well as the important things you need to sort out when building your inner circle.

Your inner circle is going to consist of different types of people. In fact, I like to encourage diversity. You have that person who is a money person. You have a businessperson. There is a fun person, and your contribution to the group. When you bring this together, you have a dynamic energy that motivates whoever is in that circle to be whatever they want to be. The media likes to show female friendships filled with unnecessary squealing, backstabbing, and boyfriend stealing. To say that this is an insult is an understatement. Female friendships are more than what has played out in the media. A lot of people will have you believe that having female friendships could be to your detriment but in truth, if you want to progress to the next stage in your life, you need genuine female friendships.

Identify Your Support Unit

Life is not a bed of roses. There will always be ups and downs and all of us need someone to be there when we are going through the hard times. That is what your support unit is there for. When you are looking at qualities in friendship, it is not enough to have people who laugh with you when the going is good. You also need people who are ready to step up when you are in no shape to be there for yourself physically or mentally. A support unit is comprised of friends and family. Every black woman needs her tribe. They not only love you, but they also respect you. They want what is best for you. Your support unit is more than just the people you call in the middle of the night to swap stories with. They are the ones you call when you sense an opportunity that will favor them. They are also the people that you support. You have to understand that a support unit should never be a one-way street. With all of this in mind, let us look at how we can build our tribe.

1. Find Yourself

My mother is often fond of saying 'like begets like.' Essentially, we naturally gravitate towards people who are like us. If you are lost, insecure, and unsure about yourself, you will attract people who are in the same boat. And people like that will find it difficult to support you and be there for you the way you need them to. Your inner circle is meant to consist of people who rub you the right way. Christians say, "Iron sharpeneth iron." You can't use plastic to get the job done. The iron would destroy the plastic. Stone can sharpen iron, but the relationship is not mutually beneficial. However, when you find a situation where iron is doing the job, both parties will enjoy it. You have to find yourself. Know who you are. Understand your values. You must determine what direction you want to take in life. When you put in the work to get this done you will naturally gravitate towards people who share the same principles and have more to offer you.

2. Be open

Many of us have developed a subconscious image of what we think an ideal friend or member of our tribe should look like. I don't know whether this is because of the media's influence. When we begin searching for people to take up spots in our inner circle, we use this image as the yardstick to measure who we think the ideal friend should be. When you do this, you miss out on opportunities to meet truly great people. People come to us in different shapes and sizes. Their personalities will be different as well. It is left for you to do the work by getting to know them. In the process of getting to know them, you will find yourself naturally pulled to some people because of the previous point I mentioned. The shared interest and similarities will be the bond that draws you to each other. However, your openness and acceptance of them the way they are will help foster that relationship and take it to the next stage. Leave the criticisms and judgment aside. Get to see them for who they are instead of who you think they should be. Understand them on a deeper level and then decide where you want to go with them. And this brings us to our next point.

3. Have a tribe for different purposes

You may be lucky enough to find one or two friends capable of meeting your needs in every way. Before you misconstrue things, here is what I mean when I say meeting your needs. When you want fun, they are down to have fun. If you suddenly crave traveling, they are up for it. If you are trying to set up a business, they will link you up. Whatever it is you are trying to pursue in life, these girls are there for you. However, if we are going to be realistic, some people are better suited for specific needs. When you are looking for fun, you need people who will support you in that venture. A business-minded friend who will always try to stop you from partaking in activities that bring the fun. It is not because they want to bring you down. The problem is, they don't share that value with you. This is why I mentioned keeping your mind open. When you are more receptive, you open yourself to more people who can serve your relationship in different capacities. It is also why understanding yourself is critical to the process because then you know what you want and can identify people who can help you get what you want.

Set Clear Boundaries

If you want to stay authentic and retain this new identity you are building for yourself, setting clear boundaries is important. People wrongfully assume that boundaries are meant to keep people out. In truth, it serves a dual purpose. It restricts unwanted movement that leads to invasion of space, and it also contains people within a specific space. I have used the word space a lot because it is an ingredient that helps foster relationships that we are not aware of. Did you know that you are not just your person? You also have a space. Have you ever wondered why you suddenly feel irritated when a stranger moves too close to you and acts too comfortable around you? They don't need to touch you or even say something to you, but that invasion of space automatically pulls your guard up. That is why we need clear boundaries. However, the boundaries are not limited to physical space, and include what you are willing to do, when you are willing to do it, and how you want to do it, and then communicating that to the people who need to know.

Whether you like it or not, we all have limitations when it comes to our mental, physical, and emotional strength. When you exert that strength 100% of the time, you end up being drained and losing the capacity to serve or be of use to anyone. A relationship that has no boundaries will leave you drained and exhausted. In such a situation, you lose your voice and your identity. After everything we have worked on so far, this is not a desirable outcome. So, what is the solution? To set boundaries of course, and here's how you are going to do it!

1. Learn to say no

This is the number one rule for any relationship. You can't be the yes person. When you are feeling exhausted or when you are just not in the mood, it is okay to say no. Another thing to understand is how to say no. You must teach yourself to say it in a way that communicates your decision without making the other party feel rejected. It is a delicate skill, but one that you will master over time with practice. For example, if your boss comes to your desk 5 minutes before closing time and asks you to stay longer for a work project, if you are not up to it or you already have plans, you can say no, state your reasons and its importance to you. At the same time, you could offer to make it up to them some other time, but make sure your message is passed across.

2. Communicate your needs

When setting boundaries, you can't just get up and dictate what you want. People need to understand not just what you want, but the reason why. When people understand why you want these boundaries set up, they are more likely to comply. But this communication is only relevant when it comes to people who form part of your inner circle. For acquaintances or people you meet randomly, you must establish your boundaries from the very beginning so they know that this is how they relate with you. An explanation is not always necessary for those types of relationships. For the people you are close to, communicate your boundaries with compassion and respect for their feelings. Don't focus on just what you want. Understand their needs and then work things out from there.

3. Apply healthy boundaries

When your boundary starts affecting a person's actions or invading their privacy, you are doing it wrong. When your boundaries make a person feel less appreciated, you are doing it wrong. Healthy boundaries focus on improving the relationship, not isolating one party. For example, if you happen to have friends who come from different religious backgrounds, a healthy boundary in that relationship includes avoiding making hurtful jokes about faith. This is particularly important if you guys haven't gotten to the point where you can freely discuss each other's religion. This way, you respect what they have and create an environment where they are also expected to respect what you have. Anything outside of this can lead to resentment and hurt feelings

Avoid Toxic Relationships

One thing that must never be entertained in your inner circle is toxicity. It creates an environment that chokes ideas, cripples confidence, and makes it difficult for you to fully express yourself. Your inner circle is the one place where you can be yourself without fear of judgment. When you invite a toxic person into that circle, they bring the very things you are trying to get rid of. Some toxic people have masked their toxicity under the label of "concern for your well-being." They make it seem as though their harsh treatment of you can be justified by their so-called concern for your well-being. They are masters at gaslighting and making it seem as though you are crazy for questioning their words and actions.

A toxic relationship is a brand of trauma enabler that can mess with your psyche for years. That is because there is a bond that is forged in that relationship, an investment that is made into that relationship, and some level of commitment. You cannot easily separate yourself from this person. The image that comes to mind when I think of toxic relationships is securing chains around your neck and then attaching those chains to the horse that drags you on rough ground. That is how bad toxic relationships are. Unfortunately, it is not always easy to spot toxic relationships. Yes, there is physical and verbal abuse (which some women still struggle with extricating themselves from). But beyond that, spotting it can take time and during that time, you suffer greatly. So here are some ways to tell that you are in a toxic relationship:

Constant stress or unhappiness

I told you before that there are no negative emotions, and this is mostly because the emotions we like to qualify as negative are a natural response to things that are not favoring you. When you find yourself constantly stressed or unhappy, especially when those emotions are linked to a specific person, it is safe to say that you are in a toxic situation. Every relationship undergoes periods of stress and struggle. But when that period becomes prolonged or your happiness is far and few in between, you might be in a relationship that is cutting you off from your happiness. When you make this discovery, wallowing in the stress or unhappiness is not going to help. Your next step should be to find out why you feel that way and determine if the relationship is worth it. If it is not, have an open conversation with that person, express your feelings and see what happens.

You feel ignored

Black women have constantly had to deal with situations where someone is supposedly good to them with the expectation that they return this goodness with loyalty. I have had friends who were in not-so-great relationships but felt they had to stay there only because their partners were taking care of them. When you talk about this with regular folks, they focus on things like "he takes care of your bills, he makes sure you have everything you need, what else could you want?" What people fail to understand and thankfully there's been a lot of awareness created about it, is that we all have our unique love languages. There are specific things that people have to do to communicate to you that you are loved and respected. They can give you the entire world but if they fail to do these things, you are going to feel ignored and unappreciated. It's even worse when you have communicated this to them several times and they insist on doing things their own way. You deserve to be heard. You deserve to be respected. You deserve to be loved. Anything less does not serve you.

You keep hoping for change

When the relationship you are in is too focused on what will happen in the future rather than what is happening at the moment, you might be in a toxic situation. Let me explain. Perhaps you are with someone who you have had a lot of good days with, and you have seen what they are when things are going good for them. But over the years, they have become this unrecognizable person that doesn't do those things anymore. Still, you hang on because you are hoping that they will revert to what they were before or evolve into something better. Somehow, you have made yourself an anchor from this future you are hoping for. You are convinced that if you leave, things are going to take a turn for the worse. Maybe they told you that. All these suppositions are just indications that you are not in the present. One major reason we avoid the present is that we are unhappy in it and when you are unhappy, it's a sign that that relationship is toxic. Toxic doesn't have to mean abuse. It could be that you are in an environment that stops you from growing.

Family is not always a choice in the sense that we are born to who we are born to. We don't choose them. But you see your inner circle? They are the ones you choose, which mean you have the power to create the supportive community you are looking for. It is going to take time and it is going to take a lot of hard work. Most importantly, it is going to require you to step up to be the kind of person you want to attract into your circle. So be diligent about it. If you already have people like that in your life, work on nurturing those relationships so they can be what you need them to be. With a supportive group standing behind you, you now have twice the resources and energy you need to tune out those negative voices that have been implanted in you by society. That is our next step on this journey.

CHAPTER NINE

Tune Out the Voices

Everyone has a past. This past comes with moments of happiness, moments of sadness, and moments that we wish we could hide away from the rest of the world forever. But one fundamental principle of this book is owning up to your truth. Hiding your past is not going to make it go away or disappear. I have a favorite workout program that I like to listen to on YouTube. In it, one of the motivators says, 'you are already in pain, why not turn that pain into profit?' That phrase always gets me through my workout regimen no matter how grueling it is. I think it is just effective in this situation. You see, your past has already happened even though it was not ideal. It may be ugly. It may contain some of your least proud moments. However, rather than wallow in the events of something that has already happened, this is your opportunity to turn that past into the platform that will launch you into your future. Sounds impossible? Well, that is exactly what we are going to do in this chapter.

We are going to confront the memories you have of your past. Both the ones that fill you with pain and regret and the ones that keep you trapped in the glorious old days. It is time for you to move forward into this amazing life you were destined for. But to do that, you must properly handle your history. Remember, you are taking charge of your narrative. This includes going back to where it all started, reframing the story (not rewriting it) so that you can grab the lessons and the blessings, and then use them as tools to push you forward. I don't know what kind of life you have had but as a black woman, I am willing to bet that it wasn't exactly a smooth sailing one. Your past being crappy does not justify your inability to have a future that is bright and excellent. You have the power in your hand and as you come into the knowledge of who you are, you must equip yourself with the skills to turn that past around.

Before we go digging around your past trauma, you need to brace yourself mentally because you may find some information that may trigger emotions you may not be ready to deal with yet. You need to hit all the right notes with this. Try as much as possible not to get sucked into the emotions triggered by the trip down memory lane. Focus on the steps you are taking, not the ones you have already taken. Limit the judgmental attitude and try to be extra kind to yourself. If things start to get a little too difficult, remind yourself that you are a queen, you are boss, and you have everything under control. Plus, the past has no power over your present unless you hand it over.

Reframe Your Failures

Nobody likes to fail. The main reason we dislike failure is that we attach our identity to our failures. We feel that failing at something automatically makes us failures. Before we start talking about our personal failures, I want to point out that most of the people we look up to and consider extremely successful are people who have a lot of failures under their belts. There is no billionaire, CEO, or inventor who got to where they are without failing. And if you talk to them about their failures, one common thread you would find among all of them is the fact that they credit their success to their failures. Surprisingly, despite this amount of history staring at us in the face, we still look at failure as a roadblock. Hopefully, we are going to change that in this segment. At the end of this, I want you to be able to look at your failures and say yes, I did that. That is how you reframe your failures. But there is more to it.

1. Retrace your steps

When you fall or you miss your way, the first thing you do is retrace your steps. This helps you figure out what you may have missed or what might have gone wrong. Retracing yourself is not for you to relive the failures. It is a logical way of analyzing how far you have come and what you would need to do to get over this barrier. Analyzing the cycle of failure and retracing your steps can be frustrating, but there is a lesson to be learnt. Every great inventor and great invention are a result of someone failing but not giving up. Instead, they analyzed their failures, retracing their steps until they got to the success point. We all have a success point and sometimes the failure we are running away from is what would take us to that success point. This is why giving up should not be your instinctive response every time you fail. Retrace your step, figure out what went wrong, and stay the course. It doesn't matter if the failure was in your marriage, relationship, business, or career, retracing your steps is always effective in helping you figure out the next step.

2. Forgive yourself

If your actions are not replicable but have changed your life, you need to forgive yourself after you have retraced your steps and figured out where you went wrong. You need to take responsibility for what you have done, or at least recognize your role in it. This is called accountability. It is a way of taking back your power especially if the mistakes you made trigger a lot of emotions, not just in you but in the people involved.

Taking back your power may sound conceited, but it is essential if you are going to learn the lessons/blessings of any failure. Failure has a way of casting doubt over your abilities. It makes you question your every action. By taking ownership of your role in that situation, you regain a bit of your lost confidence. You then need to make the effort to forgive yourself. We are usually harder on ourselves than we are on others. Correct that and make forgiveness your priority.

3. Move on

Out of all the steps involved here, I think this one is the hardest. The concept of moving on makes it sound like you are a coward or you don't care about what has happened. I don't know where we got that ideology from. Still, moving on is the final stage in getting over a failure. When you fall, don't sit there moping over it. Get up and dust yourself off. If there is a cut, clean it and dress the wound. That is what we are supposed to do every time we experience failure. You take the steps that we talked about before and then you move on. If it is a situation that requires you to try again, do so. If it was an error in judgment, forgive yourself. If there is an opportunity to make amends, do so. And that is the essence of reframing failures. Don't lie to yourself about what happened, and don't chain yourself to the past either. Learn from it and move on.

Take Control of Your Fears

Only a fool or someone with a medical condition can say they are not afraid. Fear is a human response. It is perfectly fine to be afraid. The problem begins when you permit your fear to control you. As black women, we have so much to be afraid for and afraid of. However, we can't allow those fears to take over our decision-making process. It doesn't mean we shouldn't be cautious or apply wisdom in our dealings. But fear should not dictate our choices. There are countries where it is advisable not to travel alone as a woman. We hear a lot of horror stories. Does it mean you should cut out travel experiences completely? Of course not. For every unsafe city, there are dozens more that are safe. For every opportunity that might compromise your safety and overall life experience, there are even more opportunities for you to take advantage of. The only criteria are for you to gather the courage to step up to the plate.

Another thing you should know is that sometimes the fear we experience is second-hand. It is handed to us by either our environment or through the content we consume. I am a huge fan of crime shows. They fascinate me, but there is a downside to watching crime shows. It slowly erodes your trust in people. If someone makes a wrong move, your brain automatically interprets it as a possible influence that could cause harm or danger to you. This doesn't mean that you shouldn't take your fears seriously.

Something is causing you to be concerned. Obviously, addressing those concerns will put your mind at ease but the objective here is to make sure that you are always in control. Even when you are thrust into situations that take away your control, it should not completely control how you react. The keyword in that sentence is 'react' because our reactions determine our experiences and our experiences influence the bulk of the message we feed ourselves.

When confidence is low, leaning back on your experiences can help create an environment that boosts your confidence especially if you have positive experiences. However, if those experiences are clouded by fear, it would only cause your confidence to sink even lower. So how do you combat fear in a manner that is significant and impactful? The first thing I will ask you to do is to grab your journal and write down a list of things that you would want to do. Right next to that list, write down what has stopped you from doing those things. The next step is to figure out how you can overcome those fears. The easiest path to a solution for that is to face your fears head-on. In other words, if you have a fear of bugs, set up a meet and greet. Doesn't sound exciting but after you have confronted the worst, its impact or influence over you becomes significantly reduced. The more you do it the less afraid you become. Apply this to everything on your list and you find that the only thing that has been stopping you all this while was you.

Affirm Your Strengths

When you have multiple voices in your head telling you what you can or cannot do, making a decision in the midst of that chaos becomes difficult. The worst part is that it is almost impossible to feel authentic in that environment because of the conflicting messages, which in turn ruins your confidence. You have reframed your failures and worked on picking yourself up after you have admitted your mistakes, your next step is to silence those voices or at least turn them down so that you can hear yourself think. From my experience, the most efficient way to clean out negativity is to affirm positivity. In this case, the positivity we are going to affirm is your strength. If you are not a sports fan, I am sorry because the next analogy I am going to use relates to sports.

When you watch the players on the pitch, there are people on the sidelines waving, swinging their arms, and cheering. I am not talking about the fans. I am talking about the cheerleaders. No matter how rough the game is going for their team, the cheerleaders always chant the right thing. That is what affirming your strengths does to you. However, affirmations take things a step further. They create a bubble around your confidence that cushions you from the effect of the negative voices trying to bring you down. They also create an environment that enables your sense of self-esteem to grow.

Affirmations put you in a positive light by allowing you to see the best in yourself even at your worst. Affirmations are a proactive way for you to reprogram your mind. After all that negative messaging, you are way overdue for the good stuff. So how do you affirm your strengths?

1. Accept yourself

Since we started this book, you have heard phrases like, own your truth, leave your truth, be yourself, and so on. All of this serves one purpose; to help you accept yourself the way you are. Now, accepting yourself the way you are doesn't necessarily mean you don't make any room for change or growth. It is simply setting up yourself to be the recipient of unconditional love. The kind where your love is not based on what you can or cannot accomplish. It is rooted in just being you.

2. Believe in yourself

Before you start saying your affirmations, you must start believing in yourself. The thing is, you can speak all the right affirmations from now until you are blue in the face, but if you don't have any faith in yourself and in your ability to be the best version of yourself, those words will not have any impact. Because I understand how much of a struggle this is, we are going to talk about it in subsequent chapters.

3. Compile a list

Write down the most amazing qualities that you have as well as qualities that you would like to have whether in your work area, finances, or in a relationship. Now phrase those qualities in a way that reflects your expected present circumstance. For example, if you want to be more confident, try writing an affirmation like, *I am a confident woman.* It is that simple. However, if you feel that you are struggling, you could buy a book of affirmations centered around the kind of topics you are interested in and highlight the ones that resonate with you.

After you have done all three things, you need to consistently speak your affirmations. It is that consistency that will ensure the message is internalized. If you miss a day or two, don't beat yourself over it. Simply get back into the game and continue like you never left. But if you find yourself distracted from your affirmations and the steps you are trying to take to get rid of those negative voices, it might be time for you to reassess your priorities and that is where we are going next.

CHAPTER TEN

Reassess Your Priorities

You are whatever you devote your time and efforts to. This is a message I have carried with me since I was a child. If I spend more than 70% of my time on social media, whatever content I absorb during that time will influence my thoughts and opinions. This is the part of your journey where you start putting everything you have learned about yourself into practice. When you know your interests, the things that you like, and the things that inspire you, it makes more sense to prioritize them over things that society expects you to handle. Also, reassessing your priorities is not about only focusing on the things that bring you joy. You are going to look at the life you are currently living and how it reflects your new identity. Like the relationships you have with people, do they reflect the respect and companionship you seek?

The health habits that you have right now, do they reflect the respect you have for your body? These are just the simple questions you will need to ask yourself in this part of your journey. Reassessing your priorities is not about turning your life upside down. It is just turning your attention to little things that matter to you so that you know where to apply effort for maximum results. The idea is to get yourself to a point where you are no longer active participants in the rat race. Instead, you enjoy each moment and live life to the fullest. You want to be a powerful black woman who is loved and respected. You don't do that by sticking to the things that people expect from you. If you follow that pathway, you might end up getting the power and the respect, but you'll also end up being miserable in your own life.

Misery and confidence do not work well together. One will amplify the other leading to even more misery and possibly fake confidence. There is something called imposter syndrome. This happens when you feel as though you are not qualified to have the life you currently have and one of its root causes is inauthenticity. This is usually because you are participating in things that don't represent you favorably. These range from the opinions of other people to keeping up appearances. This creates a toxic environment, and you already know how toxicity negatively affects confidence.

Stop Living For Others

Black women are experts at putting their life on hold to make other people happy. And I get it. We are communal people and when you are in a community sometimes you need to put the needs of a community over your own. But the thing with us black women is that we make it a lifestyle. We sacrifice for our parents and sacrifice for our siblings. When we get married, our husbands and children become the beneficiaries of our sacrifices. This life of sacrifice deprives you of an opportunity to live a rich and authentic life. If you are going to find your voice, what purpose will it serve if you fail to use it? You can't continue to live your life for other people. There must be a balance. This balance is where you cater to your needs and then manage the relationships that you have as well. Proper relationship management will ensure that your life is not built on the expectations of other people. We do this all the time and we don't even realize how much it affects us until it gets too late. But that is not the worst of it.

If the ball stopped with us, it wouldn't be a big deal. However, the sad reality is that we transfer this same cycle to our children. We expect them to live for us after years of sacrificing for their well-being. We feel that our reward as parents should be their sacrifices for us. We equate their love for us with their ability to cast aside their hopes, dreams, and aspirations in favor of ours. There is this joke about a mother and daughter preparing for the daughter's wedding. The mother took charge of the wedding and the daughter complained about it. The mother's response was this, 'when I was getting married, it was my mother's wedding. Now that you are getting married, it is my wedding.' This pattern of behavior hurts us, especially us black women. Living to please other people is not really living at all. To truly live is to get to the end of the line and be able to say yes, I live up to my potential. But how can you say that when you don't even put yourself in a position where you can take advantage of opportunities?

It is like we operate on a system of debt. You are made to feel indebted to other people for your existence and therefore you must pay these people. This payment can mean that your choice of study in school is determined by other people. Where you work can also be determined by other people. This is so wrong. I am not even going to touch the illusion we have built around ourselves when it comes to social media relationships. That would need a whole new book on its own. But that behavior didn't start with social media. It started in our own homes and that is where the fixing needs to start. We need to learn to put ourselves first. It sounds selfish but the truth is, when you can serve yourself, you create an emotional environment that enables you to become even better at serving other people. One thing I want you to remember from this segment is that as black women, we hold the key to the growth of our community. If we thrive, our community will thrive. If we find happiness, our community will do the same. So, by being selfish and focusing on yourself, you can unlock that life that allows you to become a better advocate/ambassador for your community.

Set Your Own Expectations

When I set up my first office, my friends gifted me with wall art with the inscription, 'be your own boss.' It was a very simple phrase, but it made me feel empowered. I decided my work and play hours. I handle 100% of the risks and 100% rewards. It was everything I wanted. But certain people ruined it for me with their snide comments. They would make little jokes about my 'small' business or how the 'little lady' was trying to make her way in a big world. They said they meant well but I could hear the sarcasm dripping in their voices. It is not like they intentionally wanted to put me down i. These people had expectations for, me and I was not meeting them. After many conversations over the background of mixed emotions, I found out that these people fell into two categories. The first group felt that I had too much potential to be wasting it on a small business and the second group didn't expect me to get this far.

What I learned from that experience is that no matter what you do, you can never completely satisfy people. You are damned if you do and damned if you don't. People will always have varying opinions and expectations. There is nothing you can do about that. But jumping the hoops and making yourself less just to satisfy those expectations will slow you down and make it impossible for you to focus on your wants and needs. Sometimes, we don't even realize what we are doing. We want to be daddy's perfect little girls, so we bend over backward even when it brings us pain. To get the approval of mommy dearest, we make compromises that hurt us in the long run. In extreme cases, we treat those expectations like oxygen. Without them, we feel empty and lost. I have heard people claim to find their purpose in these expectations. This kind of attitude is not limited to family members. You have heard of the label 'a teacher's pet.' Kids with that title are eager people pleasers, and it doesn't get better as they grow older.

If you are one of those kids, it is time to stop the circus. You can't be wasting this beautiful gift of life by waiting on other people. Healing mentally and emotionally requires making important life changes. It may not be comfortable to make those choices, but the reward is more satisfying than the initial discomfort. Girl, you can't fully kickstart your journey under the weight of the expectations of other people. They are only going to block out the sunlight and limit the joy you should be experiencing. You are a daughter of the earth. Our skin was made to glisten in the sun (literally and figuratively). That is the reason for that melanin magic. Get out from under that cloud and step into the light. And speaking of clouds, we have one more to get rid of.

Let Go of Past Regrets

Living with regrets is like driving a car with your focus on the rearview mirror. It distracts you from the journey ahead and keeps you stuck in the past that you no longer have access to. Because your focus is not where it should be, you miss out on important moments in your life. But that is not the only thing you will miss out on. There are opportunities, pleasure, and leisure activities waiting for you to experience them every day. Being preoccupied with regrets caused by past actions or inaction will either blind you to these experiences or make you hesitant about taking those leaps. So, why are you being held back by regrets? And what can you do going forward? Well, that is what we are about to find out.

Feelings of regret are not isolated events. We all experience it on some level. On the surface, it is not entirely bad. When you are trying to reframe past failures, regret can be an excellent guide as you retrace your steps. However, things start to get a little tricky when you revisit the past and instead of accepting things for what they are, you paint alternative scenarios with different outcomes. This can make you feel good temporarily, but you are not confronting the real problem. Without the truth, you are like a dog chasing your tail around in circles. You are essentially trapped in a cycle. When you are stuck, moving forward is not always easy. But it is not impossible.

For starters, stop focusing on what you could have done differently. Confront that past, face the truth (the role you played in it), learn the lessons you need, and then face forward. This sounds easy, but these are a lot of steps you need to take. Depending on your regrets, one of those steps might include making amends to the people you wronged. Another important step is forgiving yourself. Beating yourself over an incident that happened in the past won't do anything except drag your confidence down. And girl we are way past that at this point. Wondering how to move forward? Make up your mind to do so and just do it. Stop waiting for some grand sign or event to happen. Just do it. You know that there is so much out there waiting for you. Grab the proverbial bull by the horns and get ready for the ride.

CHAPTER ELEVEN

Reclaim Your Excellence

Do you know why we struggle with our confidence? That is because somewhere along the line, we forgot how awesome we are. We allowed self-doubt, other people's negative opinions, and expectations to crush our esteem. We permitted negativity into our space and let it become a domineering thought or voice in our head. When you forget who you are, it becomes easy to buy into the narrative other people are selling. We have said a lot of things up to this point. We have talked about the problems we encounter as black women. We explored our pain, opened ourselves to our passion, and I think that is enough for now. I want to introduce you to someone you may not have met before. Or maybe you have, but I think a reintroduction might help.

This person is the definition of the word beautiful. Her beauty radiates from within and shines through to the outside. When she walks, her movements are those of a powerful goddess. When she speaks, grace and elegance flow through her words. She is strong and fierce, and at the same time, she is delicate and flexible. She is wise and patient. She is kind and eloquent. She is aware and smart. She is everything she needs to be for herself and more. She almost sounds too good to be true, but that is our girl. She is a woman of excellence in every sense of the word. I am pretty sure that you already have an idea of who this woman is, but just in case, let us hear those drumrolls please…the woman is you.

How do you feel about being this woman? If your first reaction was disbelief, it is okay. Anyone would feel intimidated in the presence of such a person and the idea of comparing yourself to them? That is a lot. So, I understand the disbelief. But after you are done with the segments in this chapter, that will change. If your reaction on the other hand was excitement, congratulations girl. You are a rock star, and you know it. The rest of this chapter is going to help you embrace that message. Reclaiming your excellence is how you reposition yourself to receive all the great things coming your way.

Believe in Yourself

If you are going to become the best version of yourself, you need a team of one; you. Of course, you have your tribe backing you, but this one-man-army is going to get you started. You need to be your own cheerleader, fan, and believer. It is nice to have other people do this for you but if you can't do it for yourself, their efforts will be like trying to store water in a woven basket. Useless. Well, not entirely useless, but definitely not enough to get you through long-term situations. So, let me walk you through the 3 members of your army. Let us start with your cheerleader.

This is the second inference I am making to this preppy group of people who seem to be perpetually happy. But it is for a good reason. Life will always toss the storms your way now and then. Being your own cheerleader teaches you the ability to find healthier ways to cope when things get too tough. Rather than seeking validation in places that cultivate an unhealthy mental environment, you look inward and fortify yourself against the negative voices that want to creep in. As your cheerleader, chants like, *you've got this,* or *you can do this* should be your mantra every time you are confronted with impossible situations.

Right next to our cheerleader is your fan. You have to love your work girl and I don't mean to love it from the perspective of a person enjoying what they do. I mean having great appreciation and value for your work. Have you seen the beehive go crazy over Beyonce's work? You don't need to go that crazy, but they could be excellent pointers when it comes to how to be a fan. One thing about fans though, no matter how crazy they are, they never accept mediocrity. The goal is excellence and when it is achieved, they celebrate it. You should do the same. This brings us to the last point - you must believe that you are enough. Never compare yourself with anyone else. And if the doubts start creeping in, take things back to the cheerleader. You can do this!

Unlock Your Passions

What does excellence mean to you? Best of the best at your job? Making great sales? Generating good reviews for your brand? I think it is about adding value. Black excellence doesn't only celebrate what society considers the best and brightest. It is about the people who elevate our community through their valued contributions which are not always monetary. When you look at the people we celebrate, they come from all walks of life but there is a common thread, they are all doing what they are passionate about.

Excellence is not about who rakes in the biggest buck or who has the fame. Excellence is about contributing value. You could be working your boring desk job and still be adding value in your own way. But when we put your confidence on the table, you have to consider other options. Following your passion is one of those options. You get the chance to use your skill or talent in a way that makes you happy while adding value to society. Passion is an important ingredient in your work because when you hit a roadblock that makes you consider quitting, it (passion) will get you over that bump.

We have only one life to live. Wouldn't it be better to spend it doing things that bring us joy while providing value to society at the same time? There is so much going on in the world. So much pain. So much sadness. We can't fix it for everyone. Neither can we make everyone happy. The only people whose happiness we are completely responsible for is ours. Instead of spending each day stuck in routines that bore you and provide you with zero inspiration, why not take up things that give you joy. Your passions do not need to have monetary value, contrary to what social media motivators tell you. It should simply give you joy and value.

Dream Big Dreams

If you want to make your way in this life, you are going to hear a lot of nos before you get to the yeses. When someone says yes to your idea, it is the most refreshing thing in the world. You feel empowered. You feel loved and appreciated. But the no can be soul-crushing. If you are not mentally prepared for it, your confidence levels will tank, and it feels as though you have lost your ability to dream. No creates a vacuum in your heart for fear to roam freely. And when fear roams, you become overly cautious. You stop yourself from taking a leap because you are afraid of getting shut down again. You don't stop dreaming but you stop yourself from dreaming. A life without dreams is a life without hope. And girl, if you are going to reclaim your excellence, you need to start dreaming again. And not the safe, small dreams that keep you in your comfort zone. You need to dream big.

Dreaming big can be scary. Mostly because you are filled with the overwhelming thought of how you are going to make that dream come true or if you are capable of getting it done. This is understandable, but it is also a classic indication of fear. From my experience, fear of dreaming arises from the loss of control. You feel that you don't control all the factors needed to make those dreams a reality and because there is no control, you feel everything else will fall apart like dominoes. But you must understand that dreams are not valuable because of your ability to make them come true. They serve a higher purpose.

Dreams are a non-risky way of expanding the world around you. There are no limitations when it comes to your dream. You can be a zookeeper in Madagascar. A ballerina in France. An all-star athlete in America or even a bad-ass Bond girl in Britain. My point is, there are zero restrictions. Given that our reality consists of social rules and standards that keep us caged in, this is an excellent avenue to explore what life's alternatives are available. Think of dreams as a gap year that you can take any time you want. No consequences. No responsibilities. Just explorations. If you focus on the right dream, you feel motivated and excited to follow your passions. When you meet a black girl who has those kinds of dreams, you better believe that she can do anything. And with that, we make our move to the final chapter.

CHAPTER TWELVE

Take Care of Yourself

Self-care is you prioritizing your needs. As black women, we have been raised to put everyone else before us. We have rooted our identity in self-sacrifice so much that we feel like we are not serving if we are not sacrificing. We sacrifice our peace, sanity, and physical health for the people we love. I have met ladies who suffered domestic abuse in their relationships. They had the ridiculous notion that the abuse was an expression of love. To reciprocate that love, they felt they had to endure the pain and torture. Even in other relationships, we put ourselves at the receiving end of pain, and worse, we normalize it.

This has to stop. Another behavior I have noticed that is common among black women is the damsel in distress syndrome where we suffer in silence as we secretly wait for someone to rescue us. But at the same time, we put up a facade of strength even when we need to be and feel vulnerable. This need to present a front while hiding away our true feelings relegates us to the bottom of the list in our own lives. It is unhealthy and contributes to our inability to feel confident in who we are. Throughout this book, we have explored the various ways we can get back on our respective thrones and reclaim our crowns. We have talked about the tough stuff. Now, it is time to talk about the easy stuff.

Our focus in this chapter is nurturing our minds and body. Looking after our overall health can give us the much-needed confidence boost. When you are healthy, you feel good about yourself. You feel more competent when it comes to pursuing your goals and going after the life you want. Caring for yourself gives you permission to feel good about yourself. It is a way of communicating to your mind and body that you are invested and committed to your wellbeing and emotional growth. When it comes to investments, no type of investment can pay off like investing in yourself. I did say you are your biggest asset. Taking care of yourself will ensure that you remain in prime condition for longer. Now, let us look at the three main ways you can care for yourself.

Nutrition

I used the word nutrition here instead of diet for a specific reason. We often equate diet with nutrition when they mean two different things. Nutrition refers to getting the most from your diet. It is not about hitting a bodyweight goal or following the latest health trends. It is ensuring that your body gets everything it needs to stay healthy. Beyond that, it focuses on teaching you how to have a healthy relationship with food. As women, we are more prone to stuffing ourselves with food as a way of coping with our emotions. If I were to get a dollar every time I sat on my couch and cried my feelings into a tub of ice cream, I would be able to afford a month-long vacation in the Caribbean. While this happened occasionally for me, for some women, it is a standard routine. Whenever you feel sad, you eat. Feeling anxious? A nice chocolate cake can fix that. I must admit, when you are doing it, it feels really good. Even if its only for a short time, we still do it anyway.

When you do this, you are not giving your body the nutrition it needs. You are simply covering up the problems under layers of junk food that could pose a health risk for you in the future. Not to mention how the food impacts your body which in turn affects your confidence. On the flip side of eating junk food is focusing on specific food groups because of their purported benefits. Internet diet experts declare some foods as superfoods and highlight their benefits. People who buy into the benefits refuse to include anything outside those foods in their diet. The problem with this is that those benefits become temporary because there is no balance in their diet.

Proteins are great for bodybuilding, but you still need key nutrients from all the other food groups in order to make the most of your diet. Unless you work with a certified nutritionist in developing your diet, you may not be getting the most from your food and this might be having a negative impact on your health physically and mentally. Don't be too eager to get on any diet no matter how much hype it gets on social media. There have also been studies that link certain foods to elevated moods. And I mean the kind of mood elevators that won't impact your waistline negatively. The key to enjoying food is balance and portion control.

Rest

In today's world, a hardworking woman is someone who works 3 jobs and barely gets enough time to sleep. In the media, the ideal modern woman is seen dashing off to her office with coffee in her hands looking frazzled and constantly running out of time. Black women taking vacations and living a less frantic lifestyle are considered baby girls or sponsored girls. This image of black women needs to be changed. The overworked black woman is an image that has been glorified for too long and that needs to end.

Taking time to rest is not slacking off. It is you valuing yourself and your contribution to the team enough to give yourself time to recover. If you have read the biblical version of the creation story, you would know even God rested on the 7th day. We like to use the term 'super woman' a lot. It is a great compliment. To be compared to a fictional woman who possesses superhuman strength feels good, but it forces you to try and mimic her strength, which includes working round the clock. The truth is a lot simpler. You are human and you need rest the same way you need oxygen and food. A person who has gone a long time without rest experiences a significant reduction in their ability to perform. The bottom line? Rest is recommended and you shouldn't wait until you are completely exhausted to get it.

Part of your self-care routine should be rest. Rest doesn't mean laying down in your bed and sleeping. Treating yourself to a day at a spa or nail salon is a way to schedule some time for yourself. Meeting your girls later in the day for happy hour is another way to let off some steam. The goal is to let your hair down, relax, and unwind. I love to see black girls getting spoilt, especially if they are doing it on their own dime. Plan your vacation months ahead. Pick a cool location preferably somewhere with a perfect view of the ocean. If that is too far off into the future, grab a few buddies and go hiking. Taking a walk in nature is said to be very therapeutic. For us creative folks, it connects us to our creative muses, giving us much-needed inspiration to improve our respective art forms.

Counseling

Black people like to think that the mental health crisis is white people problem. This is a joke that we share to downplay our mental struggles. We buy into the social narrative that we are strong mentally and physically and therefore our minds cannot be influenced or twisted by the struggles we face. But the truth is, we have dealt with so much trauma that it would take a miracle for any black person to succeed or even exist without combating one form of mental health issue or other. Our men are constantly under scrutiny because of the prevalent racial biases, and this puts them at risk of going to jail or getting killed by the people employed to protect them.

The same racial biases prevent us from having access to much-needed health care facilities in our communities, leaving us dealing with preventable debilitating health challenges. Our women face different forms of abuse every single day. This creates the perfect environment for mental health issues to thrive. We need to stop trying too hard to be strong and focus more on trying to heal. To heal, we must first accept our biggest problem, which is the mental health struggle. We have a lot of negative misconceptions about mental health issues that when a person is struggling with mental health, we believe they are broken and weak. Because of this, we refuse to associate ourselves with anything related to it even when we are confronted with the truth.

We are more open to fixing our problems with pills and surgical procedures. But sometimes, our problems are more psychological than physiological, meaning that the treatment lies in talking to a specialist. It is only from there we can develop the solution that will bring about healing. Remember what I said earlier about how the success of one black woman can influence our community and bring about the success of that community? One black woman who was put in the work to heal from her trauma can instigate the same chain of action in her community and this is a great thing. We need to open ourselves to the idea of counseling. We can't expect to forge healthy relationships with people if we are still carrying the baggage of our past. In addition to all the narratives we need to change, eliminating the stigma surrounding mental health issues and their treatment would serve our community a lot.

If we put down this baggage, it will help us find ourselves, and in so doing we find our passion. And through passion, we find purpose. It is only through that purpose that we can create the type of value that will help build our community, which is the end goal. Counseling requires you to admit that there is a problem. Arriving at that conclusion takes courage and I believe you have what it takes. You are brave. You are strong and you have survived things that your peers will probably never be able to imagine. But you are also human and to fully survive your trauma, you need to heal. It is time we open up and start talking to the experts, and that I believe is the final step in this journey. You have done all the work and will continue to do the work but to take things to the next stage, you need to talk to someone.

Conclusion

Finally, we have come to the end of this book. In the process of writing this book, I had to revisit a lot of old wounds, and this took its toll on me emotionally. I can only imagine the journey that it took you on. It probably hurts. Here is the thing about pain; it is indicative of the problem. The pain you feel tells you that there is a problem and more importantly, it tells you that you are on the right track. You have boldly met your pain head-on. Don't stop now. You owe it to yourself to get to the finish line. The end of the book is simply the beginning of another chapter. What that means is entirely up to you.

Perhaps it is the chapter in your life where you diligently apply everything you have learned so far to improve your quality of life or you open a new chapter in another book so that you can build on the foundation that this book has already laid. And these are just two of many options. I hope that you realize that life is waiting for you to come out of your shell and live it. Unfortunately, time is ticking by. Each precious moment is only as valuable as we make it. It is time to make it count.

Know that when you make those queen moves, you are not only doing it for yourself. You are doing it for the little black girls who are watching. You want them to know that there is so much they can achieve if they set their minds to it. You are also doing it for the ladies who came before us. You want them to know that their efforts, struggles, and sacrifices were never in vain. They walked so that we can run. We must break those unhealthy cycles and build a new way of life for ourselves. You are the hero you have been waiting for to rescue you. Step up to the task with courage and confidence. Silence any voice that attempts to diminish your power.

I am so excited about this journey. I know that you will do great things and I look forward to hearing your story. Until then, keep shining and keep winning.

Book #2

Spiritual Self Care for Black Women

A Powerful, Holistic Workbook to Radically Love Yourself and
Heal Your Mind, Body, & Soul

Introduction

Being a Black woman has never been easy. Being a Black woman in America? Well, we all know what it's like. Our history is long and deep, and while there's been progress in the fight for equality and just to live a damn peaceful life, living in the modern world is still not easy. In fact, it's downright stressful.

As a Black woman, we're subject to so many stereotypes and expectations, and despite the changes happening and a well-fought civil rights movement, it doesn't make the experience any less stressful or traumatic. We're expected to excel in academics and our jobs, stay fit and healthy, please our partners sexually, be agreeable, a good friend, a good daughter, mother, sister, aunt, etc.

And not just good… we're expected to be the best at all these things.

As if that isn't enough, we're expected to suck up our troubles and internalize all the negative things that happen to us. When we're feeling anxious, sad, or angry, we're taught to push it all down, to force ourselves out of those negative head spaces and wear a happy face. We're supposed to put our problems and feelings aside for the sake of those around us.

This is a battle that rages within us all. It's within all cultures, races, societies, and genders. And on top of this, the rest of the world feels like a mess. From the moment you wake till the moment you shut your eyes, everything feels turbulent. We see it every day. Instagram inboxes are flooded. Posts are swarming with comments from allies and some of the most narrow-minded people you could imagine. The media drones on with their agenda. I'm sure you've been in a situation where you've been stuck in tense conversations between friends and family members. I know I have.

The world we live in and the society we try so hard to thrive in constantly strives to oppress us. It's a hard truth. We're constantly bombarded with images and messages that tell us we're not good enough, that our natural hair is unprofessional, and that our skin color isn't beautiful. Then, we assume our traumas are unique to us and our life experiences, yet we share these traumas with millions of other black women.

It's no wonder so many of us struggle with self-love and acceptance.

We've all lived through hard times. Every one of us has experienced racism, the relentless expectations of others, discrimination at work, in the street, or even from our own partners. Life can feel cruel, but all this struggle and hardship leaves us all fighting a battle so many women aren't even aware they're fighting.

The battle within themselves.

The battle within you.

We, as Black women, are more disconnected from ourselves than ever before.

Think of it this way - we're so used to being strong for everyone else that we don't know how to be weak. When was the last time you cried? When was the last time you allowed yourself to break down? To not have all the answers? When was the last time you looked in the mirror and smiled at what you saw? Did you truly feel wonderful?

Take a moment to consider how you treat your partner, family, children, and friends. Think about how you show them so much love, compassion, and empathy, and then recall the last time you did the same for yourself. Does anything come to mind?

For the longest time in my life, I couldn't remember the last time I showed myself the slightest bit of love, except for a few occasional moments when the house was quiet. The more I thought about it, the worse this problem became. Not only could I not remember the last time I truly loved myself, I couldn't even remember how.

And that's the best way to look at it. There is a reason you've picked up this book. There's a reason you're seeking powerful ways to learn how to love yourself, heal yourself, and to nurture a connection with your mind, body, and soul. You've felt that urge inside you, the same urge millions of Black women have been, and are, responding to. By opening this book, you've taken another step forward.

This book is all about this journey. Throughout the following chapters, we'll be diving into how to take so many more of these steps. From discovering your spiritual side and becoming in-tune with it to actively bringing new practices into your life that can heal, nourish, and nurture your very soul.

And that's just it. Even if you've never thought about this directly, you deserve to love yourself. You know you deserve it. You've picked up this book because you know you've had enough of how life has been so far and you're ready to make real, positive changes in your life. You're ready to start loving yourself. And it's one of the most beautiful journeys you can ever undertake.

The benefits are endless. Not only will you love, respect, and care for yourself like never before, you'll actually be able to show up to the people you love most in the best way.

You've been taught to be strong. That you need to be a rock for everyone else. These are things we should all be doing for each other, but without self love, it's unsustainable.

You can't pour from an empty cup.

So, please take a seat. Show yourself a bit of love for taking the time to get started on this journey. Get comfortable. For the next however long this takes, I want you to consider what it is that you want, need, and deserve. And, more importantly, how to go for it and offer it to yourself.

CHAPTER ONE

Black Women and Self Care

When I was 10, I was bullied immensely. I don't recall how it started, but I remember my parents got divorced and everything seemed like it was falling apart. I was picked on, hit, spat on, and called names by some of the older kids, and it made my life hell. I tried so hard to put on a brave face, and while I had friends, inside I felt completely alone. My father had left and my mother was devastated.

While I didn't see it at the time, she took out her frustrations on me, making me clean the house, the yard, run to the shops and back, which isn't bad in itself, but it was my life. Day in, day out. We lived below the poverty line, and even things like buying food was a struggle.

So, at home I was alone, struggling to survive with a toxic parent, and barely getting my basic human needs met. At school I was picked on for being different, for having hand-me-down clothes, and 'being poor.' I felt isolated and had no one to talk to about any of it. So, what did I do? I pushed it down.

I pushed it right down and couldn't bear to look at it. I had to be strong and I knew that I was in a better position than other people, so I had no right to complain. As I grew up, I tried my hardest to never think about the traumas I had been through, but of course, they affected everything I did. I found myself in one toxic relationship after another. I was lonely and without many friends, none of whom I could open up to about anything.

Of course, I broke down in my early 20s and I was forced into starting my own spiritual self-care journey. The point is, even trauma from years ago in your life will still affect you, and it will never be resolved without learning to love yourself.

Self-care is important for everyone, but it's especially crucial for black women. We often carry a lot of emotional and spiritual baggage, which can be tough to deal with on our own. That's why it's so important to take care of ourselves, emotionally and spiritually. Even if you've lived a pretty 'decent' life, this doesn't mean you're not carrying baggage.

One of my favorite writers, Dr. Inger Burnett-Zeigler, speaks about this in her 2021 book, *Nobody Knows the Trouble I've Seen: The Emotional Lives of Black Women*. She talks about how an estimated eight out of ten Black women have experienced some degree of trauma in their lives, but because being a strong Black woman has become so much of a cultural icon we all strive for, we push our traumas down and hardly address them.

Pushing it down and striving to fit the iconic mold is literally killing us. Medically, Dr. Burnett-Zeigler writes, this repression is leading to a record number of cases of anxiety, depression, diabetes, heart disease, hypertension, and so much more. Holding onto these traumatic experiences causes this.

And what are these traumatic experiences?

Literally everything. It could be loneliness, relationship dissatisfaction, discrimination, prejudice, sexism, racism, or even violence. It could be events from your past that affect how you're living now. This could be anything from unresolved childhood issues, drama within the family, abuse, traumatic experiences, not feeling good enough as a kid or teen, not getting the best grades, bullying, and so on.

Self-care is a way to explore these aspects of your life and actively come to peace with them, as well as learning to love them. If pushing down your traumas is the act of denying they ever happened, ignoring them, and even pretending they never happened, self-care is learning to bring them to the surface and loving them.

You have to learn to love these parts of you. They are you. They are your journey through life. They made you who you are today. Who you will be in the future. For me, I felt so alone and isolated because nobody listened to what I was going through. Yet, I was doing the same thing to myself.

Imagine a younger version of you standing in front of you, going through everything you've been through and turning to you, asking you to listen to them. What are you going to choose? Are you going to push your younger self away because you don't want to deal with them? Or are you going to choose to be there for them, to love them, and to help them grow from the experience?

The choice to love yourself is yours and yours alone.

I've been on this journey. I'm still on it. If you've ever met a Black woman who's confident, beautiful, proud, and who seems to exude some kind of internal bliss, I guarantee she's been on that journey too.

This is why self-care isn't about drinking cocktails, going for walks, or indulging in a bath every now and then. These activities do help, but true self-care is about knowing yourself, where you came from, where you're going, and healing your past wounds. The clarity that comes with this process gives you the ability to actually love yourself, truly and deeply.

You are worthy of this love, and the best way to show it is by investing in yourself. Through self-care, you are showing yourself that you are worth the time and effort it takes to live a better life. It is through self-care that we truly experience the depth of our worth, which in turn allows us to love ourselves more fully.

Fortunately, there are many different paths on this journey. Some people like to meditate or pray, while others find journaling or nature walks helpful. The most important thing is to find what works for you and to make self-care a priority in your life. I'm going to guide you through everything you need to know, ensuring you have all the information you need to help you figure out how you want to move forward.

Loving yourself is a revolutionary act, and it's something that you have to consciously choose to do every day. It's not easy, but it's worth it. When you love yourself, you open up to the possibility of living a life that is free from pain and full of joy.

This workbook is designed to help black women who want to improve their self-care routines. It includes powerful exercises and strategies for radically loving yourself and healing your mind, body, and soul. By taking care of yourself, you'll be better equipped to handle whatever life throws your way.

Let's begin.

CHAPTER TWO

Introducing Spirituality

"Believe in your infinite potential. Your only limitations are those you set upon yourself."
– Roy T. Bennett

As a teenager, especially when I was going through a particularly hard time, I found myself struggling to find my way. I can't remember a time when I was consistently comfortable in my body, happy with the company I kept, or thrilled about my grades or the direction my life was heading. Yet even though I could highlight a thousand things I didn't like about myself, I struggled to find purpose or direction. I couldn't identify a way out of this cycle of thinking. A cycle of thinking that dragged on for years.

I was always looking for ways to improve my mental and emotional health, but it wasn't until I reached my twenties that I started to make real, noticeable progress. I had always spent time reading a lot of self-help books and tried out different techniques in an effort to find something that worked for me. However, I would either pick up new practices for a week or so before I realized it didn't serve me or found the information I was given just too bland, generic, and almost always tailored towards white women.

One day, I stumbled upon spiritual self-care. This was a new concept for me, but it resonated with me immediately.

I started by incorporating some basic practices into my daily routine, like meditation and journaling. Over time, I began to explore other aspects of spirituality as well, such as yoga and aromatherapy. I soon realized that this was the missing piece of the puzzle; spiritual self-care helped me connect with myself on a deeper level and find peace within myself.

Since then, I've been on a journey to learn as much as I can about spirituality and how it can help us heal and transform our lives. Whether you're new to spiritual self-care or you've dabbled, I want you to sit back, take a deep breath, and open your mind. We're going to take this from the beginning because there are a lot of myths, misconceptions, and ideas that have blurred out the true meaning of spirituality.

If you've ever thought about spirituality and the first thing that came to mind was someone meditating with the hopes of transcending to enlightenment, traveling through spiritual and astral dimensions, and other ideas you don't believe in, rest assured, that's not what spirituality is. These kinds of ideas put me off spirituality for a long time, but it was these preconceived ideas that prevented me from realizing what spirituality could bring into my life.

In a nutshell, spiritual self-care is about connecting with something bigger than yourself.

It's about tapping into a source of strength and power that can help you heal your wounds and become the best version of yourself. Spiritual self-care, or what I believe to be the only real form of self-care, comes from within and affects everything you do. From the way you speak and treat other people, how you approach problems, to how you celebrate and remain grateful for the good in your life, spiritual self-care is all about connecting and nurturing your higher self.

Your higher self is a part of you that is connected to a greater power, or source. It is your spiritual self, your spirit, core, soul, or whatever you want to call it. This higher self can help you heal your wounds and become the best version of yourself. When you connect with your higher self, you become more authentic, peaceful, and empowered.

You can think of this higher self as the 'real' you. When you take away all the hurt, pain, and suffering; the experiences you've had, things you've learned, identities given to you by yourself or others, and your conditioning; what is left is the real, higher you.

What I really find interesting is that you can connect with the 'real' you right here, right now.

Just close your eyes and take three deep breaths. It's easy to skip over this and read it while saying 'oh yes, this is something I'll do.' However, you need to be proactive with these activities. It's a workbook after all, which means you need to put the work in!

So, close your eyes and take three deep breaths. Feel the sensation of your body weighing down and being supported by the chair or surface you're sitting on. That point of contact between your body and the surface. The feeling of gravity weighing you down.

You can feel it now, right?

Notice how 'you' are noticing this sensation. Your physical body is feeling the sensation, and you have an awareness of that sensation. Truth be told, you felt that sensation the moment you sat down. It's constantly been there, but you've only become aware of that feeling. This awareness is the real you.

Notice how there are no judgments. You don't hate or love the feeling. You don't try to change it, adjust it, or move it. You're just aware of the reality of your situation through your physical sensations and you're at peace with it.

This is a great example of how easy it is to connect with your true self. If you had a bad experience where you once sat on a nail sticking out of a chair (aka, a traumatic experience), you might be scared to sit down without checking the seat first, but the reality is that the chances of a nail sticking out of another chair you try to sit on are extremely low.

Being aware of the fear means you can overcome the fear. Otherwise, you're going to go through life constantly fearing sitting on chairs based on what is a pretty rare, one-off experience.

This process of enhancing your awareness, tuning into yourself, and understanding your fears, traumas, and inner beliefs is what spirituality is about; these understandings come from tuning into your higher self.

There's a place in your life for the things you've learned, the identities you have, and the experiences you've lived through, but being connected to the higher 'you' allows you to go through life with more clarity, peace, and understanding, regardless of what situations you find yourself in.

When you're connected with your higher self, you become untouchable. You can bring this connection to life, deepen it, and fully embrace it through the practices of spiritual self-care.

I believe that this kind of nurturing is more important now than ever before. Black women are faced with so much trauma, pain, and suffering. We are constantly bombarded with messages telling us that we're not good enough.

Just the other day, I found myself in a tough spot. I wasn't meeting my own standards and I felt like I was falling short. I was at work when I got a call from my mom and she started berating me about how I needed to do better. She was basically yelling at me, telling me that I was screwing up my life.

At that moment, I could have gone two ways. I could have allowed myself to believe what she was saying and felt even worse about myself OR,

I could have tapped into my higher self, remembered who I really am, and allowed that to give me the strength to keep going, even in the face of adversity.

I chose the latter and it made all the difference.

A few months ago, I ended up in a bad situation with someone I thought was a friend.

We were going to the cinema, and I was originally going to book the tickets, but I had to work overtime. So, I asked the friend to book them instead. They agreed, but they didn't book the seats on time and the theater was incredibly busy. We ended up in bad seats.

My 'friend' was basically trying to tear me down and make me feel bad about myself. They said I was useless because I hadn't explained the theater was busy and that I should have booked it myself. Essentially, this wouldn't have happened if I had just booked the seats. A petty situation, I know.

At first, I was lost in what they were saying, and I felt incredibly turbulent and emotional. I wasn't grounded, I was stressed, and I could feel myself spiraling into a negative headspace.

They were blunt, and their words were making me feel useless. I found myself naturally taking a deep breath, and I was able to reconnect with my higher self. I remembered who I was, I remembered my connection to the higher self. Very quickly, I was able to find peace.

I spiritually stepped back from the situation and realized that I was being manipulated by a so-called friend. It was a really powerful moment for me and it allowed me to see the situation for what it really was.

I know I was busy at work and there was nothing I could have done. It was a momentary decision, and the seats weren't even terrible, it just wasn't the seats my so-called friend wanted, and so she was acting out. It was no reflection on me, nor were the attacks personal. Anyone could have done the same thing and she would have reacted the same way.

In a tense moment like this, or any moment like it, I could have allowed the hurtful things this person said to define me. OR, I could have tapped into my higher self, remembered who I really was, and allowed that to give me the strength to keep going. I chose the latter and it made all the difference.

No matter what you're facing in life, no matter how hard it gets, always remember that you have the power to tap into your higher self and find peace. You are never alone, and you always have the strength to keep going.

When you're connected with your higher self, you'll find that you're able to:

- Let go of the past and move on

- Forgive yourself and others

- Heal from traumas and pain

- Find your purpose in life

- Create lasting change in your life

- Be more present and mindful

- Have more fulfilling relationships

The benefits of spiritual self-care are clear and plentiful. Like a mountain stream starting out as nothing more than a trickle, flowing across the ground until, over the years, it carves a breathtaking valley that defines the landscape around it, the more you nurture and care for yourself, the deeper and stronger your connection to your higher self will become.

Now, I know what you're thinking. Spiritual higher selves? Isn't this just religion? Well, in a way, spirituality is often seen as a religious or spiritual practice, but it doesn't have to be.

Spirituality and Religion

Spirituality is simply a connection to something greater than ourselves.

This could be your connection to a higher power, the universe, nature, or anything else that you feel connected to. For many people, spirituality is about connecting with their higher self, but others may find spirituality within their religion. It really is a broad concept, but essentially, you are connecting with a higher power in all forms of spirituality; whether that's within yourself, your God, or another entity.

It's about connecting with what works for you.

When you start forming this connection, you will find an overwhelmingly peaceful and powerful sense - the internal acknowledgment that there is something greater than yourself in this world. Something more than your physical, material self. Greater than the emotions you reactively feel from moment to moment, and greater than the experiences and thoughts you have.

The physical, sensory experience we have day by day is one thing, like sitting and feeling the sensation of sitting in a chair, but you are so much more than this. And this refers to both the contextual good and bad.

You are more than the emotions you feel during your first kiss, and you are more than the feelings of shame you feel when you overlook the red flags in a new relationship. Through all the pain, pleasure, suffering, torment, and euphoria you feel in life, there is something infinitely more vast, more powerful, more intelligent, and more eternal within you.

And that's what spirituality is - a recognition of this greater something. The recognition of a part of you that is not bound by the limitations of your physical body or mind.

We often get caught up in our thoughts and emotions and we forget that there is something much greater. We forget that we are so much more than just this human experience. But when we remember our connection to the higher self, to the universe, to God, it can bring a sense of peace and calm in the midst of chaos. It can help us to find our center and to move forward in life with more clarity and purpose.

Diving a little deeper, there is a strong connection between spirituality and religion. In fact, most religions are based on spirituality. The word 'religion' comes from the Latin root 'religare,' which means to bind or to connect. And so, religion is really about connecting with a higher power. It's about having a set of beliefs and practices that help us to connect with our spirituality.

Now, there are different types of religion, and not all religions are based on spirituality. There are some that are based on political power or social structure. But for the most part, religion is about connecting with something greater than ourselves.

There are many different paths to spirituality, and each person has to find their own path. Some people find their spirituality through religion, while others find it through nature, meditation, or other practices.

The most important thing is that you find a path that works for you and that helps you to connect with your higher self.

However, while the core connection of spirituality and religion is similar, there are some differences between the practices. For example, religion is organized and operates based on a set of beliefs. Alternatively, spirituality is internal and individual, and is founded on whatever you choose to believe in.

Religion and spirituality are similar in the ways that squares and rectangles are similar and different. This does mean, however, that you can be both spiritual and religious.

The Importance of Self-Care

The term 'self-care' is thrown around a lot these days. And while it's become somewhat of a buzzword, the concept of self-care is very important. Self-care is any activity that we deliberately indulge in to take care of our mental, emotional, and physical health.

Although it's often spoken about in relation to physical health, self-care is so much more than just going to the gym or eating healthy food.

Self-care is about taking care of all aspects of your health. It's about taking the time to do things that make you feel good, physically and emotionally. It's not even about necessarily feeling 'good' in the moment, but instead about understanding yourself, how you think, and why you feel the way you do. It's like being in a relationship and understanding your partner, being able to read them, and understanding where they're at. Except in this case, your partner is yourself.

For example, if you get a drink knocked out of your hand at a bar and you fly off the handle in a dramatic rage, this is a sign you're not connected with your higher self. You're acting mindlessly through emotion with little regard for yourself, what you're doing, or other people.

However, if you can take a deep breath and feel that same anger, but you're mindful enough to know that it comes from the fact you had a bad day, you had a hard conversation with someone you loved, or work is stressful, you know not to lash out. Instead, take a few minutes to calm down, an act which is better for everyone involved, especially yourself.

However, you won't be able to have this degree of self-understanding and awareness without practicing self-care.

However, remember that self-care is not selfish. In fact, it's quite the opposite. When you take care of yourself, you're better able to take care of others. You're better able to support your friends and family members when they need you.

We often put other people's needs above our own, especially as Black women, which seems to be a hard-wired trait. We try to be everything to everyone and end up spreading ourselves too thin. To be our best selves, we need to take care of ourselves first. This means that we need to find a balance. We need to make sure that we're taking care of our own needs as well as the needs of others.

One way to think about it is the airplane safety video. They tell you to put on your own oxygen mask before helping others. This is because if you're not taking care of yourself, you won't be able to take care of anyone else.

The same is true in life. If we're not taking care of ourselves, we won't be able to take care of those around us. We'll end up feeling burnt out and resentful. So it's important to remember that self-care is not selfish. It's actually one of the most selfless things you can do.

Of course, this isn't just any old Western self-care we're talking about. This is spiritual self-care. This is taking care of your mental and emotional health in a way that's intentional and connected to your spirituality.

So, enough theory, let's start putting things into practice.

CHAPTER THREE

The Art of Decluttering and Cleansing You

"The first step in crafting the life you want is to get rid of everything you don't."
— **Joshua Becker**

The further I got on my self-care journey, the clearer it became that I was not the only person going through hard times and waves of self-discovery. In fact, this is a journey millions of women have embarked on worldwide, and it begs the question;

How did we become so disconnected from ourselves?

The answer lies in the art of decluttering and cleansing yourself.

As we go through life, we accumulate a lot of baggage. This baggage can be physical, like actual bags that we carry around with us everywhere we go. But it can also be metaphorical baggage, like emotional trauma or past hurt that we're holding onto.

It's incredible to see how quickly things can go wrong when emotional baggage is lugged around for a long time. I grew up and went to school with a girl I became quite good friends with. I went over to her house one day when we were perhaps seven or eight, and I remember hearing her mother berate her rather viciously.

I was young at the time, so I kept quiet and didn't think too much of it. But throughout her life, especially in our teenage years, it was clear my friend had problems. She trusted no one. She distanced herself from everyone. She became emotionally unstable.

She once told me that she never felt good enough for anyone. When we were 14 or 15, she turned to alcohol and drugs in an attempt to numb the pain to cope. Unfortunately, this only made things worse. She ended up dying from an overdose at the young age of 21.

We all carry baggage that weighs us down and prevents us from moving forward in life. It can keep us stuck in the past and stop us from living our best lives. So it's important to learn how to declutter and cleanse yourself, both physically and metaphorically.

The World We're Trapped In

We live in a society plagued with information overload. We're constantly bombarded with messages telling us that we need to buy this new product or upgrade to the latest version of something. We're told that we need to look and act a certain way to be accepted. We're made to feel like we're not good enough just as we are.

This messaging can take a toll on our mental and emotional health. They can lead us to believe that we're not good enough and that we need to change to be accepted. They can cause us to doubt ourselves and our worth.

How often do you go on Instagram and see pictures of beautiful women in stunning clothes, gorgeous bodies, and living in nice houses with lovely cars? How badly do you desire these things and feel bad about your own life? How disconnected and unsatisfied do you feel about your life when you see these things?

This craving for more, this act of comparing your own life and feeling bad about what you have has led many down dark paths. It leaves you disconnected and ungrateful for what you have, leaves you feeling unsatisfied and always wanting more, and ultimately, leads to you spending more money on 'nicer' things.

It creates doubt about yourself and your ability to live a healthy and happy life. After all, if you were doing it right, wouldn't you also have all these nice, amazing things?

When we start to doubt ourselves, it's easy to become disconnected from who we really are. We start to believe the lies we're being told about ourselves and we start to forget what makes us special and unique.

This is why it's important to learn how to declutter and cleanse yourself. When you declutter, you're getting rid of all the physical and metaphorical baggage weighing you down. You're making space for the things that matter.

And when you cleanse yourself and declutter your thoughts and what you're putting into your head, you're getting rid of all the negative thoughts and beliefs that are holding you back. You're also making room for new, positive beliefs about yourself. You're giving yourself permission to be who you really are.

Take a moment to think about social media.

These platforms are amazing tools. They can be used for a lot of good things, like staying connected with friends and family, or promoting a cause you're passionate about.

Yet social media can also be detrimental to your mental and emotional health. So many studies have shown that the more time we spend on social media, the more likely we are to compare ourselves to others and feel inadequate. We start to believe that everyone else's life is better than our own and that we're not good enough.

Think about this in your own life. Is there really a time where you go on Instagram or Facebook and actually feel better than when you started scrolling? I know that most of the time I didn't. I'd always come across a photo of a happy family or a gorgeous woman. While I'm happy for them, it's hard not to question my own life and feel bad that I'm not where they are.

It's too easy to forget that social media and most of the technology we have around us didn't exist 30 years ago.

It's easy to forget that we used to live in a world where we didn't have constant access to social media and the internet. We had to talk to people face-to-face, and we needed to find things out for ourselves.

We had to use our imaginations more because we didn't have access to constant entertainment. We had to create our own fun, and we had to use our minds more. We didn't just spend hours a day (averages in the US are four hours a day spent on social media) scrolling, not really doing much.

And you know what? We survived. In fact, we thrived.

We were happy and we were content. Even through the hardships of our past, we still had a sense of community with the people around us, and true, meaningful relationships with others. Spending our time within these relationships is another form of self care.

People who lived below the poverty line have mostly said that they didn't know they were poor, so it didn't matter. They just lived life how they wanted to live it, along with their friends and surrounding communities.

Nowadays, it's easy to compare your life to the lives of others, as the lives of people from all over the world are constantly at your fingertips. This not only detaches you from your higher self, but the physical effects are just as prevalent. Science has shown a huge spike in conditions like chronic stress, chronic fatigue, anxiety, sleep deprivation, and so much more.

We're not taking care of ourselves, and we're not living in alignment with who we are. But it doesn't have to be this way. You can start making changes that will help you to reconnect with yourself and live in alignment with your true self.

This is why it's important to be mindful of how much time you spend on social media. If you find that you're spending more time than you'd like scrolling through your feed, take a break. Go for a walk, read a book, or do something that will make you feel good.

Through the process of spiritual self-care, you can learn to reconnect with your true self, discover who you really are, and ultimately learn to love who that is. After all, we can't really change the times that we're in, but how we live in it.

This is the process of cleansing and decluttering your mind. When you love yourself, completely and unconditionally, you will find that your whole world changes. You will be happier, healthier, and more at peace with yourself and those around you.

It's important to note that this is an ongoing and endless journey. Life doesn't stay the same, and the only constant is that everything changes, which means that there will be situations in your life where you lose yourself again.

You've been through breakups, losing a loved one, changing jobs, etc., and you know that it takes a bit of time to reconnect with yourself and figure out who you are after these events.

That's okay. You're constantly changing as you experience the external, physical world, but the skills you'll learn throughout this book will help you tap into your higher self over and over again, regardless of what experiences you're going through. This is because your higher self never really changes.

When you're in touch with this part of yourself, you will always be in alignment with your true purpose, no matter what happens in your life.

Beginning the Cleansing Process

When it comes to cleansing and decluttering your mind, there are many ways you can go about it, but one of the most impactful and easiest ways is by cleansing and decluttering your space.

This is something you can do in your house, apartment, office space, or even a dorm room. It's all about creating a space that supports your well-being and makes you feel good.

The first step is to start with physical clutter. This can be anything from clothes you don't wear anymore to old books, magazines, and trinkets. If it's something you don't use, love, or need, get rid of it.

You can donate items to charity, have a garage sale, or even just throw them away. It doesn't matter how you get rid of the physical clutter, as long as it's gone.

Let's say you have a photo or gift from an ex-partner in your home. If seeing it doesn't make you feel good, get rid of it. There's no need to keep something around that doesn't make you happy or that brings up negative emotions. Sure, if something has sentimental value and it brings joy into your life, keep it. The same logic applies to everything we'll explore in this book. If it brings true value to your life, that's fine.

If something has negative sentimental value, keeping it in your life is doing more harm than good. It's time to let it go so you can make space for things that will bring you joy.

Cleansing Within

Decluttering your space is a fantastic start. Cleaning your space, decluttering the belongings you don't want or need, and even just tidying up and emptying bins can make a huge difference. Not only are you consciously and proactively taking the time to care for your own space, you'll start to realize how you look at things. You start to notice how you evaluate things in your life.

For example, if you look at a photo you have around, how do you feel about it? Does it make you happy or sad? Does it make you angry? Do you have fond memories of that photo, or are you indifferent? What's interesting is taking a moment to think about how much time to spend going around your home and seeing everything you do, feeling the way you do about everything you lay your eyes on, but rarely taking the time to consider how this perception affects you and your mindset.

By taking the time to declutter and evaluate your belongings in such a specific way, you're giving yourself the opportunity to see how you feel about such things.

You'll mindfully look at areas of your life and the things you're surrounding yourself with and think 'does this bring value into my life?' and 'does this serve me?' You'll see how your belongings are making you feel, and whether they're bringing benefit into your life, or holding you back.

Just like your physical space, you can go through this process with your inner self, i.e. your thoughts and emotions. This is the second step.

This step is about decluttering your mental and emotional space. This means letting go of any negative thoughts, beliefs, or emotions you may be clinging to.

A lot of the time, we hold onto things because we think they're true, but if they don't serve us or make us feel good, it's time to let them go. This can be a really tough process, and it may take some time, but it's worth it.

The third and final step is to create a space that supports your wellbeing. This means actively filling your space with things that make you feel good, inspire you, and support your health, happiness, and overall spiritual journey.

This could be anything from plants, pictures of loved ones, to inspiring quotes. It's all about creating a space that feels like home and that makes you feel good.

The art of filling your space is an interesting one. Andrew Huberman, an American neuroscientist who researches brain development and general wellbeing, describes the importance of symbols in our lives. He reports that because there's too much information in the world to handle, our brain breaks everything down into relatable symbols. This is why brand logos work so well by sticking into our minds.

When you see a symbol, let's say a simple love heart emoji, you know it represents love and the infinite complexities of such a feeling. When it comes to creating your space, filling it with symbols that work for you is a big step to take. If you have a piece of art on the wall that reminds you to take a deep breath or a plant in your room that signifies new beginnings, these are all little things that can make a big difference.

At the core of each of these three steps is the lesson and value you must remember: Think about what you're putting into your mind and body.

There's endless information about the importance of putting the right food into your body. After all, if you just eat foods full of fats and sugars, you're going to feel bad, increase your risk of obesity, and become susceptible to weight-related health risks.

The same applies to your mind. If you're constantly bombarding yourself with Instagram posts of skinny women or people living their best lives with nice cars and houses, pictures of you and your ex, reminders of your traumatic childhood, television shows that show terror and toxic behaviors, or even news about the doom and gloom of the world, this is going to have serious consequences on your mental state.

You need to feed your mind just as much as you're feeding your body, and that means filling it with positive, inspiring, and uplifting content. This could be anything from books, audio programs, blogs, to articles. As long as you're absorbing content and information that's important and valuable to you, you're on the right track.

I'm sure we've all been in a situation where we're scrolling or watching TV or Netflix and we think to ourselves, 'Why am I even watching this? I'm not even enjoying myself,' only to find ourselves doing the same thing days or even hours later.

And finally, make sure you're making time for yourself. This is so important. We live in a world that constantly pushes us to move, and it's easy to get caught up in the hustle and bustle and forget to take care of ourselves.

But if we don't take care of ourselves, we can't take care of anything or anyone else. So make sure you're making time to do things you enjoy, relax, and just be.

Emotional Decluttering

One of the most impactful things you can do for your mental health is to declutter your emotions. This means letting go of any negative emotions you may be holding on to, such as anger, resentment, jealousy, and fear.

It's important to understand that these emotions are normal and that it's okay to feel them. However, it's not okay to let them take over your life.

If you're constantly angry, resentful, or jealous, it's going to have a negative impact on your mental health. It's also going to have a negative impact on your relationships.

So, how do you declutter your emotions?

The first step is to become aware of them. This means noticing when you're feeling these emotions and why. A lot of times, we're not even aware of what we're feeling until it's too late and they've taken over.

The second step is to understand where these emotions are coming from. Oftentimes, our emotions are rooted in our past. For example, if you're constantly jealous of your partner's success, it may be because you feel like you didn't get the same opportunities in your own life.

The third step is to find ways of letting go of these emotions. This means forgiving yourself, forgiving others, and moving on.

The final step is to replace these negative emotions with positive ones. This means filling your life with things that make you feel good, such as love, joy, happiness, and peace. Filling your life with positive emotions makes it much easier to let go of the negative ones.

Tips for Black Women to Cleanse and Declutter

In later chapters, we're going to dive a little deeper into the emotional decluttering process. For now, I'm going to help you focus on your physical space. I've put this section at the beginning of the book because if you work on these things now, it's going to have an immediate effect, and damn if that's not enough motivation to show you how impactful this work is.

With this in mind, here's the actionable guide to decluttering, and ultimately cleansing, your physical space.

First, start by gauging your space. If you've never been through your belongings before, then you're bound to find stuff that you forgot existed, and you can't sort it out if you can't see it. So, start by pulling everything out of where it is.

If you're working on your bedroom, set aside an afternoon to pull everything out of your closets and dressers. Leave nothing in its place and pile it high on the bed. Of course, if you come across rubbish, old receipts for example, or anything you know you don't want to keep, get rid of it immediately. Everything else can be piled.

Not only does this help you see exactly what you've got and what you're working with, but it also gives you the opportunity to deep clean your space before putting everything else back. It's a process of giving yourself a fresh slate to work with.

Dust the empty drawers. Wipe everything down. Clean all the windows and vacuum all the curtains and floors. Make sure you get every nook, cranny, and corner.

Next, get rid of anything that doesn't bring you joy or doesn't serve you. If it doesn't make you happy, get rid of it. This includes clothes, books, movies, furniture, and anything else that's taking up space in your home.

Only keep things that are essential. The trick here is to be as ruthless as possible with your belongings and only keep things that you absolutely need. If it helps, use the rule, 'if you haven't used it in a year, get rid of it.' You can do this by selling it, binning it, or donating it to someone or a charitable cause.

It helps to make three piles. You can have a pile of stuff you want to keep, stuff you want to get rid of, and stuff you're not sure about. When you've gone through everything, immediately chuck away everything you want to clear out, and put back everything you want to keep. You don't want to have piles of stuff hanging around longer than they need to.

That's pretty much it. The trick is to be organized with your approach. Set aside dedicated time to go through each room of your house, and make sure you take your time and don't try to do every room at once. Depending on your situation, it's going to be an emotional journey and spark trips down memory lane, so give yourself the time you need to be patient and process everything you're going through.

Maybe do a room every Sunday afternoon for the next few weeks, or an evening here and there, and sooner rather than later, you'll have decluttered and cleansed your entire space.

From here, the final step is to work on actively creating a space for yourself, and this process of filling your space is just as important as emptying it of things that are holding you back. Your space is your sacred sanctuary, where you can relax, rejuvenate, and just be. It's where you live your life. It doesn't have to be big, but it should be free of clutter and anything that doesn't bring you joy. Once you've decluttered your space, focus on filling it with things that make you happy. This could be plants, scented candles, photos, or anything else that brings you peace. And remember, this is your space. No one else's. So make sure it reflects who you are and what you want in life.

However, this isn't an opportunity to go on a shopping/spending spree to fill your home with new clutter. When I say 'fill your space,' it doesn't mean you have to buy anything at all. Rather, it refers to the process of living your life, and if you happen to have something you want to bring into your space that brings value to your life and serves you, then you can do so.

But granted, it can be nice to really breathe some life into your home, and this is the time to do so.

This is your chance to start afresh, and with that comes a whole new level of responsibility to take care of yourself and your space. So be gentle with yourself, enjoy the process, and make sure you give yourself the time and energy you need to declutter your mind, body, and soul, as well as your physical space.

CHAPTER FOUR

Forgiveness and Letting Go

"God saved my soul and spared my life for a reason: He left me to tell my story to others and show as many people as possible the healing power of His love and forgiveness."
— Immaculee Ilibagiza, Left to Tell

Immaculee Ilibagiza was born in Rwanda in 1972. In 1994, she was working as a translator at the Hotel Diplomates in Kigali when the Rwandan genocide began.

During the genocide, Immaculee's entire family was killed. She hid in a bathroom with seven other women for 91 days, waiting to be found and killed.

Somehow, against all odds, she survived. When the genocide ended, she moved to New York City, where she now works as a motivational speaker.

In 2006, Immaculee published her autobiography, *Left to Tell: Discovering God Amidst the Rwandan Holocaust.* The book tells her story of survival and how she was able to forgive those who murdered her family.

'The greatest gift I ever received was forgiveness,' she says. 'It gave me the courage to start my life again.'

When I first read Immaculee's story, I was left speechless. Take a moment to think about what it would have been like to live in a small, crowded bathroom for three months. Never leaving. Hearing the cries and horrors of genocide happening on other side of the walls. Hearing those you grew up with crying out their last breaths as they were slaughtered because of their tribe.

At one point, the house Immaculee and the other girls were hiding in was raided, pulled apart from top to bottom. She describes the experience as utterly terrifying. The only reason they weren't discovered was because the homeowner, a priest from the local church, had hidden the door to the bathroom behind a large bookcase when the militia came to town.

However, the standout scene from Immaculee's life, and the core message behind the entire book, came after the genocide. A new government took control and the militia was quashed pretty quickly. Those who had partaken in the riots and murder were convicted and sent to prison where they would spend life sentences for the vile crimes they committed.

Those who survived the genocide would visit these people in prison. In Immaculee's experience, many people from her village would travel to the local prison where they would sit opposite people they had known all their lives. Teachers. Shop owners. Friends. Neighbors. People who had once been a community now segregated and imprisoned because their tribal and religious beliefs drove them to murder their neighbors, friends, colleagues, and community members.

However, while the genocide was over, hate continued to thrive throughout the community.

People from the village, mourning the loss of their loved ones, would travel to the prisons to seek revenge on those who had taken everything from them. There, guards would stand by, supplying the visitors with batons and planks of wood, allowing them to take out their frustrations on those who had wronged them.

Immaculee, however, felt peaceful. Despite everything that had happened, she felt at peace with what had happened. She obviously felt sadness and mourned the loss of her loved ones, but it felt as though the violence, hate, and the lust for revenge was present in nearly everyone. There was no peace from the hate that had spread throughout the country.

A few months passed, and Immaculee made her first visit to the prison. She went to visit a man she had grown up with, a friend of her parents, a teacher, and someone she had been close to for much of her life. However, the tides had turned and he had been a part of the militia that had swept through Immaculee's village and had killed her parents, siblings, and almost everyone she had ever known.

Sitting opposite this man, she saw him beaten within an inch of his life. Perhaps deservedly, after everything he had done. The prison guard stepped forward with a baton, offering it to Immaculee.

'Do it,' the guard said. 'It will make you feel a lot better.'

Immaculee refused to take the baton. Instead, she took the hand of the man before her, hurting, battered, and bruised, looked deep into his eyes, saw the tears and the pain, and simply uttered three words that changed Immaculee's world.

'I forgive you.'

For the longest time, nobody understood Immaculee. How could she forgive those who brought so much pain, hurt, and terror into their lives? Even reading this snippet of the story, you're probably wondering how someone who lost so much could not hate those responsible for her anguish.

The truth is, Immaculee had learned one of the most important lessons: forgiveness is the key to finding peace, happiness, fulfillment, and promoting positive well-being within ourselves. It's critical, and without forgiveness, you're doomed to stew in negative thought patterns.

Immaculee's story may be an extreme case, but it's such a revolutionary tale because it shows us that forgiveness is still possible even in the most extreme circumstances, and it will still set you free.

To not forgive someone, to seek revenge, or to hold on to the negative feelings and thoughts stemming from how someone has treated you in the past will only make you feel worse. These feelings bring no value into your life, except holding you back.

And the longer you hold onto them, the more bitter, resentful, and hateful you will become. Think about people in your life who are bitter and resentful. Think about their attitude towards life. Think about their victim mentality in friendships or home life dramas. Notice how they will blame the people in their past and the experiences they've gone through for the way they are. Maybe you're this person and you're finding this hard to hear.

An entire identity can be created by holding on to past experiences and not being able to forgive how others have treated us in the past. It becomes who we are and when we identify with it, we don't want to let it go because without it, we don't know who we are anymore.

I've been there. I used to despise my ex-partners for the way they used to treat me. The way they beat me. The way they contributed to the destruction of my confidence and happiness, and the fact I had to work hard to build myself back up. I hated those men.

I despised them. It made me hate all men and the idea of ever having a relationship again. But, at the end of the day, waking up and actively hating these people, what did it achieve? Absolutely nothing. It made me a bitter and resentful person who treated the world as a disgusting place where good people get hurt and there's nothing you can do about it.

And what does this mindset achieve? Do you think I was going to wake up every day and aim to build the life of my dreams while truly loving myself and working on building the best life I could? Could I do that while clinging to so much bitterness and resentment? Of course not. Could you?

The reason we feel bitter and angry is not even because we hate the people who wrong us, but because we hate who we are because of them and their actions.

Say you're in a relationship and you love your partner wholly and deeply. However, they cheat on you and you break up. In such a simple and common situation, it can feel like you hate your partner for what they've done, and it's true, they may be a horrible, selfish person, but the hate isn't really towards them.

It's towards yourself. You hate yourself because you made a bad decision. You hate yourself for putting your trust in the wrong person. Now you feel incapable. You feel hurt. You allowed yourself to get betrayed and now you're paying the price, and you hate this situation.

If you want revenge and to hurt this person, it's because you feel so much pain and you want them to feel the same. Is that going to make the situation better? Of course not. It's only going to cause more pain, and you're going to feel worse because you're actively causing another person pain.

What's more, you can never control the actions of another person. If they hurt you, knowingly or unknowingly, you can never do anything about it. While you can influence other people, you can't make decisions for them. People make their own decisions and that's not a reflection of you. You have to stand up and be responsible for yourself.

This means being able to forgive and let go of these past experiences. It's the only way you can ever be free.

Forgiveness is not about condoning the actions of others, it's about freeing yourself from the anger and hurt that they've caused. And letting go is about moving on from the pain of the past so that you can live a more joyful future.

But, and this is an important but, one of the most difficult - but most essential - aspects of spiritual self-care is being able to forgive yourself.

You might not realize it, but you probably carry a lot of guilt and shame from your past. Maybe you made some mistakes that you now regret. Or maybe someone hurt you, and you feel like it's your fault.

Whatever the case may be, it's important to forgive yourself. You are not perfect, and that's okay. We all make mistakes. The key is to learn from them and move on. And once you've forgiven yourself, it will be so much easier to forgive others. Because if you can't forgive yourself, how can you expect to forgive others?

In spirituality, forgiveness allows you to release the pain of the past so that you can live more fully in the present. It's a powerful act of self-love and self-care.

It's important to remember that forgiveness is a journey, not a destination. There will be times when you feel like you've forgiven someone, and then they do something that triggers old feelings of hurt and anger. That's okay. Just take a step back and breathe. Remember that forgiveness is a process, and it takes time. Be patient with yourself, and know that eventually, you will get there.

So much of our pain comes from the fact that we're holding onto the past. We're holding onto the hurt, the anger, the resentment. But if we want to heal, we have to let go. We have to forgive.

How to Forgive and Let Go

The process of forgiving and letting go is not an easy one. It takes time, and since you're living your life at the same time, other things will come up and happen to you, and you'll need to work on these as well. However, the more mindful you are, and the more energy you put into processing and letting go, the easier it becomes.

This is because you start to build so much confidence and self-worth within yourself. You develop the ability to go into the world fearlessly because you know that whatever happens, you're capable of standing strong and can learn and grow from any situation.

Yes, some situations are painful and they're going to hurt. You're going to lose people in your life and bad things are going to happen from time to time. However, you are strong and you keep going because you're able to let go of the hurt and instead embrace everything it has to bring into your life, which is only going to help you love yourself more than ever before.

While so many of us will never understand Immaculee's struggles, I think we can all resonate with the idea of holding onto past pains and feeling unable to let them go. I've been in toxic relationships in the past, and I've certainly made mistakes, said and done things I shouldn't, and experienced that kind of behavior from others.

It's very easy to hold onto that bitterness. I've laid awake and wished the worst on the people that have hurt me. I've felt immense shame and regret for the way I've made some people feel, even if I was acting out of hurt myself. If I knew how to forgive myself and others, these would be feelings I never held onto and never reacted to.

So, how do you do it? I'll show you.

1. Acknowledge the hurt you feel.

The first step is to think about the times in your life when you've been hurt. Some of these will be very easy to bring to mind. A partner cheating on you. A father walking out on your family. A teacher giving you detention. That driver cutting you off. Someone in your neighborhood getting murdered by a gang. Some things that hurt you don't even affect you directly. They can be things about the world that really bother you.

That's not including the microaggressions that build up over time and hurt us just as much. A parent who is always putting you down. A best friend who is always talking behind your back. A partner who never seems to listen to you or isn't available when you need them.

All of these things hurt. And it's okay to hurt. It doesn't make you weak. The first part of the process is going through your life and writing down all the times you've been hurt and the feelings and emotions that you cling to from those situations.

2. Understand that the other person is human and imperfect, just like you.

The next step is to understand that the person who hurt you is human, and just like you, they're imperfect. They make mistakes. They have their own baggage and demons. And sometimes, those demons lead them to do things that hurt other people, even if they don't mean to.

It's important to remember that just because someone hurt you doesn't mean they're a bad person. It doesn't mean they don't deserve forgiveness or that they're not worth your time and energy. Everyone makes mistakes, and everyone deserves a second chance.

3. Accept that what happened is in the past and can't be changed.

The next step is to accept that what happened is in the past and can't be changed. No matter how much you want to, you can't go back and change what happened. All you can do is move forward. This doesn't mean that you have to forget what happened. You can still remember it, but you need to let go of the pain and hurt that it's causing you.

4. Forgive yourself for anything you might have done to contribute to the situation.

It can be hard to forgive yourself for anything you might have done to contribute to the situation. Maybe you were too trusting or naive. Maybe you should have seen the warning signs. Maybe you could have done something to prevent it.

Whatever it is, forgive yourself. You can't change the past, but you can learn from your mistakes and do better in the future. This is considered the most important part of the process.

5. Forgive the other person for their part in the situation.

Now, it's time to forgive the other person for their part in the situation. This doesn't mean you have to be friends with them or talk to them again. It just means that you need to let go of the anger and hurt that they caused you.

6. Let go of the grudges and resentment you've been holding onto.

The final step is to let go of the grudges and resentment you've been holding onto. These are poisonous emotions that will only hurt you in the long run. If you want to move on and heal, you need to let them go.

This could be resentment toward the other person, yourself, or the situation itself. It doesn't matter. What matters is that you let it go so you can finally move on.

7. Make a commitment to yourself to do better in the future.

The last step is to make a commitment to do better in the future. This doesn't mean you have to be perfect. It just means that you need to be more mindful of your actions and words and how they might affect other people. We all make mistakes, but it's important to learn from them and do our best to not repeat them in the future.

Take some time to reflect on these steps and see if there's anything you need to work on. Forgiving yourself and the other person can be a difficult process, but it's beneficial for your own mental and emotional health. If you're having trouble forgiving, reach out to a therapist or counselor who can help you work through it.

CHAPTER FIVE

Gratitude

"When you arise in the morning, give thanks for the food and for the joy of living. If you see no reason for giving thanks, the fault lies only in yourself."
— Tecumseh

When I read that quote for the first time several years ago, I was on the fence on whether it's something that resonated with me or not. Yes, I thought to myself, I should be thankful for the food I get to eat, the water that comes out of the shower at the turn of a tap, and the roof over my head. I know that my life could be a lot worse, and has been at times.

On the other hand, what was the purpose of being grateful for things that so many of us have? How could saying thank you for having a bed or being in a home make a difference to how I love myself? Just because I lived in a house growing up, that doesn't mean that it was a pleasant experience.

I lived with my ex-partner and despite having a roof, running water, and food, I sure as hell know being abused didn't make me happy living there with him. Being grateful was the last thing on my mind.

But that's just it.

Reading that last paragraph, you may have felt very similar to how I did writing it. It feels very ungrateful to not be grateful for all these things. Not because people have it worse around the world, although that's certainly true, but because even in the hardest and darkest times, there is still so much good to be thankful for. It's this line of thinking that allows you to access another way of loving yourself, and why it's considered one of the most important aspects of modern spiritual self-care.

You only have to read a few self-care articles to see that developing a gratitude practice is one of the best forms of looking after yourself, developing a positive mindset, healing your soul, and a step closer to the life you want to live.

Being grateful for what you have, no matter how small, is a way of showing yourself that you're worth it. That you deserve good things. It's a way of showing yourself that even despite everything you've been through, you still have so much good going on in your life, and much more to come.

That makes gratitude one of the most powerful ways to acknowledge the goodness in your life, even when things are tough. Because even when things are tough, there's always something to be grateful for.

Here's how I started.

Take a moment to think of one thing in your life you're grateful for. It really doesn't matter what it is, big or small. It can be something as simple as the sun shining today or being able to breathe. Yes, it sounds small and insignificant, but just try and come up with something.

Now sit with it. Really sit with it. Take a moment to really feel that gratitude. Feel how good it feels in your body. Maybe you feel a sense of warmth or peace. Maybe you feel your heart opening up or a smile spreading across your face.

Take a few deep breaths and savor that feeling. Do you feel it? That warmth? It's actually kind of magical when you can feel it, and even more so when you realize that this feeling of wholeness and completion is something you can tap into at any time of your life. Any day, any hour, no matter what you're up to.

Now, imagine how it would feel if you took a moment each day to feel gratitude for one thing in your life. Imagine the kind of effect that could have on your entire life long-term? Imagine how you would see the world if you took the time to feel this every day? I say imagine, yet you really don't need to. It's a reality you can access whenever you want, and benefits you can enjoy anytime you please.

This is what can happen when you make gratitude a part of your daily routine.

When you take the time to do this, the benefits do come in waves. You can look up other people's experiences online, but I'll take a moment to share my own.

On a physical level, gratitude contributes to the already extensive range of benefits that self care brings in your life. That includes things like better sleep, better control of my state of mind, better handling and resilience of harder situations and experiences, less stress, and so on. However, the biggest benefit it had was improving my control and my awareness of my emotions, and I found this so interesting.

When I started, I just focused on making gratitude a habit. I spent no more than a few minutes every day just writing down some of the things I was grateful for. I didn't think too hard about it, I just jotted down whatever came to mind. Stuff like the city I live in, having food, my friends, my parents, days out, memories I had made, the greenness of the park near my house, and so on. Just simple stuff.

However, every few weeks, and sometimes every other day, I would find myself struggling to think of anything. I would either think of something I had written previously, or just didn't have the ideas come to mind. At first I would get frustrated with myself.

'Why can I not think of anything?' I would think to myself. 'I live in the modern world and I can't even think of one thing to be grateful for. What kind of selfish person does that make me?' As you can already tell by the language I'm using, this wasn't a great expression of self love, but one of bitterness and almost anger towards myself.

However, this anger towards myself didn't simply come from not being able to come up with something to be grateful for. Oh no. Finding myself in a rut like this is a clear sign that something is up, my emotions are in flux, and there's something I need to be aware of within myself.

On days I'm happy and full of love, where the birds are singing and the sun shines bright, finding things to be grateful for is easy. The world simply looks like a beautiful place, and so I can name anything in it. On the other hand, when something's on my mind, perhaps a bad situation or negative feelings, then it's much harder to find something beautiful to be thankful for.

This is where emotional awareness comes into play.

In the past, I could have easily gone through my day in a bad mood without even realizing it. I would take things out on other people, I would make mistakes in my work, and I would generally just be reserved, quiet, and not myself. I might snap at someone, or I might ignore a friend's text message. If I went to lunch with a friend, I might just not show up as the best version of myself, but all in all, I wouldn't know why this would happen. To be truthful, half the time I wouldn't even realize it was happening until I looked back on it or was called out by a friend, or asked what was wrong.

However, by taking the time to be grateful every day, on the days where I struggled to think of anything at all, this was a sign that something was up. Even if I didn't know what it was, or even had the time to figure it out, I would then be able to go into my day armed with this knowledge, therefore capable of making more mindful decisions about how I was going to act.

Instead of marching into the office and telling everyone I'm fine when they can see that I'm clearly not, I would come in and just say I'm in a bad mood and have some stuff on my mind. This act of being honest not only helped people see me as being more authentic, it actually helped me to discover my more authentic self.

Through the basis of gratitude, I was actually starting to find myself.

Sometimes I would go through the day and just ride out the bad mood. Some days I would talk to people, and could actually talk to them because I was honest with them about how I was actually feeling, and sometimes I even solved the problem then. This was miraculous to me because never before had I taken the time to actually share myself with other people, even colleagues or coworkers who I always saw as strangers.

By just being myself, I was learning about who I was, and I started to love myself fully. I wasn't hiding who I was or how I felt, and I had so many people come up to me and tell me it had inspired them to do the same. Before I knew it, many of the circles in my life had started to shift. A ripple had been sent into the world through the small mindful stone I dropped in my own ocean.

Now, I'm not saying I'm responsible for change on a mass scale. Far from it. What I am saying is that each and every one one of us has the ability to make changes in our life. When we find out who we truly are, behind all the conditioned thinking and beliefs in ourselves that we've piled up over the years, then the real love for ourselves can start to shine through.

Gratitude is one of the most powerful self-care tools at your disposal for making that happen. It's always there for you, no matter what's going on in your life. And it's something you can do for yourself, anytime, anywhere.

So, make a commitment to yourself to start practicing gratitude every day. It doesn't have to be something big. Just take a few moments each day to think of something you're grateful for and really savor the feeling. You'll be amazed at how much better you feel when you make gratitude a part of your life.

So many of us go through life with a sense of entitlement. We think that we deserve all the good things that come our way, and we don't appreciate them nearly as much as we should. But entitlement breeds dissatisfaction. The more entitled we feel, the more we expect, and the less satisfied we are with what we have.

Gratitude, on the other hand, breeds contentment. When we're grateful for what we have, we're more likely to appreciate it and be satisfied with it. Of course, this doesn't mean that you shouldn't strive for more. It's okay to want more out of life. But it's important to be grateful for what you have even as you work towards something better.

One of the best ways to develop a gratitude habit is to keep a gratitude journal. Every day, write down three things you're grateful for. It's also important to be grateful for the tough times because they make the good times even better. So, if you're going through a difficult time, don't forget to focus on the things that you're grateful for.

Is Gratitude a Spiritual Practice?

Absolutely. There's no doubt about it, and this is why it's sometimes difficult to communicate with some people who have preconceived ideas of what spirituality is. It's not about sitting under a tree and meditating for ten hours a day in the hopes of achieving transcendence.

Spirituality is, as previously mentioned, the journey of connecting with something higher than your physical form. Connecting with the true and pure version of yourself. When you think of something you're grateful for, you're taking yourself out of your head and your problems and focusing on something positive.

Gratitude is about connecting with the good in your life, even when it seems like there's nothing good to focus on. And that connection is what will help you to heal your mind, body, and soul. So, if you're looking for a powerful, holistic self-care tool, gratitude is it.

Practical Steps for a Gratitude Practice

Connecting to the power of gratitude can be quite simple. Here are a few practical steps you can take to start incorporating gratitude into your self-care routine:

1. Keep a gratitude journal and write down three things that you're grateful for every day.

It doesn't matter how you do this, just find what works for you. You can use a notebook, an app on your phone, or even a piece of paper. Forming a new daily habit can be quite tricky, so make it as easy on yourself as possible.

Set aside time each day for gratitude. It can be first thing in the morning or last thing at night. Just pick a time that works for you and make it a priority.

I love waking up and simply taking out my little black gratitude journal to jot down a quick thought or two about something I'm grateful for that day. Other times, if I'm feeling really inspired, I'll write more. But usually, just three things are enough to shift my focus and help me start my day with a sense of gratitude.

2. Take a few moments each day to really feel the gratitude in your body.

While it's easy to write about the things you're grateful for, like the house you're in, the safety of your home, the money you have, the opportunities you have access to, and your loved ones, the gratitude experience can really change your life when you tune in to how you feel.

This means connecting to what you're grateful for because it helps to anchor the feeling of gratitude in your body. To really feel this connection, simply close your eyes and take a few deep breaths while you focus on the things you're grateful for.

3. Express gratitude to the people in your life who have helped you or been there for you.

One of the best things you can do for yourself is to make it a habit to express your gratitude to others. This can be as simple as saying thank you when someone holds the door open for you or sends you a text.

But it can also be something more significant, like expressing your gratitude to a mentor or teacher. When you show others that you appreciate them, it puts both of you in a better mood, spreading positivity.

4. Be grateful for the tough times, because they make the good times even better.

When you're going through hard times, or have been through bad times, it's easy to get bitter and resentful. It's easy to think that life is cruel and you're forever destined to float between having really good days and really bad times, but that is how life is. But, it's not a bad thing. In fact, it's really quite beautiful.

When winter comes and the world is cold, icy, and gray, it sucks. There are some good snowy days, but generally it sucks and makes us all miserable. It's why we all get so quiet and sad and say we can't wait for summer.

However, if it was summer all year round, we'd get bored of it. More importantly, we would take it for granted because it would just be summer all the time and we'd think nothing of it. It wouldn't be special. We'd just complain when it's too hot or colder than usual. It's because we have the darker times of winter that we're able to fully appreciate summer in all its beauty.

Personally, there are a few things in life more beautiful than coming out of a hard winter and seeing the world start to blossom throughout spring. I wouldn't see this beauty if it was just spring all the time. This is why it's so important to live life embracing the good and the bad.

Think about all the bad things that have happened to you. While it may have felt like it at the time, they never lasted forever. The good times, just like the seasons of our world, came around again, and understanding this will bring peace and love to your life. This is where gratitude comes in, because it gives you the opportunity to be grateful in the good and bad times, and everything they bring to our lives.

Now, I'm not advocating for shutting out all the negativity in the world and pretending it's not there, because it is. When someone you love passes away, it's sad. You're going to feel sad and you're going to miss them. There's no escaping this, and you shouldn't pretend to feel any other way. You have to process and you have to heal.

However, gratitude is critical in times like these. Being sad and mourning someone you love is a sign that you cared about that person, and had a relationship that you cherished. After all, it's better to have felt the joy of love and the despair of loss, than never to have loved at all.

CHAPTER SIX

Mindfulness and Meditation

"Mindfulness gives you time. Time gives you choices. Choices, skillfully made, lead to freedom."
— **Bhante Henepola Gunaratana**

You've probably heard of mindfulness, but I was feeling a little uneasy bringing it up. When you speak to some people about spirituality, mindfulness, meditation, and all this stuff, it can be a little off-putting to those who believe it is some kind of pseudo-science. They dismiss it even before you even get into the crux of what it's all about.

This happens with religion, where you only have to mention it and everyone has the image of an older man with a beard sitting in the sky. When you hear of mindfulness and meditation, maybe you think of something similar, like envisioning a monk sitting in a rainforest in orange robes with his eyes closed.

All the hearsay, trends, meditation apps, and endless blog posts on mindfulness and meditation can make it all very confusing. It may be easier to just switch off. I used to feel indifferent, even though at my core I loved the idea of being more mindful. Something about it spoke to me, but there was just too much noise around it.

But what was this thing that kept pulling me in? For years, I ignored the urge to find out more. I bought books on meditation, read articles online, and used an app for a week or two, but the interest tended to fade out before the habit had even formed. But the urge remained and a few months later, I'd try again.

It wasn't until years of going through this cycle that I started to realize what the problem was and why the practice wasn't clicking. It wasn't that I didn't want to meditate, I was just approaching it in the wrong way. I was always trying to use meditation as a way out. I tried to use it as an escape. When I was at my worst, I would try to use it as a solution to make everything better and to make my problems go away. I'd use it as a way to try and be happy.

However, this was just me trying to use meditation and mindfulness as a way to fix my external problems, instead of using it for what it's meant to be used for - **looking**

within yourself.

Mindfulness is the act of being present and aware of your thoughts, feelings, and surroundings without judgment.

It's about being in the moment and observing your experience without getting caught up in it. For example, when you have a panic attack or feel anxious about an upcoming event or conversation, getting caught up in these thoughts will leave you spiraling and losing control.

On the other hand, being mindful of your anxious thoughts means instead of getting sucked into a panic attack or feeling so anxious that you end up canceling an interview, breaking down, feeling sick, and otherwise feeling terrible for days or weeks, you stay grounded and make the true decisions you want to make. You are able to stop yourself from acting from an emotional state of mind.

For example, let's say someone cuts you off in traffic, takes your lunch at work, or knocks a drink out of your hand. It's very easy to feel angry and irritated. However, instead of mindlessly reacting, mindfulness calls for you to notice your emotions and then react from a stable and grounded state of mind.

This means that you're fully in control of your words and actions, rather than reacting in a way that you'll later regret or that will cause problems for those around you.

Being mindful means you notice the emotions instead of being lost in them, and make decisions based on what your higher self decides to do, which is aligned with your values and the kind of person you want to be.

Being able to give yourself this love and control over your emotions is a very powerful step on the journey to unconditional self-love.

As the quote at the beginning of this chapter suggests, mindfulness gives you time. It puts you in the present moment and instead of being lost in your thoughts, the stress of your life, or reminiscing about an overwhelming positive time to avoid the present moment, mindfulness keeps you grounded.

During bad times, it helps you to recognize what you're feeling. It's about taking a moment to think, 'Hey, I feel like I woke up on the wrong side of the bed today,' and then making choices from how you want to show up to the world, rather than acting on your emotions.

Remember how, when I lacked gratitude, I would retreat into myself or take it out on others whenever I felt lost, depressed, stressed, or sad? With mindfulness, you're able to recognize when you feel this way and acknowledge it before making your decision.

Imagine someone is being rude in the street. You can get angry at them, hurl insults their way, and get aggressive, something you are bound to regret, as most level-headed people do (like road rage). Or, you can be mindful, acknowledge the anger in the moment, and then choose to take a deep breath and move on. You're never going to see that person again, so what does it matter? Why bring more hate into the world?

So, how do you become more mindful?

Through the practice of meditation.

There are many different types of meditation, but the basic idea is to focus your attention on something, such as your breath, and to let thoughts come and go without getting caught up in them.

Meditation helps you become more aware of your thoughts and emotions and to better understand how they impact your life. They can also help you to develop a greater sense of peace and wellbeing.

There are a ton of misconceptions surrounding this practice. Many believe it's a fad of the Western world, but it's actually a cultural practice from the Eastern world that dates back as far as 5,000BC.

Many people also believe that it involves sitting and clearing your mind of all thought. However, this is a commercialized idea propagated by TV and movies, usually involving some kind of warrior trying to clear every thought from their mind to focus on an upcoming fight.

Mindfulness, practiced through meditation, is the process of acknowledging your thoughts, accepting them, and therefore better understanding yourself. The more you understand and know yourself, the deeper you can love yourself.

Mindfulness can also be a powerful tool for managing stress and anxiety. When we're mindful, we're less likely to get caught up in our thoughts or worry about things that haven't happened. We're also less likely to dwell on past mistakes or hurts. Instead, we're able to focus on the present moment and deal with what's happening right now.

I've recently been having trouble with my brother. He recently moved back in with our parents after his relationship ended and he lost his job. Whenever I visit, I notice that my brother is not functioning properly. He's lazy and entitled. He's selfish and never thinks about others.

He leaves a mess wherever he goes and never helps out; leaves lights, computers, and televisions on at all hours which racks up the electricity bills; and eats all the food in the house without chipping in to make or get more. I find this incredibly irritating.

He was the same when we were growing up, and he often left me to make difficult decisions while he just didn't seem to care. It irks me to see how little responsibility he takes for himself and his life.

This morning, I woke up and wanted to meditate. As soon as I sat down to meditate, my mind was consumed with thoughts of my brother and how much he's been frustrating me. At first, it was difficult not to feel frustrated and get lost in my emotions.

However, by applying mindfulness, I was able to step back and recognize the thoughts for what they were. I realized that my thoughts and emotions were just thoughts and emotions, they didn't define me or who I was.

I was able to see my brother as a person who is going through a tough time, rather than as a lazy entitled jerk. I saw how his current situation was impacting him and how he was reacting to it. I even felt a bit of compassion for him.

This was a huge step forward for me. In the past, I would have just gotten lost in my emotions and reacted out of anger and frustration, usually by having a nasty conversation or telling him what I thought of him. But by being mindful of my thoughts and emotions, I was able to understand them and react in a way that was more aligned with my values.

With this in mind, I'll be more aware of how I'm feeling when I talk to him. Instead of acting emotionally, putting him down, venting my frustrations, or saying something I'll probably regret, I can remain peaceful and grounded. This is the foundation I can use to build a relationship with him, if I choose to. And this will lead to productive conversations where I'll actually listen to my brother and try to understand him as a person in a compassionate and loving way, rather than just dumping my own emotionally charged opinions.

This is just one example of how mindfulness has helped me in my life.

However, I understand this is a bit broad and doesn't really feel actionable. This is something I've personally struggled with for a long time. I read about mindfulness and meditation, watched a lot of talks and went to several classes, and all the teachers repeated the concept of sitting quietly and acknowledging your thoughts.

However, it took me years to realize that this is just one part of being mindful, or at least one way of going about it. You can bring it into all areas of your life, at any time, no matter what you're up to, or where you are.

Fortunately, this doesn't mean you need to sit and do nothing for hours everyday, or sit in the woods while becoming a monk, although you certainly could if this works for you. Instead, it's about bringing meditative mindfulness practices into your daily life.

Getting Started with Your Own Mindfulness Practice

You can be mindful at any time of day, in any way. You don't even really need practice, especially as you become more experienced. You can be mindful right now simply by looking at something near you - focus on the details of the object, perhaps a shadow on the wall, the green of the leaves on the trees, or the texture of the carpet.

As you focus on these details, don't judge them; simply acknowledge their existence and pay attention to the thoughts and feelings you're having at that moment. What comes up? Do you find thoughts of work or your relationships cropping up?

Are you feeling okay? Are you happy, sad, stressed, tired, or content? Are you angry, jealous, or distracted? Once you recognize the feeling, don't try to push it away. Embrace it. Sit with it and see what else comes to mind. What thoughts or feelings arise? Watch them with unbridled curiosity.

Remember, there are no good or bad thoughts or emotions, and everything you feel is valid. It's your physical body and mind trying to tell you what's going on within yourself and how you feel about the details of your life.

Without this practice, the situation with my brother would leave me angry and irritated. Without my awareness, these emotions could leak into so many other areas of my life, creating even bigger problems. Being aware of my feelings and their source unlocked my ability to solve the problem in a much more mindful and compassionate way, and the same can work for you.

However, while you can be mindful at any time, there's no denying that you'll get so much more out of this practice if you develop and work on your mindfulness, so let's explore ways to ensure success in your endeavors.

1. Set aside some time each day for your mindfulness practice.

As with your gratitude practice, you'll achieve impeccable results if you practice mindfulness every single day, but you need to work it into your life in a way that works for you.

This means starting small, like a five-minute practice (or a set time frame you find comfortable). You can do it first thing in the morning, at lunchtime, or before you go to bed.

The important thing is that you find a time that works for you and commit to it. Once you've found your time, put it in your diary or set a reminder on your phone so you don't forget.

2. Start by focusing on your breath.

Breath is commonly used in meditation practices because it's a constant part of your existence that you can focus on at any time of day. Once you develop your practice, you'll start focusing on your breathing while you're out and about. However, it's best to start focusing on it when you're in a comfortable position.

To focus on your breath, simply sit or lie down comfortably and close your eyes. Then, pay attention to the sensation of the air as it enters and leaves your nose.

You don't need to control your breathing in any way, simply let it happen naturally and focus on the rise and fall of your stomach as you breathe in and out.

3. Engage all your senses

Once you're comfortable, start to expand your awareness to include your surroundings. Notice the sights, sounds, and smells around you. Listen to the birds singing or the leaves rustling in the wind.

If you're inside, pay attention to the hum of the fridge or the sound of the rain. If you're outdoors, notice the sensation of the grass under your feet or the sun on your skin.

These are all ways to help you focus on the present moment, reducing the chance of getting lost in the chatter of your mind. Remember, it's all about practicing these techniques throughout your daily life. You don't need to be sitting on your floor cross-legged.

For example, when you're brushing your teeth, be mindful of the taste of the toothpaste, the feeling of the bristles on your teeth, and the sound of the water running. When you're eating, take the time to appreciate the smell, taste, and texture of your food. When you're walking, pay attention to the sensation of your feet hitting the ground, and notice the sights and sounds around you.

The key is to be present in the moment and focus on your senses. By doing this, you'll gradually train your mind to be more mindful. Mindfulness doesn't need to be complicated. It can be as simple as focusing on your breath or being aware of your surroundings.

The important thing is to make it a part of your daily life so that it becomes second nature. It will take time to build up your ability to be mindful of your thoughts and feelings in the present moment, but you'll notice the differences almost instantly.

4. Acknowledge and become aware of your thoughts

And finally, when you're ready, pay attention to your thoughts and feelings. Notice them without judgment and let them come and go. This is where you'll find clarity and understanding within yourself, and you'll truly be able to understand what you're feeling and how your thoughts are affecting your emotions and actions.

When you hear that mindfulness practice is actually simple, it means that it's just a case of being aware. That is literally all there is to it. It can feel a little too simple, sure, but once you start to get the hang of it and you start to notice yourself becoming unconsciously mindful throughout your day, you'll smile to yourself.

That's right! You actually get to become mindful about being mindful!

It really is a lot of fun.

Experiment with Styles

Once you form your meditation habit and regular practice, you can start to experiment with some of the different types of meditation available, and there is a lot to discover.

From sitting in silence with a timer to following a guided meditation focusing on different well-being and self-care goals, meditation in the modern-day can take you pretty much wherever you want to go.

I've had body confidence issues over the years which affected so many aspects of my life, from my sex life and self-worth to my confidence and how I carried myself in public. I used to have a big issue seeing my stomach in a mirror or when it pushed my shirt out a little. I'd think that I was disgusting.

However, since I began building my mindfulness practice, I became aware of this thought. I decided to take a 30-day body image positivity meditation course (ten minutes or so per session), and I was able to take steps towards actually loving myself and treating myself with the respect and compassion that I deserved.

If I was not mindful, and instead went about my days calling myself disgusting whenever I saw myself, what kind of mentality would I have after months and years of these thoughts?

It's not a healthy way to live, and it's not a happy way to live. However, through mindfulness and meditation, I was able to take control of my thoughts, and now I no longer have that problem.

When it comes to meditation, you need to find what works for you. You might hate sitting down in silence with a ten-minute timer, and you might only want to do it for two minutes. That's fine.

You may try breathwork, body scans, or meditations and affirmations. That's fine. There's no right or wrong way to do things, and as long as you're making the effort to meditate, that's what counts.

Don't be afraid to experiment and see what works for you. And most of all, try to enjoy yourself. Self-care doesn't have to be serious, and can instead be fun and progressive. After all, the more you enjoy it, the more likely you are to stick with it.

It's all about you!

CHAPTER SEVEN

Being Intentional and Inspired Action

"Authenticity is a collection of choices that we have to make every day."
- Brene Brown

So far, we've discussed the practical aspects of spiritual self-care and things you can do to make real physical changes in your life. Through the practices in the previous chapters, you'll be able to make some incredible changes, but it's important to remember that your spiritual practice is about so much more than just the physical.

While the practices in the previous chapters form a great foundation, it's important to remember that your spiritual practice is about heart work too. This is the more intangible side of things, and it's what will help you to connect to your authentic self and live a life that feels true to you.

How do you begin working with the intangible?

The answer is **intention**.

Intentionality is the process of setting your focus on what you want to achieve, and it's a practice that can be done throughout the day in small ways, or as part of a larger spiritual ritual. It's a way of putting your desires and intentions into the universe, and a powerful way to help manifest the life you want to live.

Your intentions need to be clear, concise, and focused. Vague intentions such as 'I want to be happy' or 'I want to be healthy' are unlikely to amount to anything substantial.

Without intention, our efforts will be scattered and we are likely to give up when things get tough. When we're clear about our intentions, we can better focus our efforts and stay motivated when things get difficult.

Think about your why — Why do you want to start a spiritual practice? What are your goals? What do you hope to achieve? Once you have a clear idea of your intentions, you can take inspired action to achieve your desired results.

Inspired action is taking actions that are aligned with your goals and intentions. It's about taking steps that move you closer to your goal, not further away from it.

For example, if your intention is to meditate daily, inspired action would be setting aside time each day for your practice. If your intention is to eat healthy, inspired action would be cooking a healthy meal or packing a nutritious lunch.

How Intentionality is Essential in Spiritual Self-Care

It's easy to see the benefits of being intentional. From a self-care perspective, it's an essential component in achieving our goals. But what about from a spiritual standpoint?

When we're intentional about our spiritual practice, we're able to connect more deeply to it. We start to see it, not as something we have to do, but as something we want to do because we know the benefits.

When we're clear about our intentions, we can better focus our efforts and stay motivated when things get difficult. We can also be more open to guidance from our intuition and the universe because we know what we're working towards.

And finally, when we take inspired action towards our goals, we start to see results. Things begin to fall into place, and we move closer to the life we want to live.

Undergoing and developing a spiritual self-care practice is a broad concept in itself. Within it, you might work on releasing your past traumas, forgiving others, developing a more positive mindset, accepting and loving your body, acknowledging and healing your anxieties, figuring out what you want in and from your relationships, and so much more.

These are all different focuses you can have within your practice. Some days you'll work on multiple aspects, and some days you may just focus on one. The key is to be intentional about what you're doing and how you want to go about it, maximizing the benefits of what you're doing and how you're spending your time.

You could carve out an hour a week for a self-care bath, and it may be quite nice just relaxing, listening to some music, or scrolling through your phone without having to worry about anything else, but this isn't really intentional. You're just going through the motions.

With an intentional bath, you are focused on the why. Let's say you feel stressed and you want some alone time just to reconnect with yourself. With this idea in mind, you can start getting intentional. You might;

- Leave your phone in the other room so you're not distracted and can really spend time with yourself

- Put on some nice relaxing music that will help you destress

- Add oils to your bath to help nourish your skin, which will make you feel good and boost your confidence

- Use a nice smelling soap or cleanser so you can enjoy the scent and feel good about yourself

- Take deep breaths and focus on letting go of your stress

- Notice how your body feels in the water and appreciate how it supports you

- Take some time to journal about your experience. This can help you to process your thoughts and feelings and gain clarity on what you're working through.

When you get intentional about your spiritual practice, it's not about going through the motions; it's about being present, aware, and focused on what you're doing and why.

You can go deeper with this kind of thinking, which can be a very helpful process if you're trying to get the most out of your practice. For example, leaving your phone in the other room is a great way to reconnect with yourself.

If you want to change your life, you have to be proactive in creating change. Keep doing the same things and you'll keep getting the same results.

How to Become More Intentional Every Day

While the act of being intentional can be applied to big life goals (we'll dive into them in the next section), there are small, yet impactful, things you can do every single day to become more intentional in how you live your life.

Like all aspects of this book and the techniques within it, it will require some experimentation on your part. This means trying a technique for a week or a month, seeing what you like, exploring what benefits you most, and basically figuring out what works best for you. Everyone's different, but that's the beauty of life!

Let me share some tips from my own experience.

Be Deliberate with Your Morning Routine

Your morning routine sets the tone for your entire day. It's the first thing you do when you wake up, and it can set the stage for how you'll feel and what you'll accomplish the rest of the day.

A lot of people go through the motions in the morning. They wake up, have a cup of coffee, take a shower, get dressed, and then start their day. But what if you took a more deliberate approach?

Instead of just going through the motions, think about each step of your morning routine and how it makes you feel. Do you love the smell of coffee in the morning? Take a moment to savor it. Really pay attention to the taste, texture, and smell.

How does your shower make you feel? Relaxed? Energized? Revived? Pay attention to that. As you get dressed, think about how your clothes make you feel. Do they make you feel confident? Powerful? Sexy?

You may not have a lot of time in the morning, but by being more deliberate with your routine, you can start your day on the right foot – feeling good about yourself and ready to take on whatever comes your way.

Spend Your Time Purposefully

It's so easy to let time slip away. One minute you're taking a break to check social media, and the next, half an hour has gone by. Or you sit down to watch TV and before you know it, it's midnight.

When you're intentional with your time, you're purposeful about how you spend it. You're not just aimlessly scrolling through social media or watching TV for hours on end. Instead, you're using your time in a way that is beneficial to you.

This could mean reading a book, working on a project, taking a class, or anything productive to help you move closer to your goals.

It's not that you can never watch TV or relax – you should definitely make time for leisure activities!

Be Clear about Your Values

Understanding and being clear about your values can bring so much good into your life, especially when making decisions and seeking clarity about what you want and how you should be living your life.

Your values are the things that are most important to you. They guide your decisions and shape the way you live.

For example, if one of your values is family, that means that your family is important to you and you make decisions accordingly. You might not take a job that requires you to travel all the time because you value being present for your family.

If you value freedom, you may structure your life in a way that allows for a lot of free time and flexibility. You might not want to be tied down by a 9-5 job, so you choose freelancing or starting your own business.

Values are different for everyone, but it's important to be clear about yours. This drives you to make decisions that align with your values, and you can structure your life in a way that supports them.

Take time to think about what is most important to you and what you want your life to look like. What values do you want to live by?

Listen to the Voice of Your Higher Self

I believe everyone has heard the voice of their Higher Self at some point. Some people refer to it as 'gut instinct' or 'intuition.' This inner voice is always there to guide us no matter what. Your heart speaking to you from the Soul of the World.

I'm sure you've been in a situation where you were going to do something and you heard the voice. It told you to remember your goals and values, and to make a decision that was more aligned with the life you wanted to live. At that moment you heard the voice, you had a decision to listen to it, or ignore it.

From my experience, the more you listen to the voice and act on it, the louder it gets. The more you ignore it, the quieter it becomes until eventually, you might not hear it at all.

The voice is always there waiting for us to listen. It never goes away. It's always there, cheering us on and nudging us in the right direction.

How to Start Taking Inspired Action for the Bigger Things

To become intentional and to start living your life intentionally, you need to become more aware of your thoughts and actions. This means being present in each moment and paying attention to what you're doing. While you can do this every day by being purposeful in your actions and how you're spending your time, it's vital that you think long-term.

This is what it means to turn your dreams into reality and manifest the life you want.

Here are some tips and steps you can take to help you become clear with what you're going to do and how you can get focused on living the life you want.

1. Get clear on your intentions.

Ask yourself; what do I want to achieve and why do I want to achieve it?

What is it you're trying to manifest in your life?

The more specific you can be, the better. You might say, I want a better relationship, or I want to have a healthier, more stable relationship. We all know that's the dream, but just aiming for this is going to lead to a dead end. It's like saying you want to go to Paris on holiday and booking a flight to any city in France. You need to be concise with your end goal if you want to get there.

So, using the relationship example, getting clear on your intentions involves something like;

- I want someone who listens properly

- I want to become a better listener

- I want someone who's affectionate

- I want someone who matches my preferences in the bedroom

- I want to be with someone who understands my love languages

- I want to be with someone who has the same values as me

As you can see, with these intentions, it becomes easier to determine if someone would be right for you from the first time you speak to them. This will only lead to healthier, more suitable relationships based on what you want.

You can, of course, apply this way of thinking to all aspects of your life. This includes your routines, career, financial situation, the way you show up to the situations in your life, the friends you have, the way you spend your time, and so on.

Whatever matters to you in this life, have it clear in your mind. Yes, I know what you're thinking, and it's okay if things change over time. At least to a degree, it would be strange if you went through life and your wants and needs didn't change. If things change and evolve over time, then go with it. That's what it's meant to be, and the intention you have now could just be a stepping stone to help you to discover what you really want.

2. Create a plan and take inspired action.

Once you know what you want to achieve, you can start creating a plan to help you achieve it. You could do this by brainstorming a list of ideas, researching what you need to do, and taking small steps each day that will get you closer to your goal.

3. Take small steps.

Don't try to do everything at once. Start with small steps that you can easily accomplish.

When you set a goal, you're aiming to complete it. If you want to start running and want to run 5km, you want to run the full 5km.

However, around 3km, you start to hurt and get a stitch so you have to walk the rest of the way. That's fine. Too many people beat themselves up over situations like this when they don't need to.

Aim for 100%. Even if you reach 10% of what you aimed for, you're still 10% better off than you were before. Any percent is better than 0%. Growth is growth, no matter how big or small it is.

4. Be consistent.

The key to taking inspired action is to be consistent. Show up for your practice every day, and eventually, it will become a part of your routine.

5. Persevere.

There will be days when you don't feel like showing up, but it's important to persevere. Remember why you started and keep going. Whether it's with exercise, journaling, meditation, the food you eat, spending time in nature, or breaking a bad habit, it's important to not give up when things get tough.

When you persevere, you develop grit, determination, and strength of character. These are all essential qualities that will help you to achieve your goals.

CHAPTER EIGHT

Yoga and Spiritual Self-Care

"Yoga does not just change the way we see things, it transforms the person who sees."
— B.K.S Lyengar

It's funny. I always saw yoga in the same way that I saw the rest of spirituality. I was drawn to it and I felt a desire to try it. I always saw myself as someone who did it, but seeing it posted all over social media was off-putting, and it always felt like such a shame.

I think it was because of this that I believed yoga was a physical activity to help you become more flexible and relax your muscles. It was something for the beach babes of California, or reserved for the hippies. Over the years, I ended up having no interest in it whatsoever. Turns out I was very closed-minded about the whole concept, and while the trends exist, it was me who was missing out.

I never knew about the spiritual side of yoga until I started practicing it myself. Yoga is so much more than just a physical practice. It's about connecting your mind, body, and soul. It's a way to find inner peace and to connect with your true self.

Yoga is a great way to do this, as it combines physical activity with mindfulness and breath work. What's more, there are many different types of yoga, so there's definitely one that's right for you. It's all about getting started and figuring out what works best for you.

The Benefits of Yoga

It surprised me to learn that, just like meditation, yoga is a practice that has been popular with human beings for thousands of years. There are references to the practice in the Rig Veda, an Indian sacred text that dates back over 5,000 years.

I originally believed it was just a Western fad designed to make money and look stylish, but it turns out this was just the tip of the iceberg. This practice has roots settled deep into the worlds of Hinduism and Buddhism.

So, with all of this history, what are the benefits that yoga can bring to our spiritual self-care practice?

1. Improves flexibility and mobility

The clearest and perhaps most obvious benefit to most, is that practicing yoga will gradually improve your flexibility and mobility. This is fantastic news for those of us who suffer from conditions such as chronic pain, arthritis, and other inflammatory conditions.

2. Builds muscle strength

Yoga practice also improves muscle strength, especially in the core and lower back. This is because many yoga poses require you to use your own body weight. Although it's not too strenuous, it's enough to really engage your muscles, exercise them, and build strength.

This is what I love most about yoga. You can go really gently to restore your muscles, similar to resting after a workout. On the other hand, you can be really intensive with your yoga practice and engage in a really powerful workout that will push you to your limits.

For instance, you can go into a position or pose like a Warrior II and while it's quite simple in principle, when you really start to engage your core, stand up straight, and stretch your fingers out, it can very quickly become one of the most demanding poses there is. That's what makes yoga so great and so universally loved. It can be adapted to suit your needs at any given moment.

3. Reduces stress and anxiety

One of the main reasons people start practicing yoga is to help reduce stress and anxiety levels. In our fast-paced, constantly-connected world, it's important to find ways to wind down and relax.

Yoga helps you achieve this by teaching you how to focus on your breath and be present in the moment, just like mindfulness meditation! When you're focused on your breath, it's impossible to focus on anything else, which means you can't dwell on stressful thoughts or worry about the future.

4. Boosts mood and helps with depression

Science shows that yoga can be an effective treatment for depression, thanks to the release of serotonin (a happy hormone) during the practice.

What's more, the mind and body connection fostered through yoga can help you to understand and process your emotions in a healthy way, which is vital when you're struggling with depression.

5. Improves sleep quality

Do you often find yourself lying in bed wide awake, restless and stressed about everything in your life? If so, then you'll be pleased to know that yoga can help with this too!

The relaxation techniques that you learn in yoga can be carried over into your bedtime routine to help you drift off more easily. Also, the increased flexibility can help to relieve any muscle tension that might be keeping you awake at night.

6. Increases energy levels

Even though yoga is often seen as a relaxation practice, it can be quite energizing! This is because of the deep breathing that's involved in many of the poses.

This deep breathing helps to oxygenate blood and gives you a much-needed energy boost, which is ideal if you're struggling with fatigue.

7. Improves focus and concentration

When you first start practicing yoga, you might find it difficult to stay focused on your breath and the present moment. However, with time and practice, it will become easier to quieten the mental chatter and focus on what's important.

This improved focus and concentration can be applied in other areas of your life, such as work or study.

8. Balances the mind, body, and spirit

One of the main goals of yoga is to achieve balance in the mind, body, and spirit. This is why so many people who practice yoga feel a sense of calm and peace in their lives.

The physical poses (asanas) are just one small part of yoga – the breath work (pranayama), relaxation, and meditation are just as important. By working on all three elements, you can achieve a sense of balance and harmony in your life.

10. And much more!

Yoga is a great way to care for your mind, body, and soul. It's also a great way to connect with people on a similar journey.

If you're looking for a spiritual practice that's also good for your physical health, yoga is a great option!

Yoga and Spirituality

There is a strong link between yoga and spirituality, and there are plenty of reasons why the two practices go hand in hand.

First, both yoga and spirituality are about connection. Yoga is about connecting the mind and body, while spirituality is about connecting with something larger than yourself.

Both practices emphasize the importance of being present in the moment. In yoga, this is done through mindfulness and breath work. In spirituality, this is done by learning to live in the present moment and letting go of attachments to the past and future.

Finally, both yoga and spirituality emphasize the importance of self-care. Yoga helps you to care for your physical body, while spirituality helps you to care for your mind, body, and soul.

Defining Different Yoga Practices

There are many different types of yoga, and it can be helpful to understand what each one involves before choosing which one to practice.

Here are some of the most popular types of yoga:

1. Hatha Yoga: This type of yoga focuses on physical postures or asanas. It's a great option for beginners, as it's slower-paced and less strenuous than other types of yoga.

2. Vinyasa Yoga: This type of yoga is more active, as it links movement with breath work. It's a great option for people who are looking for a workout.

3. Iyengar Yoga: This type of yoga focuses on alignment and precision in the poses. It's a great option for people who want to focus on the technical aspects of yoga.

4. Kundalini Yoga: This type of yoga is focused on breath work, meditation, and chanting. It's a great option for people who are looking for a more spiritual practice.

5. Bikram Yoga: This type of yoga is practiced in a heated room. It's a great option for people who are looking to sweat it out!

No matter what type of yoga you choose, you're sure to experience the benefits that come from practicing this ancient discipline.

How to Choose the Best Type of Yoga for You

The best type of yoga is the one that's right for you. If you're new to yoga, start with a beginner class or app. I started out watching YouTube videos where people would guide me through ten-minute workouts. I just varied through a few types for a few weeks, found the ones I liked the most, and then dove into that and found more.

However, I would highly recommend getting comfortable with the basics before you start to explore other styles of yoga.

If you're looking for a physical workout, choose a vinyasa or bikram class. If you're looking for a more spiritual practice, try kundalini or hatha yoga.

And if you're simply looking to relax and de-stress, any type of yoga will do!

The bottom line is that there's no wrong way to practice yoga. Just find a style that resonates with you and go with it.

Simple Yoga Poses for Right Now

As with all aspects of spirituality, your higher self and the benefits of such a practice can be felt right here, right now. You don't need any fancy equipment, special spaces, or accessories. You can literally feel and connect with the benefits now.

When it comes to yoga, you just need to have some ideas of what you're doing. So, here are some simple practices you can perform right now to see what yoga is all about.

Mountain Pose

Mountain pose is easy yet powerful. It's a great pose to start with as you ground yourself and begin to connect with your breath.

Stand with your feet hip-width apart and your arms at your sides. Take a deep breath in and raise your hands above your head, interlacing your fingers. As you exhale, bring your palms together in front of your chest in prayer position.

Take a few deep breaths here, then release your hands and return to standing with your arms at your sides.

Camel Pose

Camel pose is a great way to open up your chest and heart. It's also a good way to stretch your back.

Kneel on the ground with your knees hip-width apart. Place your hands on your lower back for support. As you inhale, arch your back and look up toward the sky. As you exhale, release your back and return to a neutral position.

Take a few deep breaths here, then release your hands and return to standing.

Child's Pose

Child's pose is a restorative pose that can help ease stress and anxiety. It's also a great way to stretch your back.

Kneel on the ground with your knees hip-width apart. Sit back on your heels and place your forehead on the ground. Stretch your arms out in front of you, placing your palms on the ground.

Take a few deep breaths here, then release your hands and return to standing.

Tree Pose

A personal favorite of mine, tree pose is a great way to improve your balance and concentration. It's also a good way to stretch your legs and feet.

Stand with your feet hip-width apart. Shift your weight onto your left foot and place your right foot on your left ankle. Place your right hand on your right hip, then raise your left hand up toward the sky.

Take a few deep breaths here, then release your left hand and return to standing. Repeat on the other side.

Warrior III Pose

Warrior III is a great way to build strength in your legs and core. It's also a good balance pose.

Stand with your feet hip-width apart. Shift your weight onto your left foot and raise your right leg up behind you. Reach your right hand back. Raise your left arm up in front of you, parallel to the ground.

Take a few deep breaths here, then release your hand and return to standing. Repeat on the other side.

And with that, you should have everything you need to know when it comes to starting your own yoga practice.

CHAPTER NINE

Journaling for Spiritual Self-Care

"Journal writing, when it becomes a ritual for transformation, is not only life-changing but life-expanding."
– Jen Williamson

Throughout my spiritual self-care journey, I've tried and experimented with a lot of different techniques and practices, but none have ever come close to the benefits of journaling.

Journaling is a great way to connect with your higher self, as it allows you to dump out all the negative thoughts and feelings that are weighing you down. It's a form of release, where you can let go of the stress and anxiety that's been building up inside of you.

Not only does journaling allow you to release the negative emotions dragging you down, it also allows you to access your highest self. When you clear out the mental clutter, you make space for your intuition and higher wisdom to shine through.

Journaling is a powerful tool that should be part of everyone's spiritual self-care routine. This holistic practice helps you to process your thoughts and feelings, work through difficult experiences, and connect with your innermost self.

What's more, the benefits of journaling are plenty. Studies have shown that journaling can help to reduce stress, improve mental and emotional well-being, and even boost immunity.

If you're new to journaling, don't worry — it's not as daunting as it may seem. Simply start by grabbing a notebook and writing down whatever comes to mind. There are no rules when it comes to journaling, so let your thoughts flow freely.

In fact, there are many great jumping off points to journaling. Here's some ideas;

Gratitude Journaling: I've already spoken a lot about gratitude, and incorporating gratitude into your journaling practice can be a great way to make it easy to do both, giving you a sense of direction with your writing. It also helps you enjoy the benefits of a regular gratitude practice.

Emotional Journaling: Emotional awareness is a common theme throughout the chapters of this book, and it ties in perfectly with journaling. It doesn't matter where you are, what you're going through, what you're doing, whether you're happy, sad, angry, or peaceful. Journal about it.

Deep diving into your own feelings and emotions is not only an amazing way to vent, but it also helps you make sense of why you feel the way you do. You may even be able to find solutions you wouldn't have considered before.

Cathartic Journaling: If you're going through a hard time and finding it difficult to process how you're feeling and what's going on, journaling may be the solution. When you're thinking about a situation, thoughts tend to travel fast and while thinking about specific details at a time, it's hard to see the big picture, especially if emotions are also clouding your judgment.

By writing things down, you begin to understand the intricacies of the situation. You'll be able to see what's happening, why people are doing what they do, why you are doing what you do, and why you feel the way you do. Even if you're just giving yourself a safe place to vent your thoughts and feelings, this is great for your mental health and well-being.

Understanding Yourself: Other than journaling, there are few ways better equipped to help you understand and know yourself. There exist many ways you can use journaling to your advantage. Personally, I like to write a letter to myself. I can talk about my day, how I'm feeling, what's going on, and basically just 'brain dumping' anything that's on my mind.

How often in your life do you sit with someone you love and actually talk about your life? And not just saying you're okay or small talk, but actually diving into the details of your existence? If you're anything like me, very few times. Most people don't want to hear it, and close friends will only put up with it for so long.

With journaling, you can nurture a relationship with yourself by giving yourself that time. It can only be a few minutes a day. It could be an hour. Chances are, your journaling practice will change as life does. The point is, you can really get to know yourself by giving yourself the time to explore how you think and feel. All you need to do to get started is to ask yourself some questions, and then go from there. Questions could include;

- What brings me joy in life?
- What am I grateful for today?
- What was the highlight of my day?

- What did I not like about my day?

- What is something that's playing on my mind today?

- If there was something I would have loved to have done today, what would it have been and why?

- Is there anything I would like to improve on?

- What is something I love about myself?

- If I could speak to anyone today, who would it be and what would I say?

- What is something I would like to achieve today or this week?

You could even try this practice right now. Taking five minutes to check in with yourself and writing down some answers to these questions can bring a world of good and understanding into your day. Even if they're just little one or two word answers or notes. You'll feel the benefit almost immediately. However, don't feel like you have to stick with these questions. You can make them whatever you want.

And the beautiful thing about journaling is that it's your practice. No one ever has to read what you write and it's always about you. You can write however you like. One day you might write 1,000+ words that really dive into how you're feeling about a certain part of your life.

The next day you might write a few bullet points about your feelings and leave it at that. Some days you may write about what you've been up to, and some days you might dive into past traumas. Your journal can have spelling mistakes, pictures, doodles, quotes, cut-out photographs, or whatever you want.

It really is your space to express yourself as freely as you want without any judgment from yourself or the rest of the world.

Yes, it can take a while to get to the point where you can do this freely. For so long, I was so pedantic with my approach to journaling that it really sucked all the fun and creativity out of it. If this sounds like you, then I challenge you to let go and see where your words take you.

There's no right or wrong way to do this — just be yourself, be creative, and have fun with it!

How to Start a Successful Spiritual Journaling Practice

Journaling can be difficult to start. It doesn't matter if you're starting out or have been doing it for years, sometimes you just can't figure out what to write, or you find yourself judging every word. I've lost count of the number of times I've sat and stared at a blank page or screen or written a word or two without an idea how to express what I want to say. It's disheartening, and it's obvious why the habit can be dropped so easily.

It's easy to beat yourself up when you sit down to write and can't seem to piece anything together. You may wonder why you put yourself through this, but there's a simple answer to that.

It's worth it.

If you're feeling this way, it's simply a sign that you need to deepen the connection with yourself. When you're connected, there are endless things to write about, and you basically open your heart and let the words flow as they please.

It doesn't even have to be negative or a brain dump of all the bad things you feel are going on in your life. In fact, I highly recommend writing about all the positive things in your life, like what you're grateful for and all the dreams and aspirations you have for your life!

Here's a snippet from my journal entry about a year ago;

Today, I bumped into Michelle, a girl I went to school with. She was in a really happy mood and invited me to have lunch with her. I'd usually say no but I felt like she wouldn't take no for an answer, and I just kind of mumbled a load of words and that was that.

She spoke about herself and her life the whole time, which was fine, but fuck, it seems like she's living the dream. We were talking about her job and her family and having kids and just how happy she has been and how amazing things have been since leaving school. I don't know what happened, but she never seemed to have fun in school, and once she left, everything just seemed to fall into place. I tuned out after a while because this part of me just wasn't having any of it.

I feel like I should have it together and goddamn it it's all I can think about. There's this weird part of me that won't leave me alone that seems to be screaming at me that I should be further ahead than where I am now. I feel so fucking lost and I don't know what to do about it.

I don't know why I feel like I can't move forward. I know exactly who I want to be. I want to be bolder and push more. I want to be more confident and more courageous and I want to keep pushing boundaries. I want to work hard towards my dreams and make them come true. I want to be earning the wage where I can actually sustain myself. I want to keep building that life for me, my family, my tribe, friends, and all the people I care about.

It's happening but come on life, there's always something. Always bills or illness or whatever. I've tried for so many years to try and get some savings and I checked my bank balance just now and it's nowhere near where I want it to be, even though I feel like I'm trying so hard. It just feels so pointless to keep learning and moving forward but not actually getting anywhere. I'm exhausted.

I know. I keep telling myself it's a slow process. It's a grind and every day it's just about waking up and making it happen, but it's happening, slowly but surely it's happening. Not really much else I feel like I have on my mind today.

I just keep telling myself to keep up with all the good habits, keep being present, keep trying my best to make the best decisions I can. I want to keep learning and keep loving mindfully, listening, and being the best partner, daughter, sister, and friend that I can be, and just to overall be the best human being I can be. The best human being I know that I can be.

I just hope I can get there soon because I'm so damn tired.

Reading this journal entry back and editing it for this book was a surreal experience. I love to see how far I've come personally, and it makes me even more secure in my journey. Writing entries like this was tough at the time, but as you can see from the end of the entry, I even acknowledged that I was heading in the right direction, despite there being lots going on that held me down.

This kind of journaling works so well for me because it really allows me to see how far I've come, what I've been through, and how much progress I've made. It also helps me to stay focused on my goals and what I want to achieve because when I look back at my journal entries, it's like reading a roadmap of my life.

However, I've been journaling for years, and it took a long time to get to this point and a lot of practice to be able to write so freely to myself. When you're just getting started, here are some tips that really helped me.

Make it a daily habit

The best way to journal is to make it a daily habit. Carve out some time each day, even if it's just ten minutes, to sit down and write. I found it really helpful to use a timer so even if I wasn't writing, I trained myself to know that these ten minutes were for journaling. This is the best way to make sure that you're writing regularly and that your journal becomes a valuable tool for reflection and growth.

Set a specific goal or intention for your journaling

Before you start writing, take a few minutes to set a specific goal or intention for your journaling. What do you hope to achieve by writing in your journal? What do you want to write about? Are you emptying your mind, answering a prompt, or talking about something specific, like something you're going through or a feeling you have?

When you get more experienced, this will come naturally, but when starting, it can really help to be intentional with your journaling practice, because it gives you a focus and a direction.

Be honest with yourself

This is probably the most important tip. In order to get the most out of journaling, you have to be honest with yourself. No one else is going to read your journal, so you can write whatever you want, no holds barred. This is your chance to really let it all out, so take advantage of it.

This is a safe space for you to express your thoughts and feelings, without judgment.

Don't worry about grammar or spelling

This is your journal, not a novel, so don't worry about grammar or spelling. Just write whatever comes to mind, even if it's just a stream of consciousness. The important thing is that you're getting your thoughts and feelings down on paper.

Use prompts

If you're having trouble getting started, or if you feel like you're stuck in a rut, prompts can be a great way to jump-start your journaling. A prompt is simply a topic or question that you write about. You can find prompts online, in books, or make them up yourself.

Be patient

Don't expect miracles overnight. It takes time to see the benefits of journaling, so be patient with yourself! Stick with it, even on the days when you don't feel like it, and eventually, you'll see the impact that journaling can have on your life.

Experiment with different approaches

If you find yourself getting stuck, try experimenting with different approaches. You could try mind mapping, free writing, or even bullet journaling. The important thing is that you find a method that works for you.

Set up your journaling space

Find a quiet place where you can be alone with your thoughts. This could be in your bedroom, in a park, or anywhere else that feels comfortable for you. You can also journal in whatever medium that matters to you. Whether you want to write by hand, type on a computer in a special app or a Word document, it's completely up to you.

With this, you should start to see why journaling is essential to the spiritual self-care process. It allows you to get in touch with your innermost thoughts and feelings, process them in a safe and judgment-free space, and set goals for yourself.

CHAPTER TEN

Affirmations

"Every time you speak, you are either building up yourself for the better or you are limiting yourself for the worse. Words carry power, therefore before you speak out, speak in... and test your words!"
— Israelmore Ayivor

One of the most important aspects of your life goes on inside your mind. It's the conversation you have with yourself on a daily basis. This conversation shapes your reality and how you see yourself.

If this inner conversation is negative, it can hold you back from achieving your goals and living a happy, fulfilled life. But if it's positive, it can help you achieve anything you set your mind to.

This is where affirmations come in. Affirmations are positive statements that you repeat to yourself, out loud or in your head. They can be about any area you want to improve in your life.

For example, if you're trying to lose weight, you can affirm, 'I am healthy and I love my body.' Or if you're trying to attract more money into your life, you may say, 'I am a money magnet.'

If you're struggling with self-doubt, you can repeat the affirmation, 'I am worthy of love and respect.'

The point is to change your inner dialogue from negative to positive. Over time, these affirmations will become part of your belief system, and you'll start to see real changes in your life.

It all starts with finding the affirmations that work for you. The internet is rife with posts, blogs, and articles full of affirmations you can use. I personally like to use an app that pings on my phone five to seven times a day with an affirmation. This has been a great way to use affirmations for me.

In movies, have you ever noticed that when the main character is about to do something the plot has built up to, they whisper 'I can do this, I've trained for this, this is what I was built for' to themselves under their breath? Notice how coaches give their players pep talks before the big game?

These are all affirmations, and they're so popular in the media because they work so well and it's something so small and easy, yet the effect and impact it can have on your life is astronomical.

Repeating these statements on a daily basis can help to retrain your brain and shift your thinking from negative to positive.

In turn, this can lead to improved mental and emotional well-being, increased self-esteem, and greater overall happiness.

The magic here, however, is that you can create affirmations about whatever you want, or whatever aspect of your life you're focusing on. For example, you can say something like 'I am calm and react to whatever life throws at me in the most peaceful, grounded way.'

It's important to make your affirmations as specific and personal as possible. This will ensure that they resonate with you, and will actually help to guide your mind however you want.

Creating Your Own Affirmations

Now you know how affirmations can help improve your life, it's time to create your own. To do this, start by brainstorming a list of areas you'd like to focus on. You can focus on things like increasing your self-esteem, attracting more money into your life, or losing weight.

However, at this point in your spiritual journey, identifying areas in your life that you'd like to work on will give you a beautiful foundation to create affirmations that really mean something to you. Currently, one of the affirmations I'm working with is;

I am adventurous - This is important to me because there are so many changes happening throughout my life, and so many of these new opportunities involve an element of risk. Whether it's writing books and exploring new ideas, sharing increasingly personal aspects of my life with the world, or stepping into new forms of expression, there's an element of adventure that I need to dive into.

Another personal affirmation that's a little broader is 'I make decisions that respect my body.' As I've grown in life and taken up plenty of new habits, routines, and practices, life has been changing in a lot of ways. When I start writing books, I get very excited by the idea of working on a new project, so much so that I end up neglecting my sleep and nutritional needs. I can easily end up staying in my house for weeks at a time while ignoring friends and family members who try to get in touch.

This affirmation works for me because while I want to work hard and at times I need to push myself, this simple statement is a great way to remind me to consider my health and to make decisions that are good for me and my well-being. For me, there's no point in working hard if I'm just going to make myself ill.

Personally, I would recommend starting with one or two affirmations that you can zero in and focus on. Take time to really hone the words you're using and the outcome you want to create. As you go through life, you can mix up and change your affirmations depending on what you want to focus on and the changes or growth you want to make.

If you're having trouble coming up with affirmations that resonate with you, try Googling 'affirmation generator' or searching for affirmation lists on Pinterest. Just remember that you don't have to stick with the original affirmations you create, and you can edit and adjust them to serve your changing needs.

When you've come up with a list of affirmations that resonate with you, start repeating them to yourself on a daily basis, either out loud or in your head. The more you repeat them, the more they'll become ingrained in your belief system, and the more likely you are to see results.

Just like anything else in life, the more effort you put into your affirmations, the greater the results will be. So don't be afraid to put some time and energy into creating affirmations that work for you, and then repeating them on a daily basis. You deserve to live a life that's in alignment with your highest self, and affirmations can help you get there.

Here are some more tips that can help you create the most powerful affirmations:

Always make them present tense

Affirmations should always be stated in the present tense, as if they're already true. For example, 'I am abundant and prosperous.' This is because affirmations tap into the Law of Attraction, which states that whatever energy you put out into the universe, the universe gives back.

This means if you put out the energy that 'Wealth is coming,' wealth is always going to be coming, when in fact you want it here now. So make sure your affirmations are always in the present tense.

Make them short, sweet, and to the point

The shorter and simpler your affirmations are, the easier they will be to remember and repeat on a daily basis. They don't need to be long or complicated; just a few simple words will do.

Keep them positive

Negative affirmations (such as 'I am not poor' or 'I am not fat') will only serve to keep you stuck in a negative mindset. So make sure your affirmations are always positive statements that inspire you and make you feel good.

Be Specific

While an affirmation like 'I am free' can feel relevant, it's not specific enough because it doesn't say what you want to be free from, or how you want to be free. You'll notice that this kind of affirmation will always manifest in your life in some weird and wonderful ways, and once you notice it, you won't stop.

Recently, my friend and I were driving home from a nearby city and it was late. He said something along the lines of 'I love driving home with someone in front of me. It's a way to always make sure I'm going the speed limit.'

When we left the city and got onto the motorway, his energy manifested and we were stuck below the speed limit on a national highway for the entire journey with no way to overtake.

It was crazy that this kind of energy literally manifested in a matter of an hour or so. Be specific. Say 'The money that comes to me sets me free,' or 'I have the freedom to choose my boundaries in my relationships.'

Believe in them

The most important part of affirmations is believing in them. If you don't believe that what you're affirming is possible, it's not going to work. So make sure you only choose affirmations that you can see yourself achieving.

Make them part of your routine

Incorporate affirmations into your daily routine so that they become a habit. For example, you could repeat them to yourself as you're getting ready in the morning, or before you go to bed at night.

A list of affirmations to use at any time

While there are a ton of affirmations online and you can always create your own, I wanted to get you started with a sample list. These are examples you can use or customize to bring your affirmation to life.

Affirmations for Attracting Love

- I am valued and cherished

- I am the right person for the one I love

- I am someone's sun, moon, and stars

- I am worthy of a healthy and loving relationship

- I attract love into my life

Affirmations for reconnecting with yourself

- I am in control of my life and my happiness

- I love myself unconditionally

- I am worthy of love and respect

- I learn from my mistakes

- I am entitled to my own opinions

- I am allowed to change my mind

- I am good enough

- I deserve happiness

- I am creating my own reality

- I am powerful beyond measure

Affirmations for connecting with your higher self

- I am connected to the Divine

- I am a spiritual being having a human experience

- I am guided by my intuition

- I am receiving guidance from my higher self

- I am powerful beyond measure

- I listen to my heart and its guidance

Affirmations for soothing stress and anxiety

- I am safe

- I am loved

- I am calm

- I am relaxed

- I am at ease

- I am in control

- I breathe in peace and exhale stress

- I let go of all worry and concern

- I release all fears and doubts

- I am surrounded by an invisible shield of light that protects me from all negativity

Affirmations for body positivity and self-love

- I love my body

- I am beautiful

- I accept myself unconditionally

- I appreciate my body for taking care of me

- My relationship with my body is improving every day

- I am worthy of love and respect

Affirmations for healing from heartbreak

- I am open to receiving love again

- I forgive of myself and others

- I release the hurt from my past

- I am ready to move on and heal

CHAPTER ELEVEN

Connect with Nature and Community

"Nature does not hurry, yet everything is accomplished."
— Lao Tzu

Have you ever noticed how much lighter you feel after spending time in nature? Growing up in the big city, time spent in nature were few and far between. Whenever I went on a field trip during my teenage years or spent time with friends in a nearby park, I felt an immediate sense of relief. There's just something about being in nature that feels restorative for the soul.

Being in nature is one of the most basic and essential forms of self-care. It's free, accessible to everyone, and one of the best ways to de-stress and center yourself, even if you live in an urban area.

Spending time in nature has long been known as one of the best ways to care for yourself and to nurture inner peace. Modern activities that encourage people to go outside while meeting and socializing with new people, like social and community gardening, have exploded in popularity over recent years.

These are beautiful spaces for people to come together and connect with nature while also getting some exercise and fresh air.

But why is connecting with nature so important?

There are a number of reasons. Scientifically, it's one of the most effective ways to reduce stress and anxiety. Studies have shown that being in nature can lower blood pressure, heart rate, and stress hormone levels. It can also improve mood and increase feelings of happiness and well-being.

But it's not just the physical benefits that are important. There's also a spiritual element to nature. For centuries, humans have looked to nature for guidance, comfort, and answers to life's big questions.

In many indigenous cultures, nature is seen as a sacred space to be respected and honored. There are countless stories and legends of animals and plants being spirit

145

guides, helping humans on their journey through life.

What's more, we all come from nature. As much as we may feel disconnected from nature, every single one of us is a part of nature, just like the animals, trees, grass, and sky.

And when we take the time to connect with nature, we're essentially just connecting with ourselves.

Ways to Spend Time in Nature

It's essential to make spending time in nature a part of your spiritual self-care practice. It doesn't matter if you live in the city or the countryside, there are always opportunities to connect with nature. Spend time outside every day, even if it's just for a few minutes. Go for a walk in the park, sit in your backyard, or simply spend some time looking at the stars.

To some people, it may seem crazy to have a section of this book dedicated to ways of spending time in nature, but in a world of social media, smartphones, Netflix, and office blocks, properly spending time in nature is getting more difficult.

Remember that using your phone during 'nature time' negates the experience, just like scrolling your phone when spending time with a loved one would.

So, this section is about the practical ways you can reconnect with nature.

1. Go for a walk

One of the simplest and most effective ways to spend time in nature is to go for a walk. Walking is a great form of exercise, it's low impact so you can do it even if you're not very active, and it's a great way to clear your head.

There are all sorts of different walks you can go on, from a short 10-minute walk around the block to an all-day hike in the woods.

But there are a few things you can do to make sure your walk is as reconnecting as possible. First, try to leave your phone at home. If you absolutely have to bring it with you, put it on silent and put it away in your pocket or bag so you're not tempted to use it.

Secondly, really take in your surroundings. Look at the trees, the sky, and listen to the birds. If you can, walk barefoot so you can feel the earth beneath your feet. And if you can, walk in silence. Let your mind wander and don't worry about where you're going or how long you've been walking for.

2. Sit in silence

If you're not a fan of walking, or if you simply don't have the time, find a quiet spot and sit in silence. This could be in your backyard, in a park, or anywhere else that's peaceful and quiet.

Again, try to leave your phone at home, or at least put it away and leave it on silent for ten minutes or so, so you're not tempted to use it. And take a few deep breaths, letting your mind wander. Listen to the sounds of nature and feel the sun on your skin.

3. Go camping

Camping is a great way to spend a lot of time in nature and really disconnect from the hustle and bustle of everyday life. When you go camping, you're forced to unplug and really connect with the world around you.

There are all sorts of different ways to camp, from pitching a tent in your backyard to going on a week-long camping trip. And there are all sorts of different activities you can do when you're camping; from hiking, swimming, fishing, to stargazing.

4. Spend time in your garden

If you have a garden, make the most of it! Gardens are great places to relax and connect with nature. Spend some time pottering around, planting flowers or vegetables, or simply sit in silence and appreciate the beauty of your surroundings.

If you don't have a garden, you can still connect with nature by spending time in a nearby park or green space.

When you take time to practice your self-care, remain intentional with what you do and how you spend your time. If you want to be phone-free, turn off your ringer and put your phone away. If you want to be active, go for a walk or run. If you want to relax, find a comfortable spot and take deep breaths.

Connecting with Others

Socializing and connecting with other people is vital since relationships are important for your spiritual well-being.

There are all sorts of different ways to connect with others, from face-to-face interactions to online communication. And there are all sorts of different people you can meet that can open your mind to new ways of thinking and views of the world. Not too long ago, I spent some time hiking through some forests on the outskirts of my home city with a group.

I met a woman called Mel who spoke about her life and how the walking group had become one of her favorite times of the week. She spoke about her past, abusive relationships, and how she had felt stuck for so many years, slowly but surely losing her confidence, self-esteem, and her ability to communicate with others.

Mel's story had so much detail that I couldn't help but think about her life and how various aspects of it were similar to mine. There were so many lessons to be learned in what she was saying, and while I wasn't comparing our circumstances, it was such a human conversation to be a part of, and it made me feel more connected to a stranger than I had ever been.

Connecting with Mel in this way, and being outside with her and the rest of the walking group in a relaxing, beautiful, and peaceful natural space, was simply an incredible experience. While we can all read studies and hear experiences like mine, I truly believe spending time in nature with others is one of those experiences you have to indulge in to see what it's all about.

And it's not hard.

When catching up with a friend, rather than going to a bar or for lunch, make it an event and go for a walk in nature together, and then get lunch afterward.

You can also go to outdoor events like open-air concerts, markets, or festivals. Or you can join a sports team or social club that meets outdoors, like a walking group or a gardening club. There are so many opportunities available if you just take the time to dive into them.

Find something that you enjoy and that you can regularly indulge in. If you hate walking, joining a walking group isn't going to be the best solution for you. But if you love being outdoors and you're looking for an opportunity to meet new people and get some exercise, joining a walking group could be perfect.

It's all about what works for you.

CHAPTER TWELVE

Spirituality and Sexuality

"Behind every shallow sexual interaction, there hides a person who does not want to see or be seen at a deeper level."
— **Michael Mirdad**

When I sat down to first write this book, I never thought I would end up writing this chapter. Which was interesting, because I, like many Black women, have spent a lot of time thinking about my sexuality and my so-called 'role' in society. For so long, our sexuality has been used against us. We are repressed through objectification and sexualization.

So many of us feel demeaned and belittled, yet it's something no one seems to speak about. Yes, there's music that seems to further perpetuate the stereotypes, but does that represent you and how you feel?

When was the last time you sat down and actually spoke about your sexuality and how you feel, whether that was with your partner, a friend, a therapist, or even with yourself? Do you know what you like or don't like? Do you know how confident you are? Are you able to fully express yourself sexually in a way that feels right to you?

Or are you constantly bending your will to the wants, needs, or ego of others? Damn, I know I've spent at least several conscious years in that cycle. Even now, in my 30s, with an experienced partner and more confidence than I've ever had, I'm still discovering new parts of myself in terms of my sexuality. And I still find it difficult to sit down and have that conversation, in any way, shape, or form, no matter how many times I've done it before.

I know so many other women who are going through the same thing. It's almost taboo. It's almost like there's a never-ending weight from society, culture, and our history that prevents 'the conversation' from happening. But is this okay?

Is this acceptable? Is this blockage of connection with our sexualities helping us to truly connect with ourselves?

When it comes to expressing your sexuality, you probably don't even know where to start, yet everywhere we're told to be bad bitches and to give the world what we've got.

It becomes more ridiculous the more you become aware of it.

Your sexuality is a part of who you are, and therefore how connected you are with yourself depends a lot on how comfortable you are with your own sexuality. It's about not seeing sexuality as a sin, a cocktail of urges, physical feelings, and chemical drives that make us pursue all kinds of chaos. Sure, sexuality can definitely feel like all these things due to modern conditioning, but it's so much more than this, especially when combined with a spiritual practice.

This chapter is about allowing ourselves to drop the expectations and ideas imposed on us, and to instead focus on ourselves. This means getting to know yourself, understanding your sexuality, and discovering and connecting with a part of you that you may have misplaced for a very long time.

And I think that's what made this chapter so interesting to write.

For many people, spirituality and sexuality are two separate entities, at least that's what I always believed. However, they can actually be quite intertwined. In many cases, you can't have one without the other.

In my past, sexuality was often seen as something dirty or sinful. Something that brought each and every one of us into the world, a natural part of life, but still taboo nonetheless. And for many people, spirituality is something clean or pure. Something that opposes sexuality and therefore can't coexist with it.

Nowadays, however, there is a lot more acceptance of both spirituality and sexuality. And as a result, people are starting to explore the connection between the two. That means there's also a bright and vibrant opportunity for you to do the same in your own life.

So, how can you bring these two aspects of your life together?

How Spirituality and Sexuality are Connected

Sexuality is more than just sex. It's not just about being physical, getting off, having fun, or starting a family. Of course, being connected with your own sexuality means sharing the physical experiences with yourself and others. These experiences are certainly a part of tuning into your sexuality. However, these experiences are not possible without seeking and nurturing a comfortable and secure connection with yourself, nor understanding yourself as a whole.

Already, you should start to see how your spirituality and sexuality are linked. It's about having clarity on the connection you have with yourself. Therefore, the link between sexuality and spirituality is that they're both about the connection you have with yourself.

Spirituality, as I've discussed throughout this book, is all about your connection with yourself, mind, and spirit. It can easily be summarized by your connection to your non-physical self. Therefore, on the opposite end of the spectrum, sexuality is your connection to your physical body, or the aspect of you that you can touch.

There are many different aspects of you that you can connect with, and each will fall under the sexuality or spirituality category. If it's part of your physical self, it's your sexuality. If you can't, it's your spirituality. Many people also see sexuality as spirituality, just in a physical form. These aspects include;

- Biologically

- Psychologically

- Physically

- Emotionally

- Socially

- Spiritually

- Behaviourally

The modern problem with this is that sexuality and spirituality are often seen as two different things, when they're the same. You could see them as two sides of the same coin. People see sex as a taboo, bad, and sinful act, and if you were to live a 'pure' and spiritual life, then you would abstain or be celibate. This is just not the case, and finding true harmony with yourself means finding your own balance and connections between the two.

If you can be connected to your physical and non-physical self, you'll be able to live a full life, a satisfying and fulfilling life, and can find real peace in your existence, instead of the revolving and relentless feeling of conflict with your internal and external worlds.

Spiritual Sexuality Beyond the Physical

We live in a time where gender roles and how we view sex and sexuality is more in flux than ever before. Relationships are evolving faster than ever, and we're entering territory that has never been seen before. Even a century ago, it was believed that orgasms didn't exist and sex was only for breeding. Ignorance was rife and women took the brunt of it, usually objectivized as pleasures for men.

Things aren't much better today. Women are somehow expected to be free spirits while still providing pleasure for men, are expected to be free of inhibitions while feeling free and confident, orgasming every time we have sex, while men are supposed to be long-lasting stallions that have mastered all physical aspects of sex. It just doesn't add up.

The truth is that humanity hasn't always been this way. In fact, there's evidence that suggests that even ancient empires from Greek and Rome saw sex as a positive, spiritual experience. During these times, sexuality was all about abundance, connecting with spirit, higher entities, and uniting our souls and humanity with other human beings.

So, we've been there before. We, as human beings, have used sexuality as a way to connect with ourselves and others in a positive and healthy way, and it's something we've lost over the centuries. It is, however, something we can get back to when we explore how things have changed and why.

There are two parts to this.

The first part is the physical side. It's the conscious, physical side of sex and sexual energy that creates and nurtures all those intense feelings we have for our sexual partners. It's those strong, undeniable feelings that we experience when we have physical and non-physical sexual experiences with other human beings. It's these feelings that most relationships are founded on, and is what most modern sexuality beliefs are based on.

However, the second part is about sexual union, which is what most people consider the ultimate expression of sexuality. You may have experienced a state of pure bliss after some sexual experiences in your life. It's like a clarity that's hard to put into words. You can feel your state of mind enter a zone of clarity and inspiration.

This is far more important than most people think. This clarity, this pure bliss, isn't just the release of stress and chemicals. It's not just a release from your day-to-day life. It's an opportunity to connect with your true self at a higher level. You may have felt it, with yourself or with a partner. That direct experience. That refocusing and realigning of life that happens within and around you after a sexual experience.

It's so powerful, and if you're able to tune into this power, it can change your life.

Balancing Your Sexuality and Spirituality

Balancing your sexuality and spirituality can feel a little complicated. Even now, you're probably thinking about what you're even supposed to be focusing on and where you would start with such a journey. Let's break this down and make it actionable.

First, you need to tune into how you feel about both your sexuality and your spirituality. This is different for everyone, so you'll need to use the techniques within this book to dive into how you feel and what thoughts go through your head. For example, do you feel comfortable when you have sex? Do you have anxieties around it? Do you feel shame when engaged with physical, sexual activity with yourself or others?

Do you feel as though you've let yourself down? These are questions to get you started, but even spending a little time exploring these ideas should begin to unlock how you feel about yourself and your own sexuality.

Think about your own practices so far. Have you been working to connect with yourself on a spiritual level, but judge yourself sexually? Do you judge yourself for your actions, your likes and dislikes, what you look like, what partners you choose, or your past experiences? Do you feel excitement or shame? Are you aware of your values, wants, and needs, not just physically, but spiritually and emotionally?

Do you find that you lean more towards sex or more towards living a 'spiritual' or 'mindful' life? This is a great question to help you understand where you're at and how you connect with yourself. I'm sure if you look into your own life, you'll know people who are more in tune with their sexuality and seem to thrive with physical contact and intimacy (even if it's in other ways toxic or unhealthy), or people who are more mindful, spiritual, and practice activities like yoga or meditation.

If you pay attention, you may notice how people may stay the same for most of their lives, or they may bounce or sway between the two. I've noticed I'm the latter, and sometimes I feel very sexually charged and crave physical contact and sex, whereas other times in my life it feels like I'm abstaining, but my focus is more on myself and my well-being. I feel like most people fit this category, and you've probably found yourself swaying between the two.

In my own experiences, I know for a fact that I lean more into my sexuality when I'm going through a hard time. If I experience the end of a relationship, I may seek 'rebounds' or after a stressful day, I might catch myself watching pornography. On the other hand, when life is 'good,' I'm focused on work or I'm working on my health. I find myself naturally picking up the habits and routines of journaling, meditation, and even just going for more walks in nature.

However, this way of living life is so unbalanced, your wellbeing and focus swinging from one end of the spectrum to the other. The goal is to find the balance in between. Granted, you're not going to get this right all the time, and while others may beg to differ, I don't believe it's possible to find balance between the two and stay there forever.

Life is too random and there are too many things outside our own control to maintain that balance properly. Instead, I believe we should constantly aim for that balance point, and become aware when we're swinging one way or the other. It's this awareness or mindfulness of your own positioning and states of mind that will allow you to take action towards rebalancing yourself. This process of rebalancing is a life-long journey and what your spiritual practice consists of.

How to Find the Balance

Okay, with the theory out of the way, let's make this rebalancing actionable. What can you do to tip your spiritual and sexual scales to the midpoint?

Taking the thought process I spoke about in the previous section, you need to think about why your scales tip the way they do. Again, this is individual to you, so you need to spend some time figuring it out.

For example, do you find yourself resistant to masturbating? Do you think of it as a disgusting, horrible, or forbidden thing? If so, where do these thoughts come from and are they serving you? If you truly believe that masturbation is a sin and it makes you feel uncomfortable, sure, that could be you and that's fine. However, I believe for the majority of people living in the modern world, it's an essential way to connect with yourself, thus tipping the scales to the center.

Do you find yourself indulging in unhealthy sexual habits when you're going through a rough time? Do you sleep around, cheat on your partner, or in other ways abuse yourself and your body in a way you don't like? Are you intimate with others in the moment, but feel shame and guilt for allowing yourself to treat yourself in such a way?

If so, dive into these feelings to identify where they come from and why you do this. This is where you'll find the answers and the insights of how you can move forward. With myself, I had a nasty habit of seeking out porn when I was having a rough time.

If I had a bad time, felt disconnected from my partner, argued, or just felt bad in any way, I would turn to porn. Of course, I only felt better for about a minute before the negative feelings came back, so I would seek it out again. And again. Over the months and years, it turned into a bit of an addiction, and every time I felt bad or stressed, I wouldn't deal with those feelings, but would try to tune out of them using porn.

This has a huge knock-on effect in all other areas of my life. I was distracted at work. I couldn't focus at home. My sex life with myself and my partner at the time plummeted because I just wasn't interested in the physical relationship with him, which knocked our romantic and emotional relationship. I was tired all the time, unmotivated, and to cut a long story short, I wasn't respecting my sexuality, and my spirituality was suffering as well.

My scales were all over the place and I was completely out of balance. They would tip multiple times a day, sometimes hour by hour, and it was just an exhausting way to live. Through mindfulness, spiritual practices, and taking the time to get to know myself on a spiritual and sexual level, I was able to regain balance.

Advanced Tips for Connecting Your Spirituality and Sexuality

Hand in hand with the section above, here are many ways you can rebalance your sexuality and spirituality. A lot of the process will mean going through the techniques outlined in this book and diving into how you think and feel, why, and how to move forward armed with this new information. However, specifically looking into how you can balance yourself, there are some practical tips you can follow.

You don't need to dive into all of these. Just go through them and see what resonates with you. Pick, choose, and customize your approach to see what works for you, and which practices serve you best.

Be open to new experiences

As with all things in life, you'll discover new parts of yourself all the time as long as you're willing to step outside your comfort zone, and this means being willing to try new experiences. There's no need to be afraid to try new things, especially since it's the only way you're ever going to figure out what you like and don't like.

Of course, there's a respect and safety aspect involved, and if you're trying something new physically with yourself or with a partner, then you may need to take things slowly. However, even having a conversation about sex, intimacy, or your wants or needs with your partner, yourself, or even a friend could be outside your comfort zone, and this can be an incredibly rewarding place to start.

Be safe and secure

One of the most important parts of this process. Listen to your heart, your soul, and your Higher Self. If you're given an opportunity you're curious about, but you don't feel comfortable with the person, listen to your intuition. It's there for a reason. This is the literal definition of self love, respecting yourself, and respecting your own boundaries.

Consent is everything. If you're not sure about something, don't do it. Make sure you communicate with your partner and make sure that everyone is on the same page. This doesn't just apply to sexually experiences with others, but also experiences with yourself. Experiences could include anything from opening up and talking to someone or writing something down to physical experiences.

As a rule of thumb, trust in the saying that your body is a temple. If you had a physical temple that you cared for, you would keep it clean and tidy, you'd sweep the floor, polish the statues, and would be aware of what went in and what went out. This is what it means to treat your body as a temple. It's about treating yourself with that degree of respect, and this is essential throughout all self-development practices, whatever it is you're working on.

Communication is key

Communication is always so important when it comes to anything in life. It's how we understand others and their needs, as well as expressing our own. When balancing your sexuality and spirituality, communication is one of the most important foundations you'll need to work on.

This starts with communicating with yourself. Express your needs through writing or dialogue, and don't be afraid to ask questions or to question what you think and why you think it. Basically everything we've touched on throughout this chapter.

But, of course, communicating your sexuality to others is just as important. As surreal as this may sound, it doesn't matter whether you're having a one-night stand or in a long-term relationship, you have to develop your ability to step up and communicate your desires, needs, and boundaries. It's important to be on the same page in order to create a mutually satisfying experience that's built on openness and honesty.

It can take time to get there and to build your confidence. I know when I started out, it felt completely alien to communicate my wants or needs. Hell, I didn't even know what they were or where to start, but through talking and expressing where I was at, I was able to take steps towards understanding. It took time and openness, and so much vulnerability. There were good days and bad days, and it's a process that's still happening to this day.

But through it all, progress was only made when I was communicating with others, speaking and listening from the heart.

Be present as much as you can

Throughout the process of balancing yourself, exercising mindfulness is going to be a great way to connect and move forward. Whether you're engaging in an individual spiritual practice or with your partner, tune into the present moment and pay attention to your thoughts, feelings, and emotions. If your partner is talking about a past sexual experience and is being honest and vulnerable, how does this make you feel?

Are you jealous? Excited? Curious? Feeling shame? It's so important to tune into these feelings because they will show you how you're feeling and where you are currently. Again, it's with this information that you gain clarity about where you're at and can then choose where you want to go in terms of balancing yourself.

Even as you read this book, I mention one night stands and you'll have feelings come up about them. Are you grossed out by them? Do you find them inappropriate? Do you find them liberating? Whatever comes up, question it and you'll find answers about your true self.

Let go of expectations

It's very easy to fall into the habit of having expectations, especially in terms of discovering your sexuality. You might feel completely liberated sexually and you could develop this idea that you're going to courageously go out into the world and discover who you are, what you like, what your values are, and maybe even find the perfect partner for you.

These are amazing ideas to have, but they are expectations that are going to hold you back. If you have the expectation that you're going to head out into the world and everything is going to fall into place and that doesn't happen, you risk knocking your confidence down a few pegs and holding yourself back.

This applies to having experiences with yourself and with others. For example, me and my partner are experimenting with ways of being more intimate and we tried massages. I did a load of research, bought oils, and learned a load of techniques from the internet, and had this idea in my head of how perfectly the night was going to go.

However, while the night started off well, I ended up pushing down on a muscle and accidentally hurting my partner, meaning I had to stop. At first, I was devastated. The night was ruined and even though I had these grand ideas how perfect the night was going to be, it was all over.

That's the problem with expectations. Just because things didn't turn out the way I had intended, that doesn't mean anything is wrong. It's just not how I wanted it to be. I took some breaths and refocused myself, understanding that life isn't perfect, and even though things didn't go as planned, that didn't mean that anything was wrong.

Instead, me and my partner chose to laugh about it and move on, actually making the whole event a pleasurable experience. Expectations only lead to disappointment, resentment, and bitterness, and letting them go can liberate you, allowing you to fully enjoy life with all its ups, downs, and perfect imperfections.

Dare to be vulnerable

Tuning into both your spirituality and sexuality takes a lot of vulnerability, and this is going to be a journey. It means opening up and being completely honest with yourself and others, even if you don't like what you see. It can be hard to admit you have traumas or things in your past or present that hold you back, but without being able to admit them, you'll never be able to work on them.

Yeah, it's scary as hell to be vulnerable. To express your wants and needs to your partner risks them judging you and giving their opinions on what they think, and of course we fear we're going to hear the worst. It's what holds us back.

However, quite paradoxically, the more vulnerable you are, the more powerful and empowered you become. The more true to your Higher Self you can be. When you build the courage to be vulnerable and express how you truly feel, openly and honestly being yourself to others, the deeper you can make that connection with yourself.

There are fortunately plenty of ways to be more vulnerable. It could be telling people how you truly feel, especially when you're upset or hurt. It could be sharing personal experiences with others, openly expressing that you feel pride or shame towards something, setting and respecting your own boundaries, or putting yourself out into the world in any way, even with the risk of rejection.

It can take time, and you'll want to start small and build up your confidence. Try it next time someone says something that makes you feel sad, hurt, or anxious. Just say something like, 'oh, what you just said made me feel really anxious because XYZ.' You don't need to go further than that if you don't want to, but see what happens and tune into how much more connected it makes you feel with yourself and the person you're speaking with.

Being vulnerable can be your superpower to being the true version of you, rather than the weakness many people believe it is.

Let go of judgment

Having judgments is one of the most powerful ways to hold yourself back from having a rich and fulfilling life. Of course, we can't help it all the time, and when things happen, we're going to have opinions about them, but it's identifying these thoughts that can bring you so much power.

For example, I was speaking with my grandmother not too long ago and she was talking about how people don't work hard in relationships these days. Breaking up and divorce is common, and it's so different from her generation when people would stay together and would work hard to love each other. She complained that there's far too many single parents and people who have children in other relationships.

Now, it's a pretty big judgment to say that people these days are lazy and go about having relationships the wrong way. While I would agree that some people give up too easily or the idea of having a 'better' partner can be very enticing thanks to things like dating apps, the world is much more complicated than this.

For example, my partner's father was married twice, his first wife passing away from cancer when she was just 35 years old. They had three children together, and he remarried a decade or so later to a widow whose ex-husband died in war.

The point is that my grandmother's judgemental ways of thinking are very narrow-minded and don't take into account all the variables of the world. When I mentioned this to her, she simply said nothing and dismissed the thought, and this is a clear example of why we shouldn't be so quick to judge.

In this case, she was denying the possible compassion she could have for people who lost their partners at an early age. Being married for 60 years, she could have used this as an opportunity to be grateful that she was able to stay in her relationship for such a long time, and find peace with her own life, rather than putting other people down for circumstances that she knows very little about, or clearly hasn't given a lot of thought to.

We never know all the ins and outs of a situation, and there are a million ways to view a particular event or circumstance, many of which we'll never see. This limited way of looking at life can hold us back from finding lessons and discovering new aspects of ourselves, and connecting with the rest of the world, thus denying the connection we can have with our true selves.

Instead, you need to be mindful when judgments come up in your life, take the time to identify what they are and where they come from, and then take steps to let them go and be open to new ways of thinking. This is how you can truly be open to the flow of the universe and the flow of life, ultimately allowing you to become the best version of yourself.

Have fun

On a final note, applying everything you've read in this book, this journey of self-discovery you're embarking, and connecting with your Higher Self doesn't have to be seen as hard work. It's fun. It's exciting. It's damn liberating.

For too long in my life, I saw self-care as hard work. It meant grinding. It meant looking into all those hard, difficult places that I didn't particularly want to go, but I sometimes had to force myself to go. But when I switched my mindset, everything changed.

Walking this path of discovering your spirituality, your sexuality, and balancing the two is your life's work, but it's barely work. It's the process of connecting with yourself in the same way you would get to know and connect with a new friend. It's enlightening, peaceful, and an utterly beautiful experience.

So, if you take anything away from this book, let it be this.

Be free and have fun. Treat this journey as an adventure. You'll have good times and bad days, hard days and beautiful days, but above all, you'll be seeking out the greatest treasure a human being can ever discover; a love for you.

Embrace it with open arms and such an adventure will positively change your life in a way you could never imagine.

Conclusion

And there we have it, kind soul. You've made it through this workbook. I hope you've learned something new about yourself and that you feel empowered to take care of yourself - body, mind, and soul.

You are worthy of self-love, and you deserve to feel good. Remember that you always have the power to choose what feels good for you.

You are the expert on you, and no one else knows what's best for you. So, trust yourself and follow your heart. Don't be afraid to experiment and try new things. Be open to new experiences and be willing to let go of old, outdated beliefs.

I'll leave you with one last piece of advice: don't take yourself too seriously. Life is supposed to be fun. So, make sure to enjoy yourself along the way!

Thanks so much for reading, and I hope you have a beautiful day.

Book #3

365 Powerful Positive Affirmations for Black Women

Reprogram Your Mind to Boost Confidence, Self-Esteem, Attract Success, Make Money, Health, and Love

Introduction

When was the last time you woke up and felt truly excited about the life you live? Are you living and thriving or just living and surviving? Would you like to change the narrative that has defined your life? Are you ready to become the best version of yourself and live your life to the fullest? If this is you, the key to unlocking that future is now in your hands... or mouth, so to speak. Change the words you speak and the life you seek will fall into place.

"Life is hard." "I can't do it." "I am no good." "I don't deserve this" ... These are just simple phrases that many of us use in our day-to-day life. What we don't know is the powerful impact these words have on our experiences. We need to undo the harm caused by those words through positive affirmations. This book, *365 Powerful Affirmations for Black Women; Reprogram Your Mind to Boost Confidence, Self-Esteem, Attract Success, Make Money, Health, and Love,* is everything you need to get started.

In this book, you will get:

- Fundamental teachings on how words shape your mindset and create the life you want

- Effective tips for activating the power of your affirmations

- Practical information for reprogramming your mind

- Words to affirm your expectations in the areas of love, health, wealth, and many more

- Powerful affirmations you can use for every single day of the year

This is not a one-and-done type of book. This is the book for every black woman looking to make her way in the world that we live in today. As a woman of color living in a society that sees people through lenses steeped in prejudice and biases, it can feel as though the scales are tipped against you from the start. I know how disheartening it feels when you are faced with disappointment again and again. But let me tell you something I wished someone told me when I was in your shoes.

165

You are not as powerless or as helpless as you think. You are capable of greatness far beyond what you've ever dreamed or imagined. You have the tools you need to shape your life. You can wake up to the life you have dreamed of. The first step on that journey is speaking the right words. This book, *365 Powerful Affirmations for Black Women; Reprogram Your Mind to Boost Confidence, Self-Esteem, Attract Success, Make Money, Health, and Love,* is the key to unlocking the power within.

So, take a deep breath. Exhale. Relax. You've got this. All you need to do is flip over to the next page and let your journey begin.

CHAPTER ONE

Preparing Your Mind

By now, you must have heard from several sources about how powerful the mind is. So, I am not going to go into details on that. My focus instead is to help you understand how you can utilize the power of your mind to your advantage through your words of affirmation. Before we get into that let me put out a disclaimer. Speaking the right words into your life is not going to create an overnight type of transformation. It took years of negative programming for you to get to your present experience and situation. To counteract that effect, you would need to give your words time to take root in your life.

Thankfully, you don't need an extended period to manifest your dreams through affirmations. The fact that you are being very conscious and deliberate about the words you speak to yourself and into your environment makes a world of difference in the outcome and how long it takes for that outcome to manifest. That being said, while transformation doesn't happen overnight, there are changes that take place every time you speak the right words. The end result is usually a culmination of all the changes. To prepare your mind to accept the words of affirmation that you speak, there are three things you must pay attention to. These three things are conviction, consistency, and commitment.

Conviction

According to the dictionary, conviction is a firm belief or opinion. Without conviction, when you speak those words of affirmation, they are as powerful as a feather drifting in the wind. They have no direction or purpose. Your conviction is what binds the words that you speak to the dreams that you have, making it an anchor that forces it to manifest in your life. When you have a strong belief in what you are saying, you become an unshakable force so that even when you are going through the darkest times, you will have the power to maintain your affirmations. Conviction is what gives you the courage to dream big dreams even though your circumstances may want to place limits on what you can achieve. The first step in preparing your mind for your affirmation journey is convincing yourself that the words you speak are your new reality. The moment you successfully achieve this, you become unstoppable.

Consistency

One mistake you cannot afford to make on your journey to manifesting the life you want is linking your affirmations to your mood. The words you speak to yourself must be constant and independent of how you feel. You cannot say I am amazing in one breath and then in the next call yourself a failure. You must be consistent in the words that you speak regarding your situation and how frequently you say it. Consciously or unconsciously, your mind has absorbed a lot of information through experiences, the people around you, and the words that they spoke to you. Some of that information may be hindering you from making advancements in specific areas of your life and so to unlearn those things, you need to consistently speak the right words. As I mentioned earlier, speaking words of affirmations is not something you do once and then forget about it. It must be done consistently over a long period. As you grow and evolve in life, the words may be tweaked and adjusted, but you should never stop speaking those things you want to manifest.

Commitment

It is imperative to ensure that the words you speak are backed up by actions. Let us say, for example, you are trying to manifest a specific type of house. Speaking that house into existence is only one-half of the equation. You need to take the necessary steps to back up your words. Taking the necessary steps doesn't mean you have to pay for the house right away. It could be something as simple as doing an internet search to find out how much a house like the one you are trying to manifest would cost. What you are doing when you take these little steps is physically aligning your actions with your affirmations. You can't be manifesting a house and yet take actions that make it look like you are passing up opportunities to make your dreams come true. Your actions show the level of commitment you have to the words that you have spoken. It doesn't matter if you're looking for a new job, a partner, or trying to get into the best shape of your life. The words that you speak to affirm the life you want to manifest must correspond with the actions that you take to make that affirmation your reality.

Tips on How to Use These Affirmations

A quick Google search will give you tons of tips on how to use affirmations and make them work for you faster. The tips I am going to share with you here are the ones that have worked for me. But before we get into that, I want you to understand that the timeline for manifesting your affirmations varies for different reasons. I have things that I manifested within days. I have those that took me over a year to come to light and then there are things that I am still affirming to this day. Does it mean that my affirmations are not working? No. There is a process to everything. Your affirmations create an alignment. Think of it as the individual stitches that come together to make up a fabric. The number of stitches you need depend on the length of fabric required for what you are trying to make. With this in mind, let us look at some of the things we can do to make those affirmations work faster.

1. A Positive Mindset

When I say a positive mindset, I am not referring to being upbeat and full of sunshine and rainbows. What I mean is that you need to be optimistic about the outcome. Whatever you are trying to affirm, you have to believe in its outcome and reality. No matter how big your dream or vision is, you must believe in the possibility of its manifestation. There is no compromising this. If for example you believe that you are going to triple your income in the coming months or years, you must see yourself achieving this; and this brings us to the next point.

2. Visualization

If you cannot see the words you are speaking in action, those words are empty. As humans, we tend to connect with things we can relate to our senses. When you can find a connection through your senses, you find conviction. Remember what I said about conviction and how it affects your affirmation? When you say, "I am beautiful," you need to see the beauty in yourself. The struggle we have with this part of our affirmation process is seeing ourselves through the eyes of other people. You need to stop building the image of yourself based on what other people think.

3. Be vocal

One critical mistake I made during my earlier affirmation years was reading my affirmations the same way I read a book. I read it to myself in silence. The very definition of an affirmation is speaking your expectations into existence. Without speaking out loud, you can't fulfill the terms of affirmation. The truth is this; the potency of the words you affirm takes its full form when you vocalize your intentions. This happens in two ways; one, it increases your ability to internalize the message which in turn affects your convictions positively. And two, you infuse energy into your atmosphere that communicates with the environment around you, and this helps to speed up the alignment of things to bring about the manifestation you seek.

These are simple but effective tools and tips to help you make the most of your affirmations. Your next step is to put them into practice and over the next 6 chapters, you will be getting 365 days' worth of affirmations covering key areas of your life. Remember, have Conviction. Be consistent. Be committed.

CHAPTER TWO

60 Affirmations for Confidence

Confidence is the backbone of everything that you do. To live the life you have only dreamed of, you must find the courage and confidence to do so.

1. In the face of everything that this day presents to me, I am bold and full of courage.

2. I stand firmly by what I hold true with utmost confidence and grace.

3. My voice cannot be muted by societal expectations. I speak up for myself.

4. I am confident in my skills, abilities, and potential.

5. I am made of greatness and strength, and I have the courage to back up my words with actions.

6. I can, and I will successfully complete every task I set out to achieve today.

7. I command the attention of everyone in any room I step into today because of my confidence.

8. In my speech, mannerisms, and deeds, I radiate positive confidence.

9. I tackle every project with the grace and efficiency that have become the markers of my confidence.

10. I am not afraid to embrace every facet of myself no matter how flawed I perceive them to be.

11. Today, I am better than I was yesterday, and tomorrow, I will be better than I am today.

12. I am breaking limits and surpassing every expectation in all my endeavors.

13. I choose to be excellent in everything that I set out to do.

14. I am not the mistakes I have made. I learn my lessons and grow.

15. I am the best version of myself regardless of what people say.

16. I am taking steps to conquer my fears and achieve my dreams.

17. I am not going to stand in the way of my success. I believe in the power of me.

18. I am the leading lady in my own life. No one is going to upstage me.

19. My confidence is made of more than the clothes I wear or the things I own.

20. The opinions of other people can never diminish my confidence and faith in myself.

21. I trust my instincts and therefore every emotion I experience is valid.

22. I am a queen, a boss and a divine being in every way that defines those words.

23. I am confident in the person I am today and in the person I will become tomorrow.

24. I am confident enough to cast aside my insecurities to give room for other queens to shine.

25. I am uniquely built to handle whatever challenges or obstacles stand in my way today.

26. I am proud of every single thing I have achieved, whether big or small.

27. I deserve every bit of happiness and positivity that comes my way today.

28. I accept myself for who I am, and this does not make me any less or better than anyone else.

29. I am authentic and uniquely myself wherever I am and this makes me feel powerful.

30. I am not afraid to take the necessary steps to become a better version of myself.

31. I relentlessly pursue my goals with fierce determination and absolute conviction.

32. I am a woman of substance and character. I don't need to seek validation from anyone except me.

33. Life does not happen to me. I am happening to life because I am in charge of my life.

34. I am taking charge of my life today and I won't be needing anyone's permission to be amazing.

35. I am making good and morally sound decisions that prioritize my physical and mental wellbeing.

36. I am smart enough to know what is right for me and I am confident enough to pick myself first.

37. I am not afraid to prioritize my wants, needs, and expectations in whatever relationship I am in.

38. Neither my hair, my clothes, the color of my skin, nor my social status has the power to define or authenticate my person.

39. I refuse to diminish my light or dumb down my potential just to make other people feel better about themselves.

40. I am attracting people who genuinely desire to see me succeed and are not threatened by the absolute confidence I have in myself.

41. I am surrounded by a positive force field that reinforces my confidence and protects my ability to be myself.

42. I am a light that burns brightly and I am capable of illuminating my world.

43. I am protected from the antagonism and bullying that is pervasive online and offline. It does not and cannot change me.

44. I work and function in the sound knowledge of who I am; nothing can distract me from my true identity.

45. I acknowledge the fears and concerns that I have, and I take the necessary precautions to avoid a negative outcome. I refuse to let those fears control me.

46. I am always in charge of my life, even when things appear out of control.

47. There is no limit on my ability to go out into the world, conquer my fears, and live out my dreams.

48. The world is my runway and I am confidently strutting in with grace, charm, and charisma.

49. I have the power to create my dreams and deliver on them.

50. I am not going to second guess or put myself down just because I am trying to fit into the image of what other people expect me to be.

51. I am communicating my feelings and thoughts in a way that sincerely conveys the message I want to pass across to whoever is listening.

52. I deserve every accolade, compliment, or award that comes my way today because I have earned it.

53. I am done with underestimating my potential and skills. I am constantly speaking to my strengths.

54. I am stepping into my best life and I am not going to question any of the good or positive experiences I have today.

56. I am ready and qualified for the next level of greatness in my life. I close the door to mediocrity and redundancy.

57. I am rocking my role as a sister, daughter, wife, friend, business owner, worker, and as a woman generally. I am doing a great job.

58. I can make a difference in my world, and I am taking that first step today.

59. I am the woman I want to be; brave, bold, and different.

60. I believe in my dreams and in my ability to make them my reality.

61. I am delivering excellence in everything I do.

CHAPTER THREE

60 Affirmations for Self-Esteem

Your self-esteem is an echo of the perception you have about yourself. It fuels your confidence which in turn drives your confidence. A woman who knows who she is and what she is worth cannot be brought down easily. Give your self-esteem a boost and watch yourself rise/grow in every area of your life.

1. I am black. I am beautiful. I am brilliant. I am powerful. I am everything I need to thrive in this life.

2. I love the curves and lines of my body because they illuminate my womanhood and amplify my uniqueness.

3. I am me and that is enough. I don't need to be anyone else.

4. I listen to my positive inner voice. My views about myself are the only views that matter.

5. I am the new normal. I am breaking every cycle of abuse that has haunted the women in my family.

6. I am happy and I am actively focusing on my health and well-being to maintain my happiness today.

7. I am more than my circumstance or experience. I am made of more.

8. I am a victor. I am a survivor. I am a winner.

9. I am excited because I have so much to look forward to today.

10. I am free to be whoever I want and I am exercising this freedom.

11. I am proud of the woman I see in the mirror every day.

12. I believe in the work I am putting in to make myself better.

13. I am making progress in my efforts to be my best self.

14. I am attracting the kind of friendships and relationships that uplift me.

15. I am a beautiful black woman pursuing her dreams and I am well-equipped for this journey.

16. I am shutting out any voice that demeans my person and relevance.

17. I am important. I matter to the people in my world.

18. I am taking full ownership of my life. I am in the driver's seat now.

19. I am worthy of the love, respect, and affection I desire.

20. I am talented, resourceful, and emotionally capable of attaining all my goals.

21. I am my own standard of beauty. I embrace the features that differentiate me from every other woman.

22. My beauty is exquisite. My body is divine. My heart is a treasure trove of wonders.

23. I am in love with everything about me. My looks, my personality, my ambitions... they excite me.

24. I am done tolerating people who have no regard for my person or my values. I demand respect.

25. I am kind, sensitive, and vulnerable. I am willful, direct, and incredibly strong. All these different sides of myself make me powerful.

26. I am not a second option type of woman. I prioritize myself, so I expect to be prioritized.

27. I respect myself enough to avoid situations that negatively affect my mental health, physical health, or brand.

28. I am a sexual and sensual creature. I have no reason to be ashamed or embarrassed by this.

29. I am courageously walking out of any unhealthy alliances or relationships that threaten my peace and sanity.

30. I am stronger, wiser, and better than the person people have painted me out to be. I will not conform to their expectations.

31. I am the prize. I am the pot of gold at the end of the rainbow. Any person I date is lucky to be chosen.

32. I am beautiful inside and out.

33. I am perfectly okay with the fact that I am not meant for everyone.

34. I acknowledge the reality that people's perception of me is not my problem to solve.

35. My body, with its scars, changes, and stretch marks, is a magnificent piece of art. I appreciate its beauty and perseverance.

36. I am imperfectly perfect the way I am, and I love that about myself.

37. I am seen. I am heard. I am loved. I am accepted.

38. I honor my body by choosing to engage in healthy habits that promote my physical well-being.

39. My confidence in myself gets better every day. I am patient with the process.

40. I am my own special hype woman and cheerleader. I don't talk myself down.

41. I am kind and forgiving to myself, especially when it comes to the mistakes I make.

42. I am completely in love with my magnificent brown skin and how it always makes me feel beautiful.

43. I radiate light, and I refuse to add my voice to the crowd of negative voices around me.

44. I am a constant work in progress. My goal is not perfection. My goal is to be better than the person I was yesterday.

45. I am okay with being different. My identity as a woman is not based on other people's opinions of what I should look like.

46. I take full ownership of my happiness. I am done waiting on other people to make me happy.

47. I am a goddess in human form and I manifest divinity through my words, thoughts, and actions.

48. I am aware of the power behind my words and therefore, today, I am choosing to use words that build me up.

49. I am a brave queen. I can stand up to my challenges. I am not waiting for anyone to rescue me.

50. I deserve to be pampered, protected, and pleasured.

51. I am never going to quit on myself. I owe it to myself to see my goals to the finish line.

52. My failures, pain, and trauma are part of the bricks I will piece together to build my empire.

53. I am talented at what I do. I offer tremendous value to any organization I choose to work for.

54. I am uprooting every lie planted in my soul that undermines my worth. I am replacing those lies with the truth about myself.

55. I am opening up to access the power and strength I have within me.

56. I am built for this time and season. Nothing is too tough for me to handle.

57. I am not only going to survive this season, I will thrive in this season.

58. I am not going back to people or circumstances that held me back. I am moving onward and forward.

59. I am stepping up and showing up for myself today.

60. I enjoy the woman I am today.

61. I embrace uniqueness and power as a beautiful melanated black queen.

Chapter Four

60 Affirmations for Attracting Success

Success means different things to different people. Just remember, success does not mean total perfection or the absence of challenges. But at the end of the day, when you are in a space where you have mental balance, financial abundance, and strong alliances, it is safe to say that you are successful.

1. I am attracting wealth and abundance into my life.

2. I am experiencing tremendous growth in every area of my life.

3. I am forming alliances and building lasting relationships that provide me with safety and comfort.

4. I am engaging in new habits that adequately prepare me for a life of success.

5. I am moving out of my comfort zone and conquering new territories.

6. I embody success.

7. My actions, choices, and thoughts are aligned with the person I want to become.

8. I can get it all; the career I enjoy, the love that makes me glow, the family that supports me, and the abundance that brings me peace.

9. I am taking steps today to guarantee the future I desire.

10. I have the code to unlock my success story.

11. I have all the resources I need to make my dreams a reality.

12. I am taking advantage of every opportunity that comes my way today.

13. I am meant for bigger things in life. I refuse to stay small.

14. I am done eating the scraps that fall off other people's table. I am building my own table.

15. I am sharing my energy with people who aspire for greater levels of success. I refuse to engage with mediocrity.

16. My morning rituals set me up perfectly for a successful day.

17. I am speaking words that activate the goal-getter in me.

18. I am reading books and listening to content that help me build a success mindset.

19. I am taking actions that lead me to success.

20. I am open to learning from my mistakes and implementing strategies that turn those mistakes into stepping rungs on my success ladder.

21. I am deactivating those triggers that cause me to sabotage myself every time I get closer to my goals.

22. I am consistent and diligent in the habits that bring about success in my life.

23. I am upgrading my mindset to match the life I want to live.

24. I am unlearning negative patterns of behavior that have held me from reaching my full potential.

25. I am navigating life like a person who has purpose and direction. My days of stumbling around are over.

26. I am making a big investment in myself because I recognize the fact that I am my biggest asset.

27. I am readjusting my priorities and pushing strongly for my goals.

28. I am successful.

29. I am not giving up until I get the life I want.

30. I know what I am worth and what I bring to the table. I am not going to settle for less. I will get what I want.

31. I am working hard and making the necessary sacrifices for the life I want.

32. I am building a healthy space for me to thrive mentally, physically, and financially.

33. My success is positively impacting my world.

34. I am loving how positive and powerful I have become.

35. I am bigger than any anxiety, doubts, or negative opinions about my success.

36. I have the right attitude for success and I am choosing that today.

37. I am pouring my energy into building the future I desire.

38. I am selecting projects, people, and opportunities that are in alignment with my aspirations.

39. I am actively engaging in things that lead me to my success goals.

40. I deserve and have earned every success milestone I cross.

41. I am working with the knowledge that life is happening for me today.

42. I am a woman of action. I am executing my tasks more than I am making excuses.

43. I am balanced in my pursuit of success. I rest when I need to. I play when I need to, and I work when I need to.

44. I am taking responsibility for how my success story plays out. I am not giving that power to anyone.

45. I am crushing all my goals and bringing myself closer to my dreams.

46. I am attracting people who are genuinely interested in seeing me succeed.

47. I believe in myself and my ability to make my success aspirations a reality.

48. I am taking pleasure in the simple moments I find on my journey to the top.

49. I am refusing to let my emotions dictate how much work I put into my growth.

50. I am not competing with anyone when it comes to my success story. The position at the top is meant for me.

51. I am not threatened by the successes of other women. I celebrate their victories and allow them to inspire me.

52. I have the courage to outgrow my past and become the woman I want to be even if it might mean letting go of habits, people, or situations.

53. I have a plan for my future and I am going to make it happen no matter what.

54. I am walking into the most successful season of my life and I am ready for it.

55. I am ready to elevate myself and become better at what I do.

56. I open myself up to receive abundance. I accept love in abundance, wealth in abundance, and health in abundance.

57. I am in control of how much effort I put into achieving my goals. I work with this mindset every day.

58. I am not afraid, ashamed, or anxious about asking for more. I deserve it.

59. I am valuable enough to attract the level of success I want.

60. My dreams are a possible reality and I am attracting the right people, opportunities, and elements to make my dreams my reality.

61. I am wealthy in the things that matter to me.

CHAPTER FIVE

60 Affirmations for Making Money

Money is a form of wealth. The attitude we have towards money makes a world of difference in how we experience it. These affirmations can help you build a healthier and more productive relationship with money.

1. Money works for me and not the other way round.

2. I am attracting the kind of opportunities that allow me to double the returns on my investments.

3. I have a healthy attitude towards money and as a result, I use it wisely.

4. I am making the right financial choices. I am done with financial lack or absence.

5. I have created multiple streams of income for wealth to flow through. I can never be broke.

6. I am resourceful in how I create and distribute wealth.

7. I have a success mindset and this attracts wealth.

8. In all my business endeavors, I am a money magnet.

9. I am strategically positioned to create and accumulate wealth.

10. Abundance and wealth is a natural state for me.

11. I am reaping tremendous financial rewards for all the hard work I put in.

12. I am bold in my desire to be rich and I have set plans in motion to help me achieve this.

13. I am creating wealth opportunities for myself and the people around me.

14. I am breaking every financial limit in my family and exceeding our financial projections and expectations.

15. I am a wealth creator.

16. My habits have strong financial value. My daily actions have strong links to the amount of wealth I accrue.

17. I have unlocked the level of wealth that is capable of catering to all my needs.

18. The scales are tipped in my favor to ensure abundance and wealth in my life.

19. I am building the type of wealth that lasts for generations.

20. My wealth is positively impacting the people in my life, my community, and my world.

21. I am living in immense financial abundance every single day.

22. I have the financial capacity to buy whatever I want.

23. I am financially free. I have paid off all my debts.

24. I am open to receiving money from both expected and unexpected sources.

25. I am doing what I enjoy, living my best life, and creating wealth in the process.

26. I have an unending financial source that guarantees a secure income.

27. I am creating financially profitable business ventures.

28. I am rich in every resource required to help me build sustainable wealth.

29. I am building empires with high-income yields.

30. I am creating relationships that boost my network portfolio.

31. The people I have in my circle have a success mindset that inspires me to reach for my goals.

32. I am a successful wealth manager.

33. I am wise and I have the ability to convert the resources at my disposal into viable streams of income.

34. I am building the kind of financial profile that makes me an asset in any economy.

35. I am growing my wealth from a place of rest.

36. I am not chasing after money. Money is chasing after me.

37. I will enjoy the financial benefits of all my hard work.

38. My brain is wired to see the wealth creation opportunities in any situation.

39. I am making money moves today to build a stable financial future for myself.

40. I am bold in my decision to grow and acquire more wealth.

41. I am a living expression of the phrase, "smiling to the bank."

42. I am attracting the kind of jobs that give me financial freedom and job fulfillment.

43. I know how to enjoy the money that comes my way. I spend wisely.

44. Every form of promotion that comes my way today brings financial advancement as well.

45. I am not degrading or devaluing myself for financial opportunities.

46. I deserve every good thing that life has to offer, including financial abundance.

47. I am experiencing exponential financial growth today.

48. I have access to the right people who can positively impact my financial story.

49. I can afford the lifestyle that I desire with ease.

50. There is no limit to what I can achieve financially.

51. I am setting financial goals that are on the same frequency as my vision for the future.

52. I am creating a new chapter in my financial story today.

53. I am going to get the amount of money I need to live the life I desire.

54. I have the money touch. Every venture I put my hands on turns into a highly profitable business.

55. I have become the mistress of money. I have absolute control over my financial outcome.

56. My income can never be less than my expenses.

57. I am living the life I dreamed of every day because I am financially free.

58. I am making serious money off my skills, talents, and ideas.

59. I am a multi-millionaire in different currencies of the world.

60. I am intentional about how I make and spend my money.

61. I can find ways to create wealth even in unexpected places.

CHAPTER SIX

60 Affirmations for Health

Health, as they say, is wealth. Without good health, it is almost impossible to enjoy all the amazing gifts that life has to offer. Poor health puts a limit on the standard of a person's quality of life. Through these affirmations, you can manifest sound health.

1. I am healthy in body, mind, and spirit.

2. Every system, organ, and cell in my body is functioning at maximum capacity for the promotion of my well-being.

3. My body is in the best condition right now and I am appreciative of this.

4. Thanks to my sound mind and body, I am physically fit and strong.

5. I am in a harmonious place spiritually and this provides me with peace and clarity.

6. My mind is a vast fertile field beaming with positive energy and radiating positive thoughts.

7. The physical limitations placed on my body do not stop me from enjoying and living my life to the fullest.

8. My body and mind are at peak performance every single day.

9. I am experiencing spiritual enlightenment that elevates my mind and stabilizes my body.

10. I feel good about the body I am in because I am perfect by my standards.

11. I honor my body by engaging in practices that promote my physical and mental well-being.

12. I am creating the right atmosphere for me to live a healthy life.

13. I am paying serious care to my health by investing in the right things for my body.

14. I exercise right. I eat right. I also take the required amount of rest to keep myself in great shape.

15. I am partnering with the right people to help ensure that my health remains in prime condition.

16. The people in my circle are working together with me to protect my overall health.

17. My body is healing and recovering from any trauma it has suffered in the past.

18. I have a divine layer of protection that ensures my mind and body do not fall victim to any plague or disease.

19. My age, genetic makeup, gender, or social beauty standards do not define my health profile.

20. My mind and body connection is in sync and this puts me in excellent physical condition.

21. I am a medical marvel and the excellent state of my physical health as well as the high standard of my quality of life continues to baffle experts in the medical community.

22. My immune system is strong enough to fight off infections and keep diseases at bay.

23. The food I eat sustains me and provides sufficient nutrients for my body to stay healthy for longer.

24. I have a sound body and a clear mind.

25. My spiritual energy is in complete alignment with my health goals and strategies.

26. I intuitively know the right foods for my body and the right exercises to help me reach my health goals.

27. I take my health seriously. It is at the very top of my to-do list.

28. All my daily habits and activities support my mind and body goals.

29. I am consistent in the habits that are meant to keep me physically fit.

30. I love my body enough to make healthier choices every single time.

31. I am expecting an unending stream of health and vitality into my mind and body.

32. I am exercising the power I have to make good choices for my physical and mental wellbeing.

33. I am capable of managing emotions like anxiety, anger, and pain. They do not control me.

34. I am immersed in a sphere that keeps me in a safe environment for my mental health to thrive.

35. I am not subscribing to fashion fads and practices simply because they are trendy. I focus on things that actually help me.

36. I am willing and ready to put in the physical and mental work needed for me to stay in good shape.

37. The goals I create for my body are designed to appeal to me. I am not trying to please anyone.

38. My body and mind are mine to command. I do what I want and what I want is what is best for my body.

39. I am stepping up all efforts to be the best version of myself.

40. I enjoy the activities I engage in to promote my physical wellbeing.

41. I have the mental capacity to persevere through my physical routines and maintain a fit body.

42. I am a sexy black woman with a hot body and a sound mind.

43. Regardless of how I feel, I am getting out of bed and pushing myself to be physically fit.

44. I am finding the motivation within myself to be healthy in mind and body.

45. I wake up every morning with renewed strength and vigor.

46. I feel very good today. I am in the right body and mindset.

47. Today, I will choose myself. When I am presented with tempting offers that might derail me, I choose what is best for me.

48. I celebrate myself for surviving the bullets life has shot at me. I have become mentally strong because of it.

49. I am craving healthy foods and habits that improve me physically and mentally.

50. I am patient with the progress I am making on my fitness journey.

51. My body is designed to do amazing things like get me through the day, provide pleasure, birth life, and so on. I honor the work it does.

52. I am honoring the sacrifices my body makes by ensuring that I nourish it with a balanced diet, exercise routines, and content that helps me mentally and physically.

53. I have an excellent health care team that works together to guarantee that I am financially, mentally, and physically able to stay in good shape.

54. I attract like-minded people who share similar health goals and take actions that inspire/motivate me to keep chasing my goals.

55. I am transforming my body into a living, breathing version of my vision board.

56. From the clothes I wear to the food I eat, I am consciously choosing the things that make me look and feel good.

57. I am attracting the energy I need to complete my fitness routines today.

58. Putting myself first and prioritizing my health gets me very excited.

59. I am welcoming support, encouragement, and positivity into my wellbeing journey.

60. The different parts of my body that make me whole are imperfect pieces coming together to fit perfectly. I love my body.

61. My health is a part of my wealth and I have it in abundance.

CHAPTER SEVEN

60 Affirmations for Love

Everyone deserves love. Love is at the center of everything that we do. Love for people. Love for self. Passion for life. These are all different expressions of love and we all need it in our lives.

1. I welcome this day with love in my heart, warmth in my soul, and light in my eyes.

2. I am made for the safe, warm, and everlasting type of love that I crave.

3. I deserve to be loved and nurtured.

4. I have a lot of love to give and I am connecting with the kind of people who deserve my love.

5. My heart is open to giving and receiving healthy love.

6. I am attracting people who genuinely love and care for me.

7. I am healing from the pains from my past and opening up my heart to opportunities to find genuine love.

8. My love is authentic and powerful.

9. My love is pure and true.

10. I am a prime expression of love in human form.

11. I am involved in relationships that fuel my love tank.

12. I respect and respond to the dynamics of my relationship, as long as it is positive.

13. I am setting and enforcing healthy boundaries in my relationships.

14. I am experiencing the most amazing kind of love every day.

15. I love myself with fierce devotion and compassion.

16. The energy I give out today is attracting my soulmate to me.

17. I am in a season of abundant love, peace, and happiness.

18. I refuse to let the traumas of my past decide my next steps for the future.

19. I am not burdening my current relationships with the emotional baggage from my previous relationships.

20. I am establishing intimate connections that help me find love within and around me.

21. I recognize relationships that are healthy for me and I seek them out.

22. My love antenna is tuned in to a higher frequency to attract people operating at the same level.

23. I am letting go of my past emotional struggles and conquering my fears.

24. I forgive people who have hurt me deeply with their words and actions.

25. I release myself from the bondage of pain, anger, and fear that has held me back from knowing true love.

26. I am walking into the starting point of the best days of the rest of my life.

27. I am not spending my days waiting for love to find me.

28. I am giving myself the love, care, and attention that I need.

29. Today, I am falling deeply in love with myself all over again.

30. I am loving myself without conditions or expectations.

31. My love is wholesome, unconditional, and forgiving.

32. I naturally avoid people with a tendency to manipulate and take advantage of my love.

33. I am taking on projects that I love. This gives me an enjoyable work experience.

34. I am finding love in the simple things that I do every day.

35. I am exuding an aura that attracts love into my life.

36. I repel people who are negative, pessimistic, and have no good intentions towards me.

37. I am open about waiting for people to earn my love and trust before I make any commitment, especially in romantic partnerships.

38. I am not repeating the same mistakes from my past relationships.

39. I forgive myself and I choose to embrace my flaws and my strengths.

40. My life is characterized by love.

41. I am committed to living the life I love.

42. I am releasing love into the universe and the universe is giving it back to me in return.

43. I am powerful because I recognize the power of having strong self-love.

44. I know my worth and I am attracting the kind of people who know my worth too.

45. I am not settling for any relationship that offers less than what I deserve.

46. I can see the life that I want clearly, and I am actively in pursuit of it.

47. I am allowing myself to become a vessel through which love flows into the lives of the people around me today.

48. The love in my romantic life is rejuvenated and made brand new.

49. My romantic partner and I are in a stable and healthy love relationship with ourselves and each other.

50. I am experiencing renewed bonds of deep and genuine friendships.

51. I have outgrown habits that sabotage my love relationships.

52. My love grows and finds expression in different ways every day.

53. I am grateful for the kind, committed, and loving partner I have.

54. I am letting go of relationships that no longer serve me and opening myself to ones that do.

55. My love is life-giving, life-transforming, and entirely wholesome. It is a positive powerful force.

56. My journey to my happily ever after begins today, and I am completely ready for it.

57. I am the key to my happiness, and I am unlocking that door to usher in my season of abundant joy.

58. I am investing myself in the right relationships and giving my love to those who deserve it.

59. My love is changing me from the inside and transforming me into the woman I have dreamed of becoming.

60. I am done with stagnated relationships and I am choosing to seek out opportunities to grow in love.

61. Love is a constant presence in my heart, home, and life.

Conclusion

The book is almost at the end. However, you are just beginning your journey. I am honored to have started this process with you but don't let it end here. Speak your affirmations loudly and clearly until these words drown out those voices that belittle your potential and undermine the effort you have put into becoming the person that you are today. You know somewhere deep down inside that you were made for more than this. Now is the time to prove it.

Connect with your affirmations. Rewrite them to align with your expectations if you have to, but never stop speaking those affirmations. Regardless of your religious affiliation or cultural roots, the power behind the words you speak to yourself is real. Will it teleport you to your desired destination within seconds? Absolutely not. But will it get you there eventually? Absolutely yes. Become more conscious and deliberate about what you say and how you say it. The rest will fall into place.

Before I jump into the goodbyes, I want you to know that you have access to the keys that will bring you the life you deserve. All you have to do is commit to it, be consistent with it, and hold on to your convictions. Being a black woman in today's society can be a blessing or a curse. Thankfully, you get to decide on what spectrum you fall under. Pick a side, build your vision, and speak it into existence.

That said, my part here is done. I look forward to reading your success story. So don't forget to write and share the details of your journey. Until then, be deliberate about changing your life for the better.

Book #4

365 Badass Positive Affirmations for Strong Black Women

For BIPOC Women to Overcome Negative Thinking, Increase Confidence, and Self-Love

Introduction

Nobody starts out hating who they are. This is something that you are socially programmed to do. We enter this world innocent and pure. The concept of race, gender, and social norms are taught to us. In a perfect world, your beautiful inner self is acknowledged from the second you enter this world. But since we live in a cruel place that teaches love is pain and that beauty is painted, we tend to see ourselves through other people's eyes. Sadly, what is reflected is an image that is far from who we are.

In my early teens and well into my late 20s, I looked for myself in the media. It was rare to find a woman who looked like me. The aesthetic for the ideal black women included features I didn't naturally possess and because of this, I never felt beautiful enough. People in my family called me beautiful but I always thought that they were obligated to say that because they were family. I never felt genuinely pretty. At least not until I was able to afford the surgical enhancements that would transform me into the "beautiful" black women I saw on screen and in my favorite magazines.

My inability to accept myself was not limited to looks. In relationships, I felt the need to talk and behave in a certain way so that my "blackness" didn't jump out at peopleI won't even touch the racial biases at work.

I grew up thinking that I could only be the best version of myself if I was anyone but me. Does this sound familiar? It is heartbreaking, but a lot of women of color identify with the picture I just painted. We push ourselves to fit the "acceptable" narrative at a price that is too steep - our identity.

It was somewhere on this journey that I found the courage to silence the voices around me and look inward. What I found there was pretty amazing. I discovered that I actually liked myself! This was a shocking revelation for me and the deeper I delved in, the harder I fell for my quirky sense of humor, my kinky black hair, and my not so curvy body. I wish I could say that this self-love happened overnight. It was a long drawn-out process with occasional setbacks (what superhero movie doesn't have that epic setback?). The result is this powerfully confident black woman (aka Moi) blazing trails in her workplace, successfully breaking through corporate ceilings, and currently typing furiously at her computer to ensure that other black women get to live up to their true and full potential.

Affirmations played a huge role in my transformation journey. I used my words to echo the beauty I found inside and this helped me gain confidence. The more confident I was, the farther away I drifted from my comfort zone. And as you probably know, growth happens outside the comfort zone; and with growth comes success in life.

I started with one phrase at a time. Telling myself things like, "I can do this," "I am capable," and so on were helpful but very generic at the time. So, I stepped things up by personalizing those phrases and that was when the magic began.

My tough to maintain hair became my crown. My body became more than just lines and curves but a vessel to carry divinity. With this change in perception came a change in behavior and thinking. It felt sacrilegious to think, say, or do anything about or to myself that was remotely negative. It is shocking to think that a few months prior, I was ready to go under the knife. Whatever your role is in life or wherever your journey has taken you, it is never too late or too early to start disconnecting yourself from the negative social conditioning that characterized your experiences. You don't have to be who they say you are. The only person you should be is yourself.

Becoming yourself is simply that; be who you are. We don't have a template or manual to refer to, so we get the added bonus of creating the person we want to be and speaking those words to ourselves until we embody this new truth. That is exactly what we are going to do in this book. The affirmations I share here are the ones that resonated with, and worked for, me. You can use this as a starting point and then as you grow, personalize it until you have created the life you want.

You just need to make sure that:

1. You are consistent with your affirmations.

This applies to the frequency of your affirmations and your ability to stay true to the words you speak. Here is an example of what I mean; you may tell yourself that you are beautiful and a few moments later, some random dude calls you, "an ugly fat bitch." This hurts especially if you have struggled with accepting yourself. However, your job is to ensure that you counteract this by remaining consistent in affirming your beauty.

Never hold onto the lies that other people tell you. Often, it is not about you. They are most likely projecting their self-loathing and insecurities onto you. The only words that matter are the ones you tell yourself. Be consistent in speaking the right words. In the face of that "ugly fat bitch" comment, tell the world that you are a confident badass bitch with the heart, soul, and body of a goddess.

2. You believe in what you say

For the longest time, I found it difficult to accept the phrase, 'I am amazing.' It felt like I was bragging. Sometimes, I felt like I was talking about someone else... someone who looked like me. It wasn't until I internalized this message that I started experiencing its impact. Even when I was thrust into situations that made me doubt my efficiency, it was easy for me to remind myself of the fact that I am truly amazing.

When you start your affirmations, you are going to struggle with accepting what you are saying because of years of negative programming. But when you hold fast, it becomes a fact, and the moment you believe in the words you speak, your affirmations become manifestations.

3. You are positive

To create a positive environment within, you must cultivate a positive attitude especially towards your affirmations. This doesn't mean that won't have negative feelings. Those emotions come naturally to us. However, you cannot act or speak based on those emotions. When you recite your affirmations, do it from a place of positivity. Truly believe in the words you are saying and see yourself becoming that person.

One of the easiest ways I learned to do that was by picturing myself a few years from where the moment I am in. In this vision, I remove limitations and negative experiences and just focus on what it would be like to be the person I want to be. This creates a feeling that activates the positive energy you need for your affirmations.

Now that we have gotten this out of the way, let us get into the affirmations. You are free to use them however you wish. The key is to remain consistent, committed, and to stand in your conviction. Remember, the transformation is not going to happen overnight and just because you aren't seeing physical evidence of your affirmations doesn't mean that they are not working. You need to keep saying them regardless of what is going on in your life.

Having said that, let me give you a quick breakdown of the structure of the book. There are five chapters with at least 70 affirmations per chapter. Each affirmation is meant to be spoken each day. But there is no harm in repeating affirmations multiple times a day or reciting more than one affirmation a day. If it resonates with you and aligns with your vision, tap into its power. Speak them boldly. Speak them out loud. Speak them with absolute confidence.

CHAPTER ONE

Unlearn the Past

The past, they say, shapes our future. Many of us come from troubled pasts, and to move into a desired future, we need to break the chains that hold us back. One of the strongest links in the chains is the horrible lies we have been fed about ourselves. Break that link and the whole house of cards comes crumbling down.

In this chapter, you are going to unlearn every lie you have been told.

1. I am my own person. I am not the mistake of the people who came before me.

2. I live for myself. My purpose is not to meet the expectations or ideals of others.

3. I am going to be me. I don't need to be anybody else to make it in this life.

4. My dark skin and kinky hair are hallmarks of my beauty.

5. The lines and curves of my body are like sirens. They announce my presence to the world.

6. My attitude is my beauty sauce. I don't need to "act right" to be considered beautiful.

7. I decide the blueprint for who I want to be. I refuse to be defined by what society thinks I should be.

8. I am making my own path in life. I am not bound to repeat the sins of my parents.

9. I am expressing my freedom in my words, thoughts, and actions. I am not a slave to my history.

10. I am a queen. Period. No negative label defines me and the way I live my life.

11. I belong to me. I own my body. I decide what is best for me.

12. I am a winner in everything I do. I am not a victim.

13. My opinions, thoughts, and feelings matter. I deserve to be heard.

14. I am a valuable member of society. I am precious and a treasure.

15. My contribution to society goes beyond social constructs about my worth.

16. I am powerful. My gender does not put a limit on my potential.

17. Being black is not a flaw. It is a fraction of my identity that I am super proud of.

18. I am made for greatness. My current environment or circumstance does not define my future.

19. Where I come from does not dictate where I am going.

20. I will always win. I will not be defeated by the challenges stacked up against me.

21. I have absolute confidence in myself. Other people's doubts cannot bring me down.

22. I am an exceptional woman. I am not defined by the racial stereotypes imposed on me.

23. Being a black woman doesn't make me less. It gives me the edge I need to thrive.

24. I know who I am. I don't need to prove myself to anyone.

25. My actions, words, and opinions do not define the degree of my blackness.

26. I am a strong woman. I am not prey or victim for people to take advantage of.

27. I am precious. I deserve to be loved and protected by the people in my world.

28. I am wise. I make decisions that have a positive impact on me and my community.

29. I work hard. I am neither lazy nor complacent.

30. I am a heroine in my life. I am not waiting to be rescued.

31. I take responsibility for my actions. I am not a product or victim of society.

32. I am a wealth creator. I break any cycle of poverty in my family.

33. I am a wealth manager. I convert my resources into generational wealth.

34. I am a woman of principle. This does not make me difficult to work with.

35. I am passionate and vocal. I am not angry or bitter.

36. I always stand up for what is right. My gender or race will not be used to silence me.

37. I am rewriting my past, not repeating my mistakes.

38. I am bold. I refuse to live in the shadow of fear caused by society's misconceptions about me based on the color of my skin.

39. I am breaking through every glass ceiling in my work, love, and social life.

40. I am a deliberate success. I didn't stumble into my wealth. I created it.

41. I am confident in my sexuality. This does not make me promiscuous or loose.

42. I have strong family values. I am positively building my home.

43. I am actively prioritizing my mental health. I do what is right for me.

44. I am giving myself a chance to heal from past trauma. I am done lugging my pain around.

45. I choose the right relationships for me. The cycle of pain, abuse, and betrayal is over.

46. I know and recognize true love. I know that pain does not mean love.

47. I am loved. I naturally gravitate towards people who genuinely love and mean me well.

48. I am not ashamed of who I was and where I come from.

49. I am protected. I am sheltered. I am not prey to anyone who wants to harm me.

50. In the face of challenges, I am defiant.

51. I am a woman of distinct pedigree and grace. Neither my past nor my present reality can change this.

52. Life is working out in my favor.

53. I have strong willpower. I will not be manipulated into making bad decisions.

54. I am everything I said I would be, and I have exceeded every limitation placed on me by society.

55. I bear the marks and scars on my body with pride. They tell the story of my origin and how far I have come.

56. I am normalizing healthy family relationships that promote positivity and mental well-being.

57. I am breaking the silent covenant that allows abuse and pain to be the norm.

58. I am focused on healing. I refuse to bleed on people who did not hurt me.

59. I am acting from a place of love and compassion.

60. I am letting go of guilt and shame. I forgive myself for my past mistakes.

61. I am walking with my head held high. My past has lost its hold on me.

62. I am cutting ties with my abusers.

63. I live by my own code. Not some misguided sense of duty or loyalty.

64. I am choosing the people who choose me and not people who feel entitled to my time.

65. I am not governed by the pain inflicted on me.

66. I am made for love and not just someone else's pleasure.

67. I am surrounded by abundant opportunities.

68. I am proud of the woman I am and the woman I am becoming.

69. I love my features. I don't need to change them to "fit in."

70. I am choosing my happiness from this day forward.

71. I am life.

72. I am divine.

73. I am light.

CHAPTER TWO

Affirm Your Truth

The world may say terrible things about you. The people you love may say hurtful things to you about yourself - sometimes not deliberately. Even your actions may betray your true intentions, leading you to question or doubt yourself. But none of these matter as much as the words you speak to yourself.

The truth is a strong powerful force capable of breaking through walls of lies. The more you live in the light of the truth, the harder it is for darkness to dim this light. Affirm your truth and manifest your potential and desires.

1. I am powerful. I can handle the storm that rages in life.

2. I am beautiful inside and out. My beauty transcends the physical form.

3. I am courageous. I am not afraid to stand by what I believe.

4. I am a woman of integrity. I live by values that cannot be compromised.

5. I am intelligent. I make very smart decisions in life.

6. I am kind. I extend mercy and compassion to those who need it.

7. I am my sister's keeper. I love seeing the women around me succeed.

8. I am a woman of my word. I keep every promise and respect my vows.

9. I am important. I matter to a lot of people in this world.

10. I am worthy. I deserve all the love, peace, and happiness.

11. I am capable. I set out to accomplish every task I assign to myself.

12. I am dependable. I can be counted on to do my part in any situation.

13. I am forgiving. I don't hold grudges or harbor hatred for anyone.

14. I am patient. I think strategically before taking action.

15. I am loyal. I pitch my tent with those deserving of my loyalty.

16. I am royalty. I wear my crown with grace and wisdom.

17. I am talented. My creativity and resourcefulness know no boundaries.

18. I am safe. I am constantly surrounded by people who support and protect me.

19. I am present. I am not lost in past glories or chasing futile dreams.

20. I am free. My skin color, tax bracket, or past sins cannot slow me down.

21. I am assertive. I am no pushover or anyone's plaything.

22. I am in love. I love my life and the people I allow into my space.

23. I own myself. I am not controlled or manipulated by anyone.

24. I am successful. I am rich in resources and in my finances.

25. I am healthy. I experience renewed vitality in my body every day.

26. I am connected. I know my history and I am not ashamed of my roots.

27. I am magical. My skin color adds an extra layer of beauty that makes me amazing.

28. I am strong. I am built to outlast tough times.

29. I am sexy. I embrace my sexuality and acknowledge the power of my sensuality.

30. I am amazing. Every day, I conquer my fears and make great things happen.

31. I am unbreakable. I may stumble. I may fall. But I always rise back up.

32. I am irresistible. The right people are attracted to my many amazing qualities.

33. I am unique. There is only one me in the entire universe and I am proud of her.

34. I am clean. I engage in practices that honor my body physically, mentally, and spiritually.

35. I regret nothing. I learn from my mistakes, pick myself up, and move forward.

36. I am the best version of myself and the only one better than me is the woman I am becoming.

37. I am extra; extraordinary, extroverted, and extralogical.

38. I am peaceful. My words and actions are reflections of my peaceful nature.

39. I am passionate. I am very excited about my work, my life, and my love.

40. I am hopeful. I know that the future I want will become my reality.

41. I am devout. I stand for what I believe with honesty and courage.

42. I am divine. I pay homage to the goddess within by loving and respecting myself.

43. I am a nurturer. People feel loved and at peace whenever they come into contact with me.

44. I am genuine. I live a life that is true to my core values.

45. I am perceptive. I have a well-developed sixth sense and I intuitively know what is right for me.

46. I am disciplined. I am guided by principles that allow me to stay on the path leading to my goals.

47. I am in control. I have absolute power over my emotions and my tongue.

48. I am proactive. I am not reactive. I anticipate correctly and take the appropriate action.

49. I am a doer. I don't build castles in the air. I support my words with action.

50. I am a giver. I am generous with my time, my love, and my wealth.

51. I am driven. I am strongly self-motivated and strive to reach my goals every day.

52. I am ambitious. My desire to succeed takes me out of my comfort and into my area of growth.

53. I am happy. I chase my dreams, but I appreciate the joys of the present.

54. I am affectionate. I am not afraid to speak of or show my love to the people I care about.

55. I am persistent. When I set my mind on something, I go after it until it is done.

56. I am resilient. I can persevere through challenges with fierce determination.

57. I am black. For me, that means more melanin, more magic, and more magnificence.

58. I am majestic. I walk with pride, stand with confidence, and talk with grace.

59. I am positively glowing. My skin, my hair, and my body reflect my inner joy.

60. I am independent. I don't need anyone's permission to live my life.

61. I am captivating. I am not the kind of woman people meet and forget.

62. I am a rebel. I have no problem following the rules. I just appreciate my life better on my terms.

63. I am good. And I get better every day.

64. I am bold. I don't bow to my fears or give up on myself.

65. I am gold. I am valuable and I know my worth.

66. I am peculiar. I embrace and celebrate my distinction.

67. I am me. And I will never change that for anybody.

68. I am a hero. I get up every day and show up for myself regardless of the challenges.

69. I am favored. I am given preferential treatment wherever I go.

70. I am loved. The people in my inner circle have genuine appreciation and love for me.

71. I am blessed. I have everything I need to succeed in this life.

72. I am respected. My opinions and contributions at home and work are valued.

73. I am productive. I make the most of my time and my resources.

CHAPTER THREE

Embrace Your Power

Every woman is born with an innate power that makes her seem extraordinary. If you have ever seen a bear or lioness defend their cub, you know the power I am talking about. It is the kind of power that makes you look at the source of your fear in the eye and still take that bold step anyway. It changes the course of history and creates a ripple effect that lasts generations into the future.

Some of us have been raised to believe that the only power we have as black women is between our legs. Honey, that is just one aspect of our power. Over the next 73 days, you are going to acknowledge that power, channel it, and use it to manifest the life you want.

1. I have the seeds of nations within me. I birth empires and dynasties.

2. I am a kingmaker. I choose my life partner diligently.

3. I am a world-class leader. I serve with purpose and lead with confidence.

4. I am a multi-millionaire. I turn my ideas into successful brands.

5. I am the complete package. I bring abundance to the table.

6. I am exceptional. Mediocrity is not a word in my book.

7. I am a businesswoman. I recognize opportunities and successfully monetize them.

8. I am a team player. I play a crucial role in any team I am a part of.

9. I am a goal-getter. I am the one people call on when they want to get the job done.

10. I am evolving. I grow in every aspect of my life.

11. I am charismatic. I can charm and talk my way out of anything.

12. I am gifted. My skills and talents are sought after by top-rated companies.

13. I am focused. I keep my eye on the prize and my feet on the path to my dreams.

14. I am a chart breaker. I am pushing past limitations and braving new frontiers.

15. I am a woman with power. I make the decisions that matter the most in my life.

16. I am a positive influencer. I raise the stock of anything or anyone I associate with.

17. I am socially strategic. I build alliances and partnerships with the right kind of people.

18. I am spiritually sound. My faith and beliefs are firmly rooted in my convictions.

19. I am vocal. I eloquently communicate my thoughts and feelings.

20. I am enough. I do not need outside validation to build my self-esteem.

21. I am the prize. Anyone I consider good enough to date or marry is lucky.

22. I am solution oriented. I am turning every stumbling block in my way into steppingstones.

23. I am a survivor. I am thriving and rising above every attempt to ruin my life.

24. I am physically fit. I am of sound mind and body and I maintain a healthy routine that keeps them that way.

25. I am a visioner. I dream powerful dreams and put in the work to make them a reality.

26. I am a cheerleader. I love to see the people in my circle succeed and I do my part to cheer them on.

27. I am a peacemaker. I have found a way to get along with everyone, including those with biases against me.

28. I am my biggest competition. Every day presents an opportunity for me to be better than my previous self.

29. I am a changemaker. I lend my voice to the millions of voices seeking to make this world a better place.

30. I am a radical thinker. I think outside the proverbial box.

31. I am a pacesetter. I am actively paving a way for the women who come after me in this generation and the next.

32. I am a provider. I have no problems ensuring that the people I love are taken care of.

33. I am a protector. I create an atmosphere that makes people around me feel protected and safe.

34. I am a builder. I turn every resource at my disposal into desirable assets.

35. I am a global brand. I build locally but I am thriving globally.

36. I am an innovator. I am developing ideas that serve the community around me.

37. I am daring. I don't allow circumstances, past experiences, and outside opinions to shape my dreams.

38. I am a hustler. I work hard, I work smart, and I am always in the winner's lane.

39. I am an intellectual. I look for knowledge and constantly seek out ways to improve myself.

40. I am entrepreneurial. I consider the business opportunities in my environment and seize them.

41. I am virtuous. I know my values and I have no problems upholding them.

42. I am a generous giver. I never abandon anyone who needs my help.

43. I am perceptive. I have the power to accurately sense the right course of action.

44. I am a warrior. I fight for what is right to protect myself and the ones I care for.

45. I am a manager. I manage resources and relationships to maximize potential.

46. I am a winner. I am a thriving, flourishing woman of substance.

47. I am self-aware. I know who I am, and I am deliberately working on who I become.

48. I am a woman of purpose. I know why I am here, and I live for that purpose.

49. I am a listener. I pay attention to the needs and counsel of the people around me.

50. I am self-reliant. I cannot be bribed or manipulated into doing what I don't want.

51. I am a boss. I create employment opportunities and turn ideas into profitable ventures.

52. I am righteous. I have sound morals and an active conscience that keeps me in check.

53. I am a fighter. I push past my challenges to reach my goal.

54. I am a healer. I strive to maintain peak physical and mental health.

55. I love freely. The scope of my love is not limited by fear or other negative emotions.

56. I am phenomenal. My life is exceptionally amazing in every way.

57. I am sexy. I pleasure myself and my partner in any consensual arrangement.

58. I am a mentor. I have created a success template that others can replicate.

59. I am honorable. Guilt, shame, and past failures cannot stop me from living right.

60. I am dangerous. To anyone who seeks my downfall, I am a thorn in their side.

61. I am strong-willed. I have a stubborn focus that makes me formidable in any arena.

62. I am fearless. I boldly go after what I want every single day.

63. I am fierce. I love and give myself to deserving people passionately.

64. I am a multitasker. I can efficiently handle multiple projects at once.

65. I am a homemaker. I can turn any living space into a warm haven.

66. I am connected. I have a network of friends and associates who are critical to my business and career growth.

67. I am a temple. I experience divinity through my body.

68. I am a first-class citizen. I am treated well and respected in any environment I find myself in.

69. I am baggage-free. I am over any emotional heartbreak and ready to welcome love.

70. I am whole. I have everything I need to enjoy life to the fullest.

71. I am independent. I don't need anyone's permission to live life on my terms.

72. I am prosperous. I can rely on my net worth to fund my lifestyle.

73. I am perfect. I am everything I need to be to win in this life.

CHAPTER FOUR

Affirmations of Self-Love

It is almost impossible to receive and appreciate genuine love unless you find it within yourself first. In this chapter, these affirmations will take you on a journey that starts with removing the blindfolds brought on by poor self-perception so that the inner vision is activated. This will help you to see yourself in the true light and fall in love with the person revealed.

1. Life has given me a clean slate to start over. I embrace it.

2. I am not the mistakes I have made.

3. I am not the mistakes made by other people.

4. I am a brand-new person; made in my image.

5. I am setting my own standards of beauty.

6. I am done waiting for others to model beauty for me.

7. I embrace everything that makes me a woman.

8. My womanity is my biggest strength.

9. My body is sacred.

10. My heart is a treasure.

11. My pleasure is a priority.

12. Every line, curve, and scar on my body is a tribute to my womanhood.

13. My features are my identity, and I am proud of them.

14. My dark skin is my beauty mark and I treasure it.

15. My hair is my crown and glory. I respect it.

16. My style is my signature. I am bold with it.

17. My smile is captivating. It turns strangers into friends.

18. My accent pays homage to my roots. I am not ashamed of this.

19. My skin color does not determine my trajectory in life.

20. I am comfortable being me.

21. The woman I see in the mirror inspires me every day.

22. I don't aspire to be fixed. My goal is to be better.

23. I prioritize my health because I am worth it.

24. My body houses my mind, my divinity, and my identity. I treasure it.

25. I am both lucky and blessed to have this black woman's body.

26. I celebrate the diversity among my fellow black sisters.

27. My scars, folds, and bumps are not flaws. They are evidence that my body working hard to keep me together.

28. I am flawlessly gorgeous.

29. Today is me-day! I am celebrating my awesomeness.

30. I am deserving of all the good things in life.

31. I am reaching for the stars simply because I can.

32. I cannot get over how beautiful I am.

33. I choose self-expression over public approval. I choose me.

34. I am attracting the right relationships into my life. I deserve it.

35. I love the woman I am today the same way I love the woman I will become tomorrow.

36. I express self-love freely and without hesitation.

37. I am celebrating every milestone and victory; big and small.

38. I am patient with my journey of growth.

39. I am taking more chances on myself today.

40. I am shutting out any negative voice in my life.

41. I am cutting ties with anyone who takes pleasure in my pain. I deserve better.

42. I reject relationships that undermine my worth.

43. I see the best in me every time.

44. I am amazing, and nobody can make me think otherwise.

45. I am surrounding myself with positivity and love.

46. I am done tolerating people who hurt me in the name of love. I deserve wholesome relationships.

47. I am bold enough to walk away from anyone who disrespects me.

48. I embrace every facet of myself, and I find comfort in that.

49. I am working hard at being better and I am enjoying the process.

50. I am committed to this new relationship I have with myself.

51. I will never give up on myself.

52. My humanity and all that it implies does not make me less amazing.

53. I am in pursuit of dreams that help me live my best life.

54. I acknowledge the progress I am making to become better.

55. I will not put myself down to make anyone feel better.

56. I am light. I don't need to dim the light of other people just so I can shine.

57. I embrace my history; my failures, my mistakes, and my regrets. But they can never define my future.

58. I walk in absolute freedom. I am free from the burden of self-hatred.

59. I renounce every form of self-sabotage. I am committed to my success.

60. I am precious, and I show this in the way I treat myself.

61. I am taking away the right for anyone to treat me less than I deserve.

62. I want love, respect, and compassion. I refuse to settle for less.

63. I am in a healthy relationship with myself. I am putting in the work to make this relationship durable.

64. I am partnering with people who are interested in my growth.

65. I am removing every limitation I have placed on myself. I am capable of great things.

66. I am taking advantage of every opportunity that helps me elevate myself.

67. I am done taking actions that procrastinate my happiness. I am going after what I want.

68. My self-worth is not rooted in the approval of outsiders. It is in my self-approval.

69. I know who I am. And that is enough for me.

70. I am satisfied with who I am right now. But I am also invested in the person I want to be tomorrow.

71. I am content with not "fitting in" as long as I am authentic.

72. I am living my life with all my might.

73. I am stepping out of my shell and living as my true self.

CHAPTER FIVE

Affirmations for Confidence

The courage to live your life to its fullest potential requires extraordinary confidence. If you are fortunate enough to have a primary support unit that has fed you with words that affirmed your confidence since your early years, that is fantastic. You are several steps into your journey already. If this is not the case for you, that is okay.

In this chapter, you will unlock your confidence and build yourself to a point where you become immune to the negative messages that make up your programming.

1. I am that badass bitch that everyone wants in their corner.

2. In the arena of public opinion, I choose to focus on myself.

3. I am selfish with my time. I refuse to waste it on things that don't serve me.

4. I am effortlessly achieving my goals today.

5. No number of naysayers can break me down.

6. I am rocking my skin and everything it incorporates with pride.

7. Nothing can stop me from winning today.

8. I am Ms. Capable. I get the job done no matter what.

9. I am ready for today. I was built for it.

10. I can achieve whatever I set my mind to.

11. I am a woman on a mission. I cannot be stopped.

12. I am irreplaceable. My work and results can only be replicated by me.

13. I am the standard. I am not trying to be anyone else.

14. I am made unique and distinct. There is no one else like me.

15. I am an exceptional black woman. I am far from ordinary.

16. I am done putting in the minimum effort. I am all about maximizing.

17. I am confident in who I am, and I am not afraid to stand out as long as I stay true to myself.

18. I refuse to be small. I unleash every potential hidden within me.

19. I am living beyond the boundaries and limitations of societal expectations.

20. My time has come. I am conquering every fear that has held me back and stepping into the light.

21. I dream big dreams and I am daring in my attempts to make them my reality.

22. I am not afraid to succeed. I am adequately built to handle the life of success.

23. I am not living to survive. I am committed to thriving and flourishing.

24. My existence is essential. I am not an accident or a mistake. I am destined to play a critical role in life.

25. I believe in who I am and in the purpose that backs my existence. I will fulfill my destiny.

26. I accept total responsibility for how I use the resources at my disposal. I am choosing to use them to achieve my dreams.

27. The failures in my past cannot mask or deny the potential I have. I choose to focus on my potential.

28. I am channeling my energy and mental resources into personal development. The more I grow, the more confident I become.

29. I silence any voice that promotes my failures and weaknesses over my triumphs and strengths.

30. I am mentally programmed for success. I am built to live a life characterized by exceptional brilliance.

31. The only person capable of denying my dreams is me and I am done being my own obstacle. Therefore, nothing stands in my way.

32. Today, I am confidently taking the right steps to achieve my goals. I am checking off my to-do lists effortlessly.

33. I am boldly charging onward and forward. The fear that imprisoned and immobilized me has lost its power.

34. I refuse to settle for mediocrity. My mind and mental prowess are expanding beyond the limits placed on me by fear, negativity, and social expectations.

35. I am not settling for the glories of the past. Every day, I am pushing myself to be better so that I can achieve even greater things.

36. My journey is not about perfection. It is about making progress. Every day, I am getting better.

37. My race, my gender, and my age cannot stop me from maximizing my potential. I am made of more.

38. My propensity for attaining greatness is not locked in my DNA or ancestry. It is a mindset thing and I have the right mindset to achieve the level of greatness I aspire to.

39. I was born for a time like this. I was created for days that demand excellence and maximum effort.

40. I am carrying out my tasks diligently and efficiently. I strike with precision and follow with determination.

41. I refuse to give up my goals because of social or environmental restrictions. I am pushing past any obstacles to claim my prize.

42. Today, I choose to give my all… to express myself fully in terms of my work and to go beyond the expectations of others in my delivery.

43. I embrace my capacity to do and be more than what is expected of me. I refuse to live a life that is influenced, altered, or determined by the opinions of others.

44. I refuse to devalue or demean my worth by comparing myself with anyone else. I am my only competition, and my goal is to be better than the person I was yesterday.

45. I am stepping out of the shadows where social biases based on my gender and race have kept me. I am entering into the light of who I truly am.

46. In my quest to fulfill my potential as a black woman of excellence, I am not leaving any stones unturned.

47. There are not enough "Nos" in the world to knock me off my A-game. I have a titanium-grade confidence that simply brushes it off and keeps moving.

48. I embrace my failures. They highlight the flaws in my methods and unlock the next step I am supposed to take.

49. I know what I want, and I am confident enough to strategically pursue it to its expected conclusion.

50. Today, I am boldly venturing into new territories to explore new possibilities for myself. I am stepping out of my comfort zone.

51. I embrace the changes that come with each season in life because I know that I am capable of adapting.

52. My outward experiences cannot dictate my internal atmosphere. I find happiness, love, and courage within.

53. My ability to succeed today is not determined by my past experiences. I win because I have decided to.

54. I am casting aside anything and anyone that attempts to diminish my confidence.

55. I am altering my value system, principles, and priorities to reflect my new direction in life.

56. I am attracting and connecting with the kind of people or circumstances that elevate me mentally, physically, and financially.

57. I am letting go of habits, thoughts, practices, and beliefs that poison my ability to believe in myself.

58. I am taking the time to rebuild my confidence and establish my self-worth. No one can ever take this from me.

59. I have absolute faith in myself and what I am capable of. This inspires the confidence I need to succeed.

60. I have a strong network of friends and family who support my growth without feeling threatened by my confidence.

61. I know the resources I have for reaching my goals and I am not hesitant in making the most out of them.

62. I am not a helpless woman waiting to be rescued. I am a mistress of strategy and master of implementing it to change my fate.

63. I will never allow fear, shame, guilt, anger, or past failures to prevent me from doing what is right by law and by my conscience.

64. I am the best thing that has ever happened to me, and I celebrate this fact every single day.

65. I am blessed with the body and mind of a goddess. I am endowed with features that pay homage to the deity within.

66. I am a talented woman with unique gifts and skills that make me a valuable addition to any organization or team.

67. Regardless of people's opinions, social conditioning, or personal circumstance, I choose to celebrate myself.

68. I am cultivating the right atmosphere for my confidence. I surround myself with positivity and excellence.

69. I am backing my dreams with the work needed to make them my reality.

70. I am not afraid to work and think outside the box. As long as it guides me to my goals, I am down for it.

71. I am boldly defying all the odds that have been stacked against me. I will win no matter what.

72. I recognize those who want my downfall no matter how well they disguise themselves. I recognize them and cut them off.

73. I am living my best life every day. My happily ever after is a continuous experience.

Closing

And just like that, we have come to the end of one phase of your journey. You know what they say, "the end of a book is the beginning of another." I personally don't believe in endings. I believe we simply transform. You started this journey with the objective of building up your confidence and changing your mindset. After 365 days of affirmation, there is no way you are the same person you were when you started this journey.

The transformation has begun, and it is your job to keep it going until you become the person you want to be and more. I may not be able to hold your hand and guide you through the next 365 days but know that I am rooting for you girl. I want to see you winning as a badass queen living and loving her life. I want to witness your awesomeness on full display for the entire world to see. You have such a bright light inside you and with your permission, the world will see it too.

You can choose to repeat the affirmations in this book for another year. You can make alterations to suit your narrative and expectations as you grow. Whatever you decide to do, ensure that you are consistent and committed in your affirmations. Keep your chin up. Hold your head high. And when those turbulent storms come your way, gently brush the dust off your melanated skin, do the fro flip and affirm you were born ready to face them. Don't forget; you are a Queen, and this life is yours to do with as you please.

Keep winning!

Book #5

One Year Self-Discovery Journal for Black Women

365 Eye-Opening Questions to Discover Yourself, Raise Self Esteem, and Embrace Your True Beauty

Introduction

Asking questions is the best way to learn something. You do this on a daily basis without realizing it. It's the quickest method to receive the knowledge you need to get by, accomplish your goals, or understand your loved ones.

But what about your own self? Are you as interested in learning about yourself as you are in learning about others?

Self-reflection inquiries are similar to peeling an onion. New questions occur every time you believe you've discovered the solution. If you're intrigued by what's below, there's always another layer to remove.

Self-awareness is a lifelong process that is unique to each individual. The questions in this journal may or may not have definitive answers. However, they'll serve as a compass to guide you through your journey of self-discovery. You'll learn to accept who you are and love yourself unconditionally over the course of a year of daily self-reflection.

You cannot be self-aware or discover your true self without taking note of important questions and answers. Once you answer these questions, you should take it a step further by journaling.

Journaling is your best friend when it comes to solving important questions. You connect to your experiences differently when you write about them. When you put words on paper, your thinking shifts. Because handwriting is slower than typing, your mind is forced to slow down and pick words more carefully.

When you answer self-reflection questions in writing, you will get different results than when you answer them verbally. Don't filter what you write if you want to gain meaningful knowledge. Allow yourself to write without altering a single word in your journal.

This book contains some thought-provoking questions to help you become more self-aware. No one else will be able to answer these questions for you.

Remember: As a Black woman, you carry intrinsic power everywhere you go, and no one can take that away from you. So, remind yourself of this when you encounter difficult questions that require painful or intense self-reflection.

Day 1

As a black woman, the need to control everything is so deeply ingrained in us that surrendering is quite tough. We have been conditioned to believe that we must work things out on our own, yet this could not be farther from reality. Surrendering is recognizing that you have this amazing power (God, spirit, or the universe) at your side at all times to assist and support you.

"What do I need to surrender to the universe?"

_____
_____
_____
_____
_____
_____
_____
_____
_____
_____

Day 2

Sometimes it is okay to worry. We'd be more prone to make errors that might harm us, endanger our health, and wreck our future if we merely went through life aimlessly. However, "normal" worry can become troublesome if it persists and is difficult to manage.

So ask yourself:

"What do I need to stop worrying about? What can I do to stop worrying about these things?"

_____
_____
_____
_____
_____
_____
_____
_____
_____
_____

Day 3

"What stereotypes do people have about me?"

There are numerous stereotypes about black women, including that we are always angry, irritated, and loud. Write down two instances where you have been stereotyped and how this made you feel.

_____
_____
_____
_____
_____
_____

Day 4

"What three adjectives best characterize my personality?"

Knowing what describes your character could assist you in knowing if you need to further develop or consciously work on these traits. Doing this will help you become the best version of yourself.

_____
_____
_____
_____
_____
_____

Day 5

"What is the one thing that terrifies me the most right now? Why does it terrify me?"

Each time you learn something new and even go the extra mile in trying it out, you might be uncomfortable, but you are learning something. Putting yourself out there is not bad.

_____
_____
_____
_____
_____
_____

Day 6

"What do I think about my current mental health?"

"What activities can I do to improve it?"

"How often should I undertake these activities?"

Experiencing racism and sexism as black women have messed with our mental health for decades. We are expected to be there for everyone. Despite the temptation to be a superhero, we are more likely to feel depressed, lonely, and nervous.

Some of us have been conditioned to believe that seeking mental health help is a taboo. Some Black women are unaware that their feelings are symptoms of anxiety or depression. This might make it difficult to determine whether or not assistance is required. The above questions will make you conscious of your mental health struggles and how to overcome them.

_____

_____

_____

_____

_____

_____

_____

Day 7

"How do I rate my physical wellbeing?"

"What can I do to make my physical wellbeing better?"

Most times, with all the responsibilities we have, we forget to take care of our physical health. We have been conditioned to care for others and neglect ourselves. You cannot function optimally if your physical health is jeopardized. Take a moment to evaluate your physical health and find ways of improving it.

_____

_____

_____

_____

_____

_____

_____

Day 8

"How can I handle my emotions properly?"

A cultural icon is a powerful Black lady. However, if we cling to that image instead of accepting and resolving the stress and trauma that so many have endured, our emotions will remain messed up. You need to examine how to handle your emotions in a healthier and more constructive manner.

_____

_____

_____

_____

_____

_____

Day 9

"What about me makes me happy?"

Your happiness begins with you. Look inwardly and find out things about yourself that make you happy.

_____

_____

_____

_____

_____

_____

Day 10

"Which three characteristics about myself do I believe make me sad?"

If you do not love yourself, you will have self-esteem issues. If these characteristics can be worked on, then work on them.

_____

_____

_____

_____

_____

_____

Day 11

"What is the most important thing to me right now?"

Answering this question helps you know what you should focus your energy on.

_____
_____
_____
_____
_____
_____
_____
_____

Day 12

"What would be one thing I'd want to do less of, and why?"

When you have an answer to this question, you will know what you need to let go of.

_____
_____
_____
_____
_____
_____

Day 13

"What would be something I'd want to do more of, and why?"

Doing something you find pleasure in will help you physically, emotionally, and mentally.

_____
_____
_____
_____
_____
_____
_____
_____

Day 14

"When was the last time I helped someone else?"

One secret to happiness is helping someone.

There is a Chinese saying, "If you want happiness for an hour, take a nap. If you want happiness for a day, go fishing. If you want happiness for a year, inherit a fortune. If you want happiness for a lifetime, help somebody."

Helping others is the key to a richer, happier, healthier, more productive, and meaningful existence. What is important is that you don't hurt yourself while giving.

_____
_____
_____
_____
_____
_____
_____
_____
_____

Day 15

"What keeps me up in the middle of the night?"

Due to trauma you might have endured while growing up or the struggles of everyday living, there are things in your adult life that spark worry and keep you up at night. You need to figure out what keeps you up at night and deal with it.

_____
_____
_____
_____
_____
_____
_____
_____
_____
_____

Day 16

"Have I been stifling my creativity in any way?"

Everyone has a creative side. We can develop undesirable habits as we get older that act as mental barriers to our creativity. Like other bad habits, they can be broken if you are prepared to put in the effort.

You have to know how you have been jeopardizing your creativity. Answering this question puts you in a better position on your self-discovery path.

_____
_____
_____
_____
_____
_____
_____
_____
_____

Day 17

"What are the roadblocks to my happiness?"

As a woman of color, you should know that no matter how hard you try, life will occasionally give you lemons. You might be at the point in your life where nothing seems to make you happy. This question will give you an insight into what is keeping you from being a happy black woman.

_____
_____
_____
_____
_____
_____
_____
_____
_____
_____
_____

Day 18

"What are my most valuable assets?"

It does not have to be money or any material item. In fact, if your most valuable assets are material things, you will notice that you are never satisfied. You can also lose everything very fast.

Take time to answer this question. If your answer is a positive one, then you should focus on those assets.

_____
_____
_____
_____
_____
_____
_____
_____
_____

Day 19

"What can I do to make myself happier?"

By now, you should know that you are the only one that can guarantee your happiness. As a black women, we have been conditioned to prioritize other people's happiness over ours. When you figure out what you can do to make yourself happy, as long as you are not hurting anyone, go for it!

_____
_____
_____
_____
_____
_____
_____
_____
_____
_____
_____

Day 20

"What does it mean to me to be self-assured?"

When you are self-assured, you are self-confident. When you are confident, nothing can deter you.

_____

_____

_____

_____

_____

Day 21

"How can I turn a humbling situation into a good lesson and development opportunity?"

It is okay to fail at something. What is most important is that you learn from your mistakes. Black women are rarely given the opportunity to fail at something and try again. There may be snide and hurtful remarks. However, do not let that deter you. You need to remember that you've got your own back.

_____

_____

_____

_____

_____

_____

Day 22

"What does personal and professional success mean to me?"

Success means different things to a lot of people. You need to figure out what it means to be successful. This will help you avoid the pitfalls of comparing yourself to other people.

_____

_____

_____

_____

_____

Day 23

"How frequently do I have doubts about my own abilities?"

Imposter syndrome is one of the unfortunate consequences of systemic oppression or conditioning that we are less-than or undeserving of achievement. By identifying how often you doubt your own abilities, you are in a better position to find ways of challenging these limiting beliefs and faulty conditioning.

_____

_____

_____

_____

_____

_____

Day 24

"Am I a leader or a follower?"

With all the ordeals we have had to face, it is possible to act as a follower even when you should be leading. This question lets you know which category you are in and if you should change.

_____

_____

_____

_____

Day 25

"Am I getting closer or farther away from my goals? What must I do to remain on track?"

It is very easy to be derailed from our goals because of the challenges and distractions we face daily. This question allows you to know what you need to do to remain on track and successfully achieve your goals.

_____

_____

_____

_____

_____

_____

Day 26

"Do I know anybody who exudes the kind of confidence I desire?"

"How can I be more like that person?"

If you are not confident enough, you need to find someone whose confidence you can emulate and, in time, make your own.

_____
_____
_____
_____
_____
_____

Day 27

"What steps do I need to take to conquer one of my fears?"

You need to take active measures to conquer your fears if you want to be a better person. By choosing one fear, even the most innocuous one, and conquering it, you slowly gain the courage to tackle the bigger fears.

_____
_____
_____
_____
_____
_____

Day 28

"What are some of my favorite quotations or phrases?"

This question allows you to understand which quotes best resonate with you and what keeps you going.

_____
_____
_____
_____
_____
_____

Day 29

"Who are the individuals who make a difference in my life?"

"How do they make an impact?"

We need to take cognizance of the role important people play in our lives and how they impact our lives positively. Recognizing them will enable us to appreciate them more.

_____

_____

_____

_____

Day 30

"How frequently do I succumb to the views of others?"

It is very easy for people, including black men, to discard our opinions. Most times, unconsciously, we might be succumbing to other people's views. This is not a good sign, especially if you do it frequently. By recognizing when you're being influenced by others, you can take the necessary steps to become more grounded and confident in your own abilities and beliefs.

_____

_____

_____

_____

_____

Day 31

"What is it about my physique that I admire the most?"

Part of accepting yourself for who you are is being able to love yourself. This question allows you to know what physical features you admire.

_____

_____

_____

_____

_____

_____

_____

Day 32

"What activities make me feel energized, satisfied, and alive?"

_____
_____
_____
_____

Day 33

"How frequently do I have doubts about my professional or personal abilities?"

_____
_____
_____
_____

Day 34

"Is my self-confidence a result of positive self-talk (or the opposite)?"

What is the foundation of your self-confidence?

_____
_____
_____
_____

Day 35

"Am I always confident regardless of the situation I find myself in?"

For some reason, our confidence level may not be high. At times, because of what we have faced in life, we do not feel confident. You need to remind yourself that you can stay confident irrespective of what life throws at you.

_____
_____
_____
_____
_____
_____

Day 36

"How can I fix the things in my life that make me feel uneasy?"

This question allows you to take charge of your life.

_____

_____

_____

_____

Day 37

"As a black woman, how do I treat people who make me happy?"

_____

_____

_____

_____

Day 38

"Who are the individuals in my life that bring me down?"

"What exactly are they doing that makes me feel this way?"

_____

_____

_____

_____

Day 39

"What does setting boundaries mean to me?"

Setting boundaries is the one process of building courage. Boundaries help us form and sustain relationships that are critical and help us unlearn negative thought habits and myths about power dynamics.

_____

_____

_____

_____

_____

_____

Day 40

"Do I set boundaries?"

"How do I enforce them?"

"How do people feel when I set boundaries?"

_____
_____
_____
_____

Day 41

"What results have boundaries given me?"

_____
_____
_____
_____

Day 42

"Who am I easily accessible to?"

"Who do I feel safe with?"

Being a black woman can make you doubt people. Growing up, it is possible to have had even the most trusted family member fail us. If the people we were supposed to trust constantly failed us, how is it possible to learn to trust anyone? Past trauma can make you build a strong wall even with people closest to you.

_____
_____
_____
_____
_____
_____
_____
_____
_____
_____

Day 43

"What can I do to surround myself with individuals who will support me?"

In many situations, we find ourselves being the only black woman in our immediate environment. Finding good people that share our struggles can be hard—because of this, having a support system or a village is very important.

Day 44

"Which black woman that I admire worked on their low esteem?"

"How did they do it? Am I ready to try what they did?"

Day 45

"What compliments or recognition have I received from others?"

"What comments did they make?"

Day 46

"Why am I important?"

_____
_____
_____
_____
_____

Day 47

"What makes my life, my job, and my presence so important?"

_____
_____
_____
_____
_____

Day 48

"What can I do today to make myself proud?"

"How can I be proud of being a black woman?"

_____
_____
_____
_____
_____
_____

Day 49

"On what previous occasions in my life have I acted like a queen?"

_____
_____
_____
_____
_____
_____
_____

Day 50

"In which previous instances did I act like a warrior?"

_____

_____

_____

_____

_____

Day 51

"On which previous occasions have I acted like a hero?"

Being a hero in some situations can be good. But remember that you need to save yourself first.

_____

_____

_____

_____

_____

Day 52

"What do people do that makes me feel happy and excited?"

_____

_____

_____

_____

_____

Day 53

"What skills do I have that I could teach others?"

_____

_____

_____

_____

_____

_____

_____

Day 54

"What superpower do I have?"

As a Black woman, navigating the world poses distinct obstacles that need a certain skill set, including adaptability, steadfast resolve, discipline, confidence, and so much more. To achieve success over our privileged rivals, we must be able to pivot quickly and multitask while preserving our mental health.

_____
_____
_____
_____
_____

Day 55

"What would I change about myself if I had the chance?"

_____
_____
_____
_____

Day 56

"What makes me an extraordinary black woman?"

_____
_____
_____
_____

Day 57

"What adjustments can I make to improve my alone time?"

No matter how you try to be there for others, you need to make time for yourself. When you get the time, you have to make the most of it.

_____
_____
_____
_____

Day 58

"What hobbies spark my interest?"

"What can I do to make the next 48 hours more enjoyable and exciting?"

_____

_____

_____

_____

Day 59

"Which of my favorite hobbies make me happy?"

_____

_____

_____

Day 60

"What behaviors do I need to change this year in order to increase my happiness and confidence?"

_____

_____

_____

_____

Day 61

"What would it be like to do something for myself every day?"

_____

_____

_____

Day 62

"What difference would being committed to a hobby make in my life?"

_____

_____

_____

_____

Day 63

"Will my hobbies change my life positively for the next six months?"

_____
_____
_____
_____

Day 64

"What would it take for me to be able to love myself regardless of the trauma I have endured as a black woman?"

The trauma you have faced all your life can make you hate yourself. Self-hate can cause various things, including self-harm. You need to love yourself.

_____
_____
_____
_____
_____
_____
_____

Day 65

"How open am I about my emotions?"

"Who do I share them with?"

Emotions are not something that most black women are encouraged to show. Changing this narrative will be good for you.

_____
_____
_____
_____
_____
_____
_____
_____
_____

Day 66

"What are my strategies for dealing with tough but important conversations?"

"When I have these conversations, do I get positive results?"

_____
_____
_____
_____
_____

Day 67

"What demotivates me?"

"How can I re-motivate myself?"

Remember that you only have yourself. Even if you have people constantly motivating you, you still need to prepare your mind to push you to keep going.

_____
_____
_____
_____
_____
_____
_____
_____

Day 68

"When was the last time I felt betrayed or wronged?"

"How did I react?"

_____
_____
_____
_____
_____
_____
_____
_____

Day 69

"In what ways do I stand in the way of my own happiness as a black woman?"

You might be the one hindering your happiness. So take time to think and reflect on your answer.

_____
_____
_____
_____
_____
_____

Day 70

"When I first wake up and when I go to bed, how do I usually feel?"

Waking up or going to bed feeling tired, drowsy, or down? Do you need to figure out what is going on?

_____
_____
_____
_____
_____
_____

Day 71

"When I get into relationships, am I primarily motivated by love or by fear? What really motivates me?"

_____
_____
_____
_____
_____
_____
_____
_____

Day 72

"Do the folks I hang out with make me feel better or worse?"

Do you need to change your circle?

_____

_____

_____

_____

_____

Day 73

"How frequently do I show myself love and respect?"

You need to be deliberate about showing yourself respect and love.

_____

_____

_____

_____

_____

Day 74

"What is it that makes me feel limited?"

_____

_____

_____

_____

_____

Day 75

"Is there someone I need to forgive who has wronged me in the past?"

What did the person do to hurt you? Holding on to it does not help.

_____

_____

_____

_____

_____

Day 76

"What have I been putting off because I am afraid of failing?"

_____

_____

_____

_____

Day 77

"Have I had any quote-worthy moments recently? What made me feel this way?"

_____

_____

_____

_____

Day 78

"What makes me feel uneasy in social situations?"

"How can I prevent these things from happening?"

_____

_____

_____

_____

Day 79

"What are some regrets from my past and my concerns for the future?"

As a black woman, are there things and mentalities you need to let go of if you want to be a better person?

_____

_____

_____

_____

_____

_____

_____

_____

Day 80

"What are some things people around me do that irritate me?"

_____

_____

_____

_____

Day 81

"What was the happiest moment you had in the last month?"

You need to be conscious of the little things that make you happy. Record them to have a mental replay.

_____

_____

_____

_____

_____

Day 82

"What do I generally think about when I can't sleep at night?"

"Do I think about these things very often?"

_____

_____

_____

_____

Day 83

"When I look in the mirror, what do I see? How do I feel?"

Do you see a confident black woman? Do you see someone who is deserving of good things?

_____

_____

_____

_____

_____

Day 84

"In my personal interactions, what excellent attributes do I bring?"

_____
_____
_____
_____

Day 85

"What duties and obligations do my colleagues entrust to me?"

Are they things you enjoy doing? Do you want to change anything?

_____
_____
_____
_____
_____

Day 86

"What are some of the ways in which I give back to my family, organization, or community?"

_____
_____
_____
_____
_____

Day 87

"What activities make me happy, energetic, and satisfied?"

How often do you do them? Do you need to create time for these things?

_____
_____
_____
_____
_____
_____

Day 88

"In the next five years, what skills do I wish to learn?"

How do you intend to achieve this feat?

_____

_____

_____

_____

_____

_____

Day 89

"What are my plans for getting back on my feet following a setback?"

_____

_____

_____

_____

Day 90

"What risks and possibilities do I perceive in my life right now?"

_____

_____

_____

_____

_____

Day 91

"What are some of the things I do that take up too much of my time?"

Are these things productive?

_____

_____

_____

_____

_____

_____

Day 92

"What are some of the things I don't spend enough time doing?"

_____
_____
_____
_____

Day 93

"What do I think I need to do for better time management?"

_____
_____
_____
_____
_____

Day 94

"What topic can I give a 30-minute speech impromptu?"

You need to take time to think about the answer to this question. Your answer could unlock something.

_____
_____
_____
_____
_____

Day 95

"What negative traits do people think I have?"

Why do you think people feel this way about you?

_____
_____
_____
_____
_____
_____

Day 96

"What do family and friends frequently ask for when they come to me for assistance?"

_____

_____

_____

_____

Day 97

"What do I generally ask for when I seek assistance from others?"

_____

_____

_____

_____

Day 98

"What do I think about when I am alone?"

Do you have sad and depressing thoughts when you are alone? Do you need to change some thoughts you have when alone?

_____

_____

_____

_____

Day 99

"What are three questions I wish I knew the answers to?"

Will the answers to these questions put you in a better place or hurt you?

_____

_____

_____

_____

_____

_____

_____

Day 100

"What are my greatest strengths and weaknesses?"

_____
_____
_____
_____
_____
_____

Day 101

"What's one choice from the past I would alter if I could?"

_____
_____
_____
_____
_____
_____

Day 102

"What limiting ideas do I think I have?"

_____
_____
_____
_____
_____
_____

Day 103

"What do I need to say to myself right now?"

_____
_____
_____
_____
_____
_____
_____

Day 104

"What is something I would never give up?"

_____
_____
_____
_____
_____

Day 105

"What is the stupidest choice I have made?"

What steps do you need to take to not find yourself in this situation again?

_____
_____
_____
_____
_____

Day 106

"What is the wisest choice I have made in my life?"

_____
_____
_____
_____
_____

Day 107

"What was the most beneficial thing I did for myself today?"

You need to be deliberate about self-love and self-care. Every day, you should take conscious steps to take care of yourself, no matter how small it may seem.

_____
_____
_____
_____
_____

Day 108

"When was the last time I caught myself off guard?"

_____
_____
_____
_____
_____
_____

Day 109

"When was the last time I learned something new?"

Just like any other gender or race, we black women have to learn new things so that we are not left behind. Even if it is a new word, try to learn it.

_____
_____
_____
_____
_____
_____

Day 110

"Who do I compare myself to constantly?"

Self-esteem issues can make us compare ourselves to others. For your own good, you need to stop.

_____
_____
_____
_____
_____
_____
_____
_____
_____

Day 111

"What was the most difficult life lesson I had to learn?"

How did it make you feel?

_____
_____
_____
_____
_____
_____
_____

Day 112

"Do I ask enough questions or rely on what I already know?"

Summon the courage to ask questions about things you don't understand, no matter how meaningless you think the question is.

_____
_____
_____
_____
_____
_____
_____

Day 113

"Is sobbing a show of strength or weakness?"

What is the reason for your answer?

_____
_____
_____
_____
_____
_____
_____
_____

Day 114

"How long would I keep a friend who talks to me in the same manner that I constantly speak to myself?"

_____

_____

_____

_____

_____

_____

Day 115

"Am I clinging to anything I should let go of?"

"What is the thing(s)?"

Will you feel better if you let go of it?

_____

_____

_____

_____

_____

_____

_____

_____

Day 116

"What will be most important to me when I am 80 years old?"

_____

_____

_____

_____

_____

_____

_____

_____

_____

Day 117

"When is it time to quit weighing risks and benefits?"

Do you get a sign? What is the sign?

_____
_____
_____
_____
_____
_____
_____
_____
_____
_____

Day 118

"Can I violate the law to rescue someone I care about?"

How does this make you feel?

_____
_____
_____
_____
_____
_____
_____
_____
_____

Day 119

"How do I show respect to myself?"

_____
_____
_____
_____
_____
_____

Day 120

"How would I conduct my life differently if I was to die at the age of 40?"

Life is very short. Do things you do not have the courage to do. Take that trip; speak to that person. You never know what will come out of it.

_____
_____
_____
_____
_____
_____
_____

Day 121

"What advice would I offer to an infant if I could only give one piece of advice?"

_____
_____
_____
_____
_____

Day 122

"Is it more important to do things right or to do the right things?"

_____
_____
_____
_____
_____

Day 123

"What has life taught me lately?"

_____
_____
_____
_____
_____

Day 124

"Where do I get my ideas from?"

Day 125

"What kind of impression do I want to make on the whole world?"

Day 126

"What am I missing out on in my day-to-day rush?"

Sometimes you need to relax and pay attention to little things in your busy life.

Day 127

"When life gets me down, what cheers me up?"

Day 128

"Have I ever regretted not saying or doing something?"

_____

_____

_____

_____

_____

_____

Day 129

"What kind of interpersonal issues do I have (with family, friends, and coworkers)?"

_____

_____

_____

_____

_____

_____

Day 130

"How do I relate with my family?"

_____

_____

_____

_____

_____

_____

Day 131

"What can I change about myself now that I will see results in in the next 48 hours?"

_____

_____

_____

_____

_____

_____

Day 132

"Have I ever had my worst nightmare come true? What caused the incident? Was it an internal or external cause?"

_____
_____
_____
_____
_____

Day 133

"Who do I think about the most?"

"What impact do they have in my life?"

_____
_____
_____
_____
_____
_____

Day 134

"Would it help or damage me if I faced the consequences of my major decisions?"

_____
_____
_____
_____
_____

Day 135

"If I could alter one thing if I had the opportunity to travel back in time, what would it be?"

_____
_____
_____
_____
_____

Day 136

"Is there a distinction between innocence and ignorance?"

_____

_____

_____

_____

_____

Day 137

"What did my gut tell me today?"

_____

_____

_____

_____

_____

Day 138

"Is it possible to be perfect?"

How will you feel if you discover that the person you admire the most has lots of imperfections? So stop being hard on yourself girl!

_____

_____

_____

_____

_____

_____

Day 139

"How much control do I think I have had over the path my life has taken?"

_____

_____

_____

_____

_____

Day 140

"Where would I want to travel the most, and why?"

Do you need to take some steps to make traveling a reality?

_____
_____
_____
_____
_____

Day 141

"What do I see myself doing in 10 years?"

_____
_____
_____
_____
_____

Day 142

"What was the last act of kindness I received that I will never forget?"

_____
_____
_____
_____
_____

Day 143

"Which of my childhood memories is the happiest?"

"What distinguishes it from the rest?"

_____
_____
_____
_____
_____

Day 144

"Do I own my possessions, or do they own me?"

"What puts me in this position?"

_____

_____

_____

_____

_____

_____

Day 145

"Would I rather lose all of my past memories or be unable to create any new ones?"

Remember that memories are unique.

_____

_____

_____

_____

_____

_____

Day 146

"As a black woman, how do I deal with a powerful person who wants me to fail?"

If you are unsure of your answer, try speaking to your mentor, therapist, or someone with such experience.

_____

_____

_____

_____

_____

_____

_____

Day 147

"What is something I can't live without?"

Is your whole existence built on this thing? What will happen if you try to get yourself away from this thing?

Day 148

"What is one thing I haven't done yet that I really want to?"

Day 149

"What do I have to lose if I do what I really want to do?"

Day 150

"How would you define 'freedom'?"

Day 151

"What is the essential thing I can accomplish in my personal life right now?"

_____

_____

_____

_____

Day 152

"Who would I ask if I could only pose one question to someone I admire, living or dead?"

_____

_____

_____

_____

Day 153

"What is your most important objective over the next six months?"

_____

_____

_____

_____

Day 154

"Would I ever put my own life on the line to help someone else? Will it be a random person or not?"

_____

_____

_____

_____

_____

Day 155

"Am I content with who I am?"

What do you think fuels this feeling?

_____
_____
_____
_____
_____
_____
_____
_____

Day 156

"If my life was a movie, what would it look like?"

Will it be sad, boring, interesting, fun, or depressing?

_____
_____
_____
_____
_____
_____
_____

Day 157

"What time of day do I feel the most like myself?"

_____
_____
_____
_____
_____
_____
_____
_____

Day 158

"Do I ever wonder, 'What's in it for me?' when I assist someone?"

_____
_____
_____
_____
_____

Day 159

"Would I want to know the precise day and hour I am going to die if someone could tell me?"

_____
_____
_____
_____
_____
_____

Day 160

"Which day of my life would I choose to experience again?"

_____
_____
_____
_____
_____

Day 161

"What would I do if I had the chance to experience the next 24 hours, delete everything and start over?"

_____
_____
_____
_____
_____
_____

Day 162

"When I discover the truth or true meanings and way of things, will I accept it?"

When we are used to a specific way of doing things and we gain new knowledge, it can be hard to welcome and accept change. We learn every day. We should be open to unlearning, learning, and relearning.

_____

_____

_____

_____

_____

_____

_____

_____

_____

_____

_____

Day 163

"What comes to mind when _I_ think of the word 'home'?"

Is it a safe space? Is it toxic?

_____

_____

_____

_____

_____

_____

_____

Day 164

"What's the difference between accepting things as they are and settling?"

_____

_____

_____

_____

_____

_____

Day 165

"Do I have any friends I trust my life with?"

Do you believe that they feel the same way about you? What is the reason for your answer?

_____
_____
_____
_____
_____
_____

Day 166

"Who is standing in the way of my happiness?"

_____
_____
_____
_____
_____

Day 167

"What factors contribute to a person's attractiveness?"

_____
_____
_____
_____

Day 168

"Is there a moment when it's better to give up?"

_____
_____
_____
_____

Day 169

"What do I take pride in?"

Day 170

"When was the last time I worked hard and enjoyed every second of it?"

Day 171

"When does silence speak louder than words?"

Day 172

"What do I do with most of my leisure time?"

Day 173

"When I think about success, what (or who) comes to mind?"

_____
_____
_____
_____
_____
_____

Day 174

"When I was a kid, what did I want to be when I grew up?"

_____
_____
_____
_____
_____
_____

Day 175

"In five years, how will today's events be remembered?"

_____
_____
_____
_____
_____
_____

Day 176

"Do I believe to see or see to believe?"

_____
_____
_____
_____
_____
_____

Day 177

"When does love become a flaw?"

What recent love have you seen that changed your mindset?

_____
_____
_____
_____
_____
_____

Day 178

"What has been the most horrifying experience I have had thus far in my life?"

_____
_____
_____
_____
_____
_____

Day 179

"How am I currently pursuing my goals?"

_____
_____
_____
_____
_____
_____

Day 180

"What have I accomplished in the previous year that I am proud of?"

_____
_____
_____
_____
_____
_____

Day 181

"What have I learned over the years that have positively transformed the way I live my life?"

_____
_____
_____
_____
_____
_____

Day 182

"What is my most memorable experience over the last three years?"

_____
_____
_____
_____
_____
_____

Day 183

"What are the most important aspects of a happy life?"

_____
_____
_____
_____
_____

Day 184

"What can I do right now with the resources I have to get closer to my goal?"

_____
_____
_____
_____
_____

Day 185

"What is the finest thing I have ever received from someone?"

_____

_____

_____

_____

_____

_____

Day 186

"When I gaze into the future, what do I see?"

_____

_____

_____

_____

_____

_____

Day 187

"What simple pleasures do I like the most?"

_____

_____

_____

_____

_____

_____

Day 188

"What do I do to make a conscious effort to impress others?"

_____

_____

_____

_____

_____

_____

Day 189

"What is the most intense peer pressure I have ever experienced?"

Day 190

"What's the greatest lie I used to believe as a black woman? What made me realize it was a lie?"

Day 191

"What have I done in my life that has caused someone else harm?"

Day 192

"What is the most enjoyable aspect of becoming older?"

Day 193

"Am I content with my current situation? Why or why not?"

_____
_____
_____
_____
_____
_____

Day 194

"What is the most significant roadblock I am currently facing?"

_____
_____
_____
_____
_____
_____

Day 195

"What do I pretend to comprehend when I really don't?"

_____
_____
_____
_____
_____
_____

Day 196

"What's something you have discovered about yourself recently?"

_____
_____
_____
_____
_____
_____

Day 197

"What was the most pivotal event in my life during the last 12 months?"

_____
_____
_____
_____
_____
_____

Day 198

"When was the last time my initial impression of someone was incorrect?"

_____
_____
_____
_____
_____
_____

Day 199

"How many hours do I spend online each week?"

_____
_____
_____
_____
_____
_____

Day 200

"'What is the most important characteristic of a good leader?"

_____
_____
_____
_____
_____
_____

Day 201

"What negative habits would I want to get rid of?"

_____

_____

_____

_____

_____

_____

Day 202

"What is my favorite spot in the world?"

Do you believe if you put yourself out there, go out more, or travel more, your answer will change?

_____

_____

_____

_____

_____

_____

_____

_____

_____

_____

_____

_____

Day 203

"What's the status of my regrets in my life?"

_____

_____

_____

_____

_____

_____

_____

Day 204

"What, if anything, would I alter in my life right now if I had the chance?"

_____

_____

_____

_____

_____

_____

Day 205

"Have I forgiven my parents/family members for their mistakes?"

Forgiving is very important in healing. Forgiving others is for your own good, not theirs.

_____

_____

_____

_____

_____

_____

Day 206

"Have I embraced my childhood for what it was?"

_____

_____

_____

_____

_____

_____

Day 207

"Am I content with who I am as a person?"

_____

_____

_____

_____

_____

Day 208

"Is the tiny kid I once was proud of who I am now?"

Will your old self be proud of who you are now? What will your old self be proud of? What do you want your old self to be proud of?

_____
_____
_____
_____
_____
_____
_____
_____
_____

Day 209

"In every aspect of my life, am I living as healthily as possible?"

In your self-discovery journey, do not forget to stay healthy. Do you need to change your diet or lifestyle?

_____
_____
_____
_____
_____
_____
_____
_____

Day 210

"Have I begun to see my parents as individuals with ambitions, dreams, and flaws?"

_____
_____
_____
_____
_____

Day 211

"Do I understand how to live in the moment?"

_____
_____
_____
_____
_____

Day 212

"Do I recognize my flaws?"

"What are these flaws?"

_____
_____
_____
_____
_____

Day 213

"Do I recognize my finest qualities?"

_____
_____
_____
_____
_____

Day 214

"Do I have at least one person in my life who will always tell me the truth about myself, no matter how painful it is?"

_____
_____
_____
_____
_____

Day 215

"Do I have any idea how to make peace with my past?"

_____

_____

_____

_____

_____

_____

_____

_____

Day 216

"Do I have a life that I am happy with?"

_____

_____

_____

_____

_____

_____

_____

_____

Day 217

"Do I have a group of individuals that are emotionally and psychologically supportive of me?"

_____

_____

_____

_____

_____

_____

_____

_____

Day 218

"Are my ties with my family fulfilling to me?"

Just because they are family doesn't mean that they will make you happy. If they are toxic to your general wellbeing, what do you need to do to make sure they do not interrupt your self-discovery journey?

_____

_____

_____

_____

_____

_____

_____

_____

_____

_____

Day 219

"Outside of societal expectations for what a woman should look like, am I content with the body I have?"

_____

_____

_____

_____

_____

_____

_____

Day 220

"What is beauty to me?"

_____

_____

_____

_____

_____

_____

Day 221

"Is it possible for me to identify my core beliefs?"

Day 222

"Is it possible for me to feel confident in my beliefs even when others disagree with me?"

Day 223

"Does my behavior reflect my personal beliefs and values?"

When there is a disconnect between your beliefs and values, you will be living an inconsistent life. Right now, write down the bad habits you have. Then write down your most important values and beliefs. Afterward, begin to root out the inconsistencies.

Day 224

"Do I spend time with folks who have opinions that are diametrically opposed to my own?"

_____
_____
_____
_____
_____
_____

Day 225

"Do the individuals I spend time with like and respect me?"

_____
_____
_____
_____
_____
_____

Day 226

"Do I understand what it's like to be alone?"

_____
_____
_____
_____
_____
_____

Day 227

"No matter what my relationship situation is, am I content with myself?"

_____
_____
_____
_____
_____
_____

Day 228

"Do I offer enough of myself and my possessions to the people I care about?"

_____
_____
_____
_____
_____
_____
_____
_____

Day 229

"Do I want to change to try something new or to get away from issues that I don't want to deal with?"

_____
_____
_____
_____
_____
_____
_____
_____

Day 230

"Is my living condition and space exactly what I want?"

"Do I need to make changes?"

_____
_____
_____
_____
_____
_____
_____
_____

Day 231

"Is this the correct location or town for my life right now?"

Being in the wrong place or location can hinder growth in any area of your life.

_____
_____
_____
_____
_____
_____

Day 232

"Is the way I spend my money a reflection of who I am or aspire to be?'

_____
_____
_____
_____
_____
_____

Day 233

"Is my employment satisfying to me?"

You need to know if you're in a toxic work environment or not. Do you have colleagues or bosses that make you feel good or worthless? Assess the general conditions of your workplace.

_____
_____
_____
_____
_____
_____
_____
_____
_____

Day 234

"Is what I'm doing right now a job or a career?"

Does your current job put you on the right track to achieving your goals?

_____
_____
_____
_____
_____
_____
_____
_____

Day 235

"Am I developing the abilities and forming the connections that I require?"

_____
_____
_____
_____
_____
_____

Day 236

"Do I know how to build a mutually beneficial network?"

_____
_____
_____
_____
_____
_____
_____
_____

Day 237

"What is my favorite personal non-physical characteristic?"

_____
_____
_____
_____
_____
_____

Day 238

"What social customs would I want to see vanish?"

_____
_____
_____
_____
_____
_____

Day 239

"What is one thing I've learned that the majority of people aren't aware of?"

_____
_____
_____
_____
_____
_____

Day 240

"What is the role of love and affection in my life?"

_____
_____
_____
_____
_____
_____

Day 241

"Do I have any self-confidence issues?"

_____
_____
_____
_____
_____
_____
_____

Day 242

_____
_____
_____
_____
_____
_____
_____

Day 243

_____
_____
_____
_____
_____
_____
_____

Day 244

"What is/was my longest-lasting friendship, and how did I keep it going for so long?"

_____
_____
_____
_____
_____
_____
_____

Day 245

"Do I believe I can have more than one best friend?"

_____
_____
_____
_____
_____
_____

Day 246

"Do I regard my parents as the best?"

_____
_____
_____
_____
_____
_____

Day 247

"Do I believe that people of opposing genders can have a friendship without falling in love?"

_____
_____
_____
_____
_____
_____

Day 248

"What is an unforgivable act to me?'

_____
_____
_____
_____

Day 249

"What recommendations would I provide to those who have long-distance friendships?"

_____
_____
_____
_____
_____
_____
_____

Day 250

"Do long-distance relationships work?"

Have you ever been in any long-distance relationship? If you could do something different about your last relationship, what would it be?

_____
_____
_____
_____
_____
_____
_____

Day 251

"Do I believe it's preferable to invest or save money?"

Your thoughts about what to do with your money is important. So what do you do with any spare money and income?

_____
_____
_____
_____
_____
_____
_____

Day 252

"What qualities do I search for in a partner?"

_____
_____
_____
_____
_____
_____

Day 253

"What is the most crucial aspect of a relationship?" (For example, trust, respect, and so on.)

_____
_____
_____
_____
_____
_____

Day 254

"How frequently should a couple fight in order to keep their relationship healthy?"

_____
_____
_____
_____
_____
_____

Day 255

"How do I face life's challenges?"

_____
_____
_____
_____
_____
_____

Day 256

"Do I like to attempt new things in order to impress others?"

Day 257

"Would I put in more effort or seek assistance if my task became too much?"

Day 258

"What would I alter about myself if I had the chance? Why?"

Day 259

"What can I do to help myself feel more secure?"

Day 260

"Do I have a secure location to escape from things and pressures in my life?"

What's the point of having one? Is it possible to face what you think you should run from?

_____
_____
_____
_____
_____
_____
_____
_____

Day 261

"What do I do when I am worried?"

_____
_____
_____
_____
_____
_____
_____

Day 262

"What is my proudest accomplishment?"

Your answer can be based on any area of your life.

_____
_____
_____
_____
_____
_____
_____
_____
_____

Day 263

"Has anything impacted my perspective on life?"

_____
_____
_____
_____
_____
_____
_____

Day 264

"Do I consider myself to be a good decision-maker?"

"What can I do to improve?"

_____
_____
_____
_____
_____
_____
_____
_____
_____

Day 265

"What is the most significant item in my life?"

_____
_____
_____
_____
_____
_____

Day 266

"Am I focused?"

"What can I do to improve?"

_____
_____
_____
_____
_____
_____
_____
_____
_____
_____

Day 267

"How do I react when angry?"

_____
_____
_____
_____
_____
_____
_____

Day 268

"How honest am I in my everyday life?"

_____
_____
_____
_____
_____
_____
_____

Day 269

"What is my fear-management strategy?"

_____
_____
_____
_____
_____
_____

Day 270

"How frequently do I let my creative side shine?"

_____
_____
_____
_____
_____
_____

Day 271

"What irritates or disturbs me the most?"

_____
_____
_____
_____
_____
_____

Day 272

"How good am I at communicating?"

_____
_____
_____
_____
_____
_____

Day 273

"What is my opinion of my work ethic? Is there room for improvement?"

_____
_____
_____
_____
_____

Day 274

"What makes life worthwhile?"

_____
_____
_____
_____
_____

Day 275

"How would I rate my capacity to endure and persist on a scale of 1-10?"

_____
_____
_____
_____
_____

Day 276

"Am I a quitter?"

"How can I be better?"

_____
_____
_____
_____
_____

Day 277

"Is it easy for me to admit my mistakes?"

Give reasons for your answer.

_____

_____

_____

_____

_____

_____

_____

_____

_____

Day 278

"What do I believe I should spend more time on in my life?"

"What am I most thankful for?"

_____

_____

_____

_____

_____

_____

_____

_____

_____

Day 279

"What do I really want?"

_____

_____

_____

_____

_____

_____

_____

Day 280

"Have I discovered a balancing ritual?"

Rituals help us build routines by giving our days and lives shape and context. If you already have one, how well do you adhere to it? Be honest with yourself. If you are not following it strictly, work on it. If you do not have one, it may be time to create one.

_____

_____

_____

_____

_____

_____

_____

_____

_____

_____

_____

_____

Day 281

"What makes me happy about myself?"

_____

_____

_____

_____

_____

_____

Day 282

"What makes me feel horrible about myself or guilty?"

_____

_____

_____

_____

_____

_____

Day 283

"When do I get a sense of my true self?"

_____
_____
_____
_____
_____
_____

Day 284

"What causes me to get enraged?"

_____
_____
_____
_____
_____
_____

Day 285

"How do I handle my rage?"

_____
_____
_____
_____
_____
_____

Day 286

"What makes me happy when I am down?"

_____
_____
_____
_____
_____
_____

Day 287

"How well do I adjust to life's changes?"

_____
_____
_____
_____
_____
_____

Day 288

"What is my go-to method for coping with tense situations?"

_____
_____
_____
_____
_____
_____

Day 289

"How do I maintain my composure in the face of adversity?"

_____
_____
_____
_____
_____
_____

Day 290

"Do I have a well-balanced mindset? What can I do to improve?"

_____
_____
_____
_____

Day 291

"Do I find myself envious of others? Why?"

_____

_____

_____

_____

_____

_____

Day 292

_____

_____

_____

_____

_____

_____

Day 293

"Do I ever feel bad about situations that are beyond my control?"

_____

_____

_____

_____

_____

_____

Day 294

"Did I have a good chuckle or grin today? What made me do that?"

_____

_____

_____

_____

_____

_____

Day 295

"Do my feelings have an impact on my actions? Is the outcome favorable or unfavorable?"

_____

_____

_____

_____

_____

_____

_____

_____

_____

Day 296

"Do I get mood swings?"

"What are my strategies for dealing with them?"

_____

_____

_____

_____

_____

_____

_____

_____

Day 297

"Do I find it easy to express my feelings?"

_____

_____

_____

_____

_____

_____

Day 298

"Do I find myself being dissatisfied with my life on a regular basis?"

"What are my plans for dealing with it?"

Day 299

"Do I have any regrets in my life?"

"What are my plans for dealing with it?"

Day 300

"Do I get worried and tense all the time?"

"What is the reason behind this?"

Day 301

"Do I consider myself to be a brave person? Why?"

_____
_____
_____
_____
_____
_____
_____
_____

Day 302

"Which of my emotions would I want to be free of? Why?"

_____
_____
_____
_____
_____
_____
_____
_____

Day 303

"Have I ever felt in command and powerful?"

Write instances of when this happened. How did you feel when it happened?

_____
_____
_____
_____
_____
_____
_____
_____
_____

Day 304

"How do I cope with psychological trauma?"

Day 305

"Can I derive enjoyment from the smallest of things?"

Day 306

"Which of my feelings do I find the most pleasurable?"

Day 307

"Have I ever experienced numbness? What was the cause for it?"

Day 308

"Have I ever had the sensation of being completely free?" Give specifics.

_____
_____
_____
_____
_____
_____
_____
_____

Day 309

"Do I consider myself to be a positive person?"

_____
_____
_____
_____
_____
_____
_____

Day 310

"What effect does ambiguity have on me?"

What are your plans for dealing with it?

_____
_____
_____
_____
_____
_____
_____
_____
_____
_____

Day 311

"What is my greatest life regret?"

_____
_____
_____
_____
_____
_____

Day 312

"What would I say to someone I have previously wronged?"

_____
_____
_____
_____
_____
_____

Day 313

"What should I say to someone who has previously harmed me?"

_____
_____
_____
_____
_____
_____

Day 314

"What makes me the most dissatisfied?"

_____
_____
_____
_____
_____
_____

Day 315

"What makes me feel the most respected and appreciated?"

_____
_____
_____
_____
_____
_____

Day 316

"What was the most enjoyable period of my life? Why?"

_____
_____
_____
_____
_____
_____

Day 317

"What is one thing I have always wanted to accomplish but aren't sure whether I can?"

_____
_____
_____
_____
_____
_____

Day 318

"What is one thing I believe I can only achieve with the help of others?"

_____
_____
_____
_____
_____
_____

Day 319

"What is one item I have been putting off for a long time?"

_____

_____

_____

_____

_____

Day 320

"What is the one thing about the future that excites me?"

_____

_____

_____

_____

_____

Day 321

"What is the perfect job for me?"

_____

_____

_____

_____

_____

Day 322

"What are some ways I feel I might improve my self-care?"

_____

_____

_____

_____

_____

_____

Day 323

"What tasks do I constantly have on my to-do list that I keep procrastinating?"

Why do you keep procrastinating? How can you stop?

_____
_____
_____
_____
_____
_____
_____
_____
_____

Day 324

"What part of my future do I dread the most?"

_____
_____
_____
_____
_____
_____
_____
_____
_____

Day 325

"What is the one characteristic in others that I can't stand?"

_____
_____
_____
_____
_____
_____
_____
_____

Day 326

"What is the one attribute in others that I appreciate the most?"

_____
_____
_____
_____
_____
_____

Day 327

"What does it mean to love?"

_____
_____
_____
_____
_____
_____

Day 328

"Who is the one person I am certain will always have my back?"

_____
_____
_____
_____
_____
_____

Day 329

"How would I presently communicate with someone I previously mistreated?"

_____
_____
_____
_____
_____
_____

Day 330

"What qualities do I want in a best friend?"

"Do I possess such characteristics?"

_____
_____
_____
_____
_____

Day 331

"How do I express my love for someone?"

_____
_____
_____
_____
_____

Day 332

"How attentive am I to others?"

_____
_____
_____
_____
_____

Day 333

"Who is my go-to person in case of an emergency? Why?"

_____
_____
_____
_____
_____

Day 334

"What do I want others to say about me?"

_____
_____
_____
_____
_____
_____

Day 335

"Who are the individuals in my life who mean the most to me?"

_____
_____
_____
_____
_____
_____

Day 336

"Who do I adore the most?"

_____
_____
_____
_____
_____

Day 337

"What characteristics would I want to see in a friend?"

_____
_____
_____
_____
_____

Day 338

"Do I desire to rekindle a relationship with someone from my past? Why?"

_____

_____

_____

_____

_____

_____

Day 339

"Who do I have the greatest faith in? Why?"

_____

_____

_____

_____

_____

_____

Day 340

"Is it possible for another person to make or ruin my life?"

_____

_____

_____

_____

_____

_____

Day 341

"Who is the one person who has improved my life even at their own expense?"

_____

_____

_____

_____

_____

_____

Day 342

"Do I lend a hand to those I care about?"

_____
_____
_____
_____
_____

Day 343

"When was the last time I felt the need for a real friend? Why?"

_____
_____
_____
_____
_____

Day 344

"Who is my closest companion?"

"Are we a lot alike?"

_____
_____
_____
_____
_____

Day 345

"What are the components that make a friendship successful?"

_____
_____
_____
_____

Day 346

"Do I express gratitude to others? How?"

_____
_____
_____
_____
_____

Day 347

"Do I have a plan for dealing with toxic people?"

"How do I handle toxic people even if they are black like me?"

_____
_____
_____
_____
_____

Day 348

"How can I get along with individuals who have opposing views?"

_____
_____
_____
_____

Day 349

"Do I like to hang out with many people or a small group of people?"

_____
_____
_____
_____

Day 350

"How frequently do people misunderstand me?"

"What are my plans for dealing with it?"

_____

_____

_____

_____

_____

_____

_____

_____

Day 351

"Have I ever been through a heartbreak?"

"How did I handle it?"

_____

_____

_____

_____

_____

_____

_____

_____

Day 352

"What is my approach to dealing with conflict?'

_____

_____

_____

_____

_____

_____

Day 353

"Do my loved ones support me in all I do?"

Do their opinions matter to you? If they do not support you, will it affect you?

_____

_____

_____

_____

_____

_____

Day 354

"Do I feel at ease meeting new people?"

_____

_____

_____

_____

_____

Day 355

"Do I worry about what other people think of me? Why?"

_____

_____

_____

_____

_____

Day 356

"Is it easy for me to accept folks for who they are?"

_____

_____

_____

_____

_____

Day 357

"What are some of the behaviors and activities that make me feel good?"

_____
_____
_____
_____
_____
_____
_____

Day 358

"Do I get enough sleep?"

"What can I do to get enough sleep or maintain a healthy sleeping schedule?"

_____
_____
_____
_____
_____
_____
_____
_____
_____

Day 359

"Do I feel energized enough today?"

What is the reason for your answer?

_____
_____
_____
_____
_____
_____
_____
_____

Day 360

"Am I at ease when I move my body?"

"Do I easily feel tired?"

_____
_____
_____
_____
_____
_____
_____
_____
_____
_____

Day 361

"Do I feel better when I exercise?"

_____
_____
_____
_____
_____
_____
_____

Day 362

"Am I scared of dying? Why?"

_____
_____
_____
_____
_____
_____

Day 363

"How do I deal with stress?"

_____
_____
_____
_____
_____
_____
_____

Day 364

"Do I recognize when my body needs rest?"

"How does my body tell me to rest?"

"Do I pay heed to my body?"

_____
_____
_____
_____
_____
_____
_____
_____

Day 365

"Is time devoted to self-care a waste?"

"Will I take out time from my schedule for self-care?"

_____
_____
_____
_____
_____
_____

Conclusion

Thank you for taking out time for yourself. With this book, you have asked and answered 365 questions tailored to knowing yourself better. I hope that it was a beneficial, exciting, and fulfilling experience that allowed you to gain clarity about who you are.

As you have discovered your true identity and answered profound self-discovery questions, you will continue to see the richness of your talents, purpose, and beliefs.

Even after dedicating a year to this journey, I encourage you to return to this book consistently.

Best wishes

-Layla

Thank you

Those who help others without any expectations in return experience more fulfillment, have higher levels of success, and live longer.

I want to create the opportunity for you to do this during this reading experience. For this, I have a very simple question... If it didn't cost you money, would you help someone you've never met before, even if you never got credit for it? If so, I want to ask for a favor on behalf of someone you do not know and likely never will. They are just like you and me, or perhaps how you were a few years ago...Less experienced, filled with the desire to help the world, seeking good information but not sure where to look...this is where you can help. The only way for us at Dreamlifepress to accomplish our mission of helping people on their spiritual growth journey is to first, reach them. And most people do judge a book by its reviews. So, if you have found this book helpful, would you please take a quick moment right now to leave an honest review of the book? It will cost you nothing and less than 60 seconds. Your review will help a stranger find this book and benefit from it.

One more person finds peace and happiness...one more person may find their passion in life...one more person experience a transformation that otherwise would never have happened...To make that come true, all you have to do is to leave a review. If you're on audible, click on the three dots in the top right of your screen, rate and review. If you're reading on a e-reader or kindle, just scroll to the bottom of the book, then swipe up and it will ask for a review. If this doesn't work, you can go to the book page on amazon or wherever store you purchased this from and leave a review from that page.

PS - If you feel good about helping an unknown person, you are my kind of people. I'm excited to continue helping you in your spiritual growth journey.

PPS - A little life hack - if you introduce something valuable to someone, they naturally associate that value to you. If you think this book can benefit anyone you know, send this book their way and build goodwill. From the bottom of my heart, thank you.

Your biggest fan – **Layla**